FOR THE
BENEFIT OF THE NATION

THE NATIONAL TRUST FOR SCOTLAND:
THE FIRST 70 YEARS

FOR
THE BENEFIT
OF THE NATION

THE NATIONAL TRUST FOR SCOTLAND:
THE FIRST 70 YEARS

DOUGLAS BREMNER

FOREWORD BY
HER MAJESTY QUEEN ELIZABETH THE QUEEN MOTHER
PATRON

The National Trust
for Scotland

PREVIOUS PAGE PHOTOGRAPH
Beinn Alligin across Loch Torridon

LIST OF PHOTOGRAPHERS
Judith Anderson, Sue Anderson, John Batty, Alexander Bennett, Donald J Bennet,
Michael Blacklock, John Boak, Gordon Borthwick, Ian Boyter, Douglas Bremner, Laurie Campbell, Mr Castle, Paul Chandler,
Brian Chapple, Churchill Photography, Kathy Collins, Douglas Corrance, Cowie and Govan, Anthony Crickmay,
Camera Press Ltd London, Trevor Croft, Jack Crombie Photography, George A Dey, Julia Downes, Anne Ellis, Ian Evans,
Allan Forbes, John Forgie, David Gowans, Stewart Guthrie, Jim Henderson, Barry Hicks, Kenbarry Productions,
Location Photography, John McConnell, Douglas MacGregor, David McIntyre, Lea MacNally, David K Mardon,
R Matassa/Scotland in Focus, Anne May, John Mayhew, Ian Mitchell, Martin Moar, Derek Munn, Jim Nicholson,
Ben Notley, Abbie Patterson, Ruaridh Pringle, Jim Ramsay, Gordon Riddle, Bill Robertson, Isla Robertson, Tom Robertson,
Joe Rock, RSPB, Paul Sandground, Robin Satow, Glyn Satterley, Gille Schofield, Scotland in Focus, The Scotsman Publications Ltd,
Tom Scott, William Shand, Neal Sharp, Sidney Shear, John Sheerin, Alasdair Smith, Jonathan Smith, Gavin Sprott,
Peter Stewart, Charles Strang, Christopher Thornton, Iain Turnbull, Robin Turner, Verity Walker,
Paul Walton, Derrick Warner, David Wear, Whitehouse Studios, John Wilkie, Harvey Wood.

© The National Trust for Scotland, 2001

Firtst published by the National Trust for Scotland in 2001

THE NATIONAL TRUST FOR SCOTLAND
Wemyss House
28 Charlotte Square
Edinburgh EH2 4ET

TELEPHONE: 0131 243 9300
FAX: 0131 243 9301
WEB: www.nts.org.uk

A CIP Record for this book is
available from the British Library

ISBN 0 901625 69 8

Designed by Mark Blackadder
Typeset in Ehrhardt

Printed and bound in the European Community

Sir James (Jamie) Stormonth Darling

CBE MC TD WS

1918–2000

Jamie was the inspiration and motivation behind the
Trust's achievements from 1949 to 1983. His death deprived us of
continuing stimulation and encouragement, always given with kindliness,
understanding and good humour. His modest character would hardly have
appreciated this dedication but it seems in every way appropriate that the
history of this great organisation should be directly associated with the
man, whose influence will always be seen throughout Scotland.

CONTENTS

Opposite.
Eryngium giganteum –
Sea Holly

CLARENCE HOUSE
SW1A 1BA

As Patron, I offer the National Trust of Scotland my warmest congratulations on its 70th Anniversary.

This book is an excellent record of the history of one of our most treasured institutions for it gives a clear insight into the organisation and the way the Trust has developed.

Much of Scotland's heritage has been secured for the Nation by the vision, care and dedication of the Staff and Volunteers who have given so much of their time to the Trust since its inception in 1931. I have no doubt that those who read this history will appreciate the extent to which we are indebted to them and I send to all those who are associated with the National Trust for Scotland my best wishes for the continuance of their valuable work.

Elizabeth R

2001

PREFACE

Trevor Croft

DIRECTOR 1997–2001

'For the Benefit of the Nation'. These words, of stirring simplicity, underline everything that is dear to the heart of the National Trust for Scotland. They underpin everything that the Trust does and set the parameters for those who work for it, whether as paid staff or volunteers.

This history of the Trust derives essentially from the outcome of the vision of its founding fathers, men of principle and commitment such as Sir John Stirling Maxwell Bt of Pollok and Sir Iain Colquhoun Bt of Luss. They came from privileged backgrounds but were not afraid to commit themselves to the public good. Their ideal was to serve the community and to preserve important elements of our national heritage for all time and for all of the people of Scotland.

This ideal has lived on through the 70 years of the Trust's life to date. It is a story of many things but above all of a partnership between different people and organisations. It is a partnership between the staff and the many volunteers who work for and with the Trust. It is a partnership between the Trust as a body corporate and the many different organisations with which it works – other voluntary bodies, government and its agencies, local authorities and commercial firms. Above all it is a partnership between the Trust and all those who support it in different ways.

There has sometimes been a tendency for people to think that working for a charity is not a real job and that somehow the Trust is not exposed to the 'real' world. Nothing could be further from the truth. The common thread running through all charities is the commitment of those involved. We have a saying in the Trust that it gets hold of you and is in danger of becoming overwhelming. There is an overarching belief that people are doing something for the public good, admittedly gaining pleasure at the same time, but being of service to the wider community in a way that can sometimes seem a little old fashioned today.

This book traces the origins of the Trust from its early days, highlighting the way in which the imagination of private individuals continues to be captured as it was at the very start. It has always been an organisation that has depended on public support, no less today than when an early legacy enabled the Trust to purchase Culross Palace.

It is of course a very different organisation from the infant body of the 1930s – but only in its scale and organisation. Growth brings with it the

Opposite, left to right: Trevor Croft, Maurice Wilkins, Bill Torrance at the opening of the Reception Centre, Arduaine Garden in 1998

need for change and this has been skilfully handled through the seven decades of the Trust's history. It is a growth which has been as exciting as it has been dynamic, with a feeling that somehow it cannot go on, but yet it always does, the next letter or telephone call always presenting the possibility of a new challenge to the Trust.

There are many common threads throughout this book but the underlying theme is the continual need for more members and a greater income. At a time when there is a tendency for Government to push more responsibility on to the private and voluntary sectors, the need for bodies like the Trust becomes more and more relevant. Pollok Park, the home of Sir John Stirling Maxwell, would almost certainly have been built over without the protection of the Trust's Conservation Agreement. Today it provides a valuable green lung for people on the south side of Glasgow, one of the greatest areas of open green space in any of the conurbations of Europe. This must be as significant today, if not more so, as it was when the Trust was founded.

I am often asked which is my favourite property. Apart from being impossible for me to choose just one, the fact is that every property has its unique significance which makes it special and generates a reason for visiting and enjoying its attractions, whether buildings, gardens, battlefields or open country. I derive great pleasure from being at a property and watching the visitors enjoying themselves. This makes all the hard work of the staff, volunteers and supporters worthwhile.

This is a fascinating record and is only made possible by the hard work of all those people who have served The National Trust for Scotland over the last seventy years. Writing this foreword allows me the opportunity to give my special thanks to everyone who supports the Trust. However difficult our task might be at times, it is the dedication and partnership of the staff and volunteers which enables the Trust to succeed, as it has for seventy years. The book itself has been a partnership between the author, Douglas Bremner, and all those who have helped in the task and who are acknowledged elsewhere in the book. I hope that all who read it will enjoy it and truly appreciate *the benefit to the nation* afforded by The National Trust for Scotland.

ACKNOWLEDGEMENTS

I should like to begin by expressing my sincere thanks to everyone who has contributed in any way to the creation of the Trust's history.

At the beginning of the commission I was very fortunate to have fruitful discussions with Sir Jamie and Lady Stormonth Darling at Dirleton and, shortly afterwards, more than one informative session with Jamie and George Russell in the latter's home in Edinburgh. George was kind enough to allow me to quote freely from his history of *The Formative Years* of the Trust, making available his fascinating record of newspaper cuttings, carefully annotated and bound in sturdy volumes and covering many years of its activities. George has taken a keen interest in the progress of the book, providing prompt and accurate responses to each chapter as it was written.

I have had the guidance, constructive criticism and encouragement of a small editorial committee consisting of Ainslie Thin as chairman, Trevor Croft, Dr David Munro and Roger Smith who has been my copy editor throughout the two years it has taken to research and to write the history. Roger has also willingly provided the index for the book.

In addition, Professor David Walker, Findlay McQuarrie and Donald Erskine have kindly read and commented on each chapter and the final manuscript. David Walker, with the Trust's Curator, Ian Gow's assistance, composed the section on Geilston, and selected chapters have been read by Ronnie Cramond, Donald Helm, Lorna Waddell and Lester Borley. Philip Schreiber, Conservation Manager West Region, kindly wrote the paragraphs on Holmwood House. I am grateful to Verity Walker and Myra Lawson who have constructively read and commented on draft copy at all stages and to Hilary Horrocks, the Trust's Publications Editor, who painstakingly read the draft manuscript, marrying my style with that of the Trust's – no mean achievement! Jackie Henrie efficiently proofed the final text. Carolynn Bain (Trust Archivist) and Isla Robertson (Photo Librarian) have generously made available the resources of their departments as well as their expert knowledge. Thanks are also due to the individual property and Head Office staff who have loaned their slides, supplementing those available from the Photo Library.

Jean Bissett, a volunteer from the Trust's Edinburgh Members' Centre, spent many hours in the basements of Nos 5 and 28 Charlotte Square extracting useful information for me from the property archives.

I am grateful for initial comments about the pitfalls of writing and style given to me by experienced authors Elisabeth Beazley, Colin and Ann Clipson, Lynne Arnott and The Rev Malcolm Goldsmith. I was pleased to be able to interview nearly 50 people, recording their experiences of the Trust, while some 25 took the trouble to thoughtfully complete and return my questionnaire on its future.

Anderson Strathern, lawyers to the Trust since its foundation, have generously sponsored the history. The Trust and I are both indebted to Mary Reckitt and Sarah Bradley, Trustees of the Albert Reckitt Charitable Trust, for continuing to channel a yearly donation in my direction for NTS. During the last three years this has helped to defray the costs of production of the book.

Finally, I am indebted to my wife Vivien for her transcription of many of the tapes produced. She also word-processed my notes from Trust archives, acted as my correspondence secretary and read and helpfully commented on chapters.

DOUGLAS BREMNER

CHAPTER ONE
MEN OF PURPOSE
1931–1944

*'The National Trust for Scotland serves the
Nation as a cabinet into which it can put some of its
valuable things, where they will be perfectly safe for
all time, and where they are open to be seen
and enjoyed by everyone.'*

SIR JOHN STIRLING MAXWELL, 1932

FROM SMALL BEGINNINGS

The Trust's founders would be astonished and gratified to learn of the progress the Trust has made in its first 70 years. When in 1931 they provided the vision which established the Trust they could not possibly have foreseen that by the 21st century 239,000 people would share that vision by becoming its members. If you are a supporter of the Trust this book will, I hope, underline the value of your membership in the preservation of Scotland's natural and built heritage. Your contribution is vital. If you are a more general reader, I hope it will give you a general insight into the work of this most remarkable organisation.

Men and women permanently employed by the Trust in 2001 number nearly 500 and provide specialist knowledge in, for example, administration and finance; building conservation and planning; countryside and gardening; education; archaeology; commerce; or as managers and curators caring for the contents of the properties.

The essential finance from members' subscriptions and donations helps to support most NTS properties which cannot make enough money to survive independently. Members also provide Trust 'clout' when defending the cause of conservation, whether on its properties or on a wider canvas. For many of its members it is the marvellous range of 126 properties held by the Trust *for the benefit of the nation* which attracts their allegiance. For others a specialist interest or the opportunity for personal involvement in practical conservation is satisfied. A Trust cruise could evoke support, or

Chapter opening picture. Sir John Stirling Maxwell by W B E Ranken © The Stirling Maxwell Collection

simply the recognition and concern that, without the Trust, much of Scotland's heritage would not be preserved and some of Scotland's most beautiful land and valuable buildings would have been abandoned or destroyed.

From its beginnings, the Trust has been led and supported by enthusiastic volunteers who now number over 10,000 – from its President and members of committees to the Members' Centres, Conservation Volunteers and individuals who give freely of their time in many capacities. They fully merit the chapter devoted to their special contribution.

THE FOUNDING

How satisfying it would be to conjure up an exact vision of the moment of founding of The National Trust for Scotland: intelligent, passionate men, intensely discussing Scotland's beauty and history in some smoke-filled, oak-panelled room, when the after-dinner conversation turns to 'what if …' and an embryonic Trust stirs in their imaginations. Unfortunately, there is no such single place or day to which the true genesis of The National Trust for Scotland can be traced.

Fortunately, a remarkable memoir of the time, *The Formative Years*, written by George Russell OBE (Trust Law Agent 1951–82), enables us to catch a glimpse of the personalities and surroundings of the early evolutionary stages of the Trust. The full text of *The Formative Years* appears in Appendix 1.

Sir John Stirling Maxwell, the owner of the Pollok Estate in Glasgow, was the leader of the small group of far-sighted Scots who believed

The Cedar Room,
Pollok House, Glasgow

that their country merited its own National Trust for Scotland with objects similar to those in England. It is thought that the Cedar Room, in his home at Pollok House, was the venue for its formation. The Council of the Association for the Preservation (later Protection) of Rural Scotland (APRS) generously agreed that their offices at 3 Forres Street, Edinburgh and the services of their Honorary Secretary, Frank Mears, should be made available to the fledgling Trust. The APRS lawyer, Arthur Russell, was instructed to draw up papers to establish the new company.

On 10 November 1930 an eminent group of people met and constituted themselves as the first provisional council of the Trust with the 8th Duke of Atholl acting as Chairman. An established Perthshire landowner, he had a distinguished war record. Sir David Young Cameron, the well-known Scottish artist, moved that the Trust be registered as a company limited under guarantee. The Duke was appointed as President, a position he held until his death in 1942. Sir Iain Colquhoun, a Lord Lieutenant for Dumbartonshire, was made Chairman of Council and served until 1946; thereafter, he was Vice-President until his death in 1948. Sir Iain's vision, courage and driving force helped to establish The National Trust for Scotland. The Company was incorporated on 1 May 1931. It was born, fully acknowledging the crucial role played by the APRS in these early years. The first Ordinary General Meeting was held on 21 July 1931 and those present were invited to become annual members by subscribing '10 shillings' (50p) or more.

Today, the seed they planted has taken root and borne fruit. This quiet yet revolutionary organisation now owns 74,200 hectares (183,500 acres) of Scotland's land-mass and has 239,000 members.

REFLECTING THE SPIRIT
OF A NATION

So why this keenly-felt need to create a National Trust for Scotland in the first place? Inspiration for the concept of a 'National Trust' may be traced back even beyond the existence of the National Trust in England, to the formation, as early as 1891, of the Trustees of Public Reservations in Massachusetts in the United States, 'for the purposes of acquiring, holding, arranging, maintaining and opening to the public under suitable regulations beautiful and historic places and tracts of lands'. This American body provided the basis for the constitution of the National Trust in 1895. A Committee for Northern Ireland was set up in 1936 and for Wales in 1945.

The English Trust's concern both to recruit members and to acquire suitable properties occupied the years before the First World War. By then there were 725 members and 63 proper-ties covering nearly 2,428 hectares (6,000 acres). There was clearly need for a more aggressive approach with concerted action to avert urban and industrial threats to the English countryside. Twenty local organisations together with 41 affiliated societies formed the Council for the Preservation of Rural England in 1926.

In Scotland, there was a parallel development when the Royal Incorporation of Architects in Scotland and the Edinburgh Architectural Association, inspired by Frank Mears, one of the country's greatest planners of the time, promoted the Association for the Preservation of Rural Scotland, established in 1926 and formally constituted in 1927.

The National Trust for Scotland was established at a seemingly unpropitious time in history. Of all the countries on the winning side following the First World War, Scotland was the slowest to show signs of recovery. Between a sixth and a fifth of men who had joined up had been killed. The average age of the population rose as a result of the emigration of younger age groups to countries such as India, Australia, New Zealand, Africa, Canada and America. There was a movement of people within Scotland from the country to the towns and cities which were ill-equipped to receive such an influx.

The war had cost Scotland a vast sum of money and the cost of living had risen dramatically. Living conditions were appalling, with more than a third of houses without a bath and a majority of people living in single rooms. The engineering industry, which had served the country superbly well both before and during

Interpretative display at J M Barrie's Birthplace, Kirriemuir

the war, was now in severe decline. On the Clyde, ship-breaking rather than shipbuilding became the order of the day. A national recession was also responsible for disastrous unemployment in Scotland, which was much worse than in comparable areas in England.

By the end of the 1920s into the early 1930s, however, the Scots were beginning to regain their confidence. They had recovered to a large extent from the ravages and depredations of war and were looking ahead once more. Both nationalism – and Nationalism – were on the increase and a pride in all things Scots was growing. The Scottish nation needed symbolic gestures of remembrance, renewal and faith in the future.

Although much talent had been lost to Scotland in the First World War, and others had been lost to the country through emigration, nevertheless there were talented people left who made very significant contributions in science and the arts. In drama, the Scottish National Players were founded in 1921 and many theatres were constructed in the post-war period. James Barrie (1860–1937) established himself in the fields of play writing and stagecraft. Barrie's Birthplace in Kirriemuir was also destined for Trust ownership. The times were favourable to the ethos of the Trust and to the passionate and imaginative men and women who were inspired to lead and support it.

EARLY DEVELOPMENTS AND ACQUISITIONS

During its formative years, particularly in the ten-year period until the Second World War, the Trust operated with a much-reduced staff and a low level of activity. Hardly any property was acquired during the period 1939–42 but early decisions taken by the Trust's first leaders were to influence a great many of its future actions.

Eight life members and 64 annual members were recorded by name and contribution in 1932. Congratulations were expressed even then, by the APRS in their Annual Reports, on the sound financial position and the substantial measure of approval and public esteem already accorded to the Trust both in Scotland and by Scottish men and women beyond its borders. Council was very grateful for the Trust's first major bequest of £5,000 (worth more than £168,000 in the year 2001) from Mary Lumsden towards administration of the young organisation. This was an important lifeline and allowed the Trust to engage in attracting membership and acquiring and managing its first properties. Miss Lumsden also made a handsome donation during her lifetime towards preliminary expenses of the Trust.

To further help in funding its administrative costs, the Trust also received donations from the Pilgrim Trust, founded in 1930 by Edward Stephen Harkness of New York. This benefi-cence was prompted by Harkness's admiration for what Great Britain had done during the 1914–18 war and by his affection for the land from which he drew his descent. The Trust's first approach to the Pilgrim Trust, also to help with administra-tion costs, resulted in £1,500 made payable in three annual instalments of £500. These were the first of many generous donations.

CROOKSTON CASTLE

When Sir John Stirling Maxwell handed over Crookston Castle, in Glasgow, to the Trust in 1931 as its first property, he made sure that what had been a ruined structure was already repaired and made safe. It was estimated at the time that the modest entry fee of tuppence (2d) would be sufficient to make the property self-supporting, which apparently it was. Sir John continued to take a personal interest in Crookston Castle, later repairing the caretaker's cottage. A Trust local committee supervised the property until 1963 when it joined others in being brought under the guardianship of the Ministry of Works.

The Castle is thought to have been built by Sir Alan Stewart, on land he bought with the authority of Robert the Steward, afterwards Robert II, in 1350. The Castle and lands were still in the possession of the Stuarts in the late 15th century, when the owner, another Sir Alan, was created the first Lord Darnley, in about 1473. In the early reign of King James IV the Castle was held by some of the rebellious lords led by Lord Darnley and the Earl of Lennox, but was besieged and captured by royal forces under the king's command. The large cannon Mons Meg was brought from Edinburgh by a bullock team to help to breach the walls. Tradition asso-ciates the Castle with Queen Mary and Lord Darnley, and at a later date with Robert Burns.

Crookston Castle,
Glasgow

BURG

Bequests and donations have been vital to the Trust's existence throughout its 70 years, reflecting the faith that individuals have in the permanence and good management ability of the Trust. Four other properties came to the Trust almost immediately, one as an intended bequest during the lifetime of the donor, two as gifts and one as an outright purchase.

Mr A Campbell-Blair of Dolgellau, North Wales offered to bequeath to the Trust a wilderness area on the Ardmeanach Peninsula on the west coast of Mull, known as Burg. This generous offer was accepted in 1932 and the site recognised as a sanctuary for animal and plant life, but also valued for its dramatic coastal geological features and the unusual remains of the Fossil Tree, first noted by the distinguished

geologist John McCulloch. In 1937 the property at Burg came under the scrutiny of Dr David Russell, a member of the Trust's Executive, when the severe problem of bracken infestation of once fertile meadows became his concern. The Russell family, who had a consuming interest in its affairs, were extraordinarily generous in the financial aid they gave to the Trust. Dr Russell sought the advice of Principal Paterson of the West of Scotland Agricultural College. The Pilgrim Trust once again helped the NTS by initially contributing £1,000 towards the project on Mull. The Pilgrim Trust and the David Russell family through the Russell Trust are two of the most significant general benefactors of The National Trust for Scotland throughout its existence.

The experiments to regenerate the farming

Above:
The Ardmeanach
peninsula from the
Ross of Mull

Right:
Burg: the Fossil Tree

Far right:
Chrissie McGillivray

economy of Burg were regarded as a possible solution on a much wider scale in Scotland. The Agricultural College brought in two Holt machine bracken-cutters and adjusted the proportion of sheep and cattle to further help in its elimination. Buildings, fences and gates were repaired and a jetty built to facilitate sea transport to and from Burg. Public demonstrations of the techniques used were held, involving local crofters on Mull and Iona, the standard of stock was raised as the land was cleared of bracken and the experiment was hailed a success. Unfortunately, by 1948, shortage of petrol, severe climate, sheep diseases and a small crop of lambs combined with a high wage bill for farm workers, forced the Trust to reconsider. Dr Russell generously paid off the liabilities of £3,000 and the experiment ended by leasing the farm to the manager, Duncan (Burg) McGillivray.

Much later, Duncan's sister Chrissie, who acted as Trust Representative at Burg for many years, received the coveted George Waterston Memorial Award from the NTS in recognition of her service. I recall watching Chrissie barefooted at her spinning wheel outside Burg Cottage, and many visitors have happy memories of her pancake tea after a long expedition to the Fossil Tree. Adventurous souls can now live in relative luxury and glorious isolation in the converted bothy in which Chrissie was born.

BANNOCKBURN

In 1930 the field of Bannockburn, site of the battle in which Robert the Bruce defeated Edward II's forces in 1314, was threatened with obliteration by housing developments. This

Bannockburn: aerial view with Rotunda and flagpole in the background

Bruce's Stone, Galloway

stimulated the formation of a national committee under the presidency of the Earl of Elgin and Kincardine, to raise funds for the battlefield and to maintain the site as open space. The purchase price of £2,500 had still to be raised and the Trust contributed £500 immediately with the promise of the same amount to complete the transaction. The property was not finally handed over to the Trust until 1945.

BRUCE'S STONE

Bruce's Stone in Galloway marks the site of Robert the Bruce's successful encounter with the English forces. The Earl of Mar, in giving Bruce's Stone to the Trust, wisely included a right of access to it from the public road as there was danger of the site being submerged by the proposed hydro-electric scheme. In more recent

years, the view to Clatteringshaws Loch has been maintained and the site interpreted.

CULROSS

Purchase in 1932 of property in the Royal Burgh of Culross in the Kingdom of Fife signalled the start of a process of conservation, which is still continuing, for that 'gem' of Scottish burgh life, with its 17th-century buildings characterised by crow-stepped gables, pantiled roofs and cobbled streets. The first property purchased was the Palace or Colonel's Close. The Earl of Dundonald offered to sell it to the Trust for £700 and the Trust accepted, dependent upon agreement with H M Office of Works that they should accept the guardianship of the property, relieving the Trust of the expenses of repairing and maintaining the rich painted ceilings in the

The Study, Culross

Palace. The purchase used up nearly half of the Trust's first legacy. This arrangement with the government body was the first of several subsequently entered into by the Trust. The advice and support of H M Office of Works was singled out for gratitude as an excellent example of co-operation without overlapping of interests: 'all too common a feature of Scottish institutions'.[1]

The Office was especially helpful in connection with the Trust's expanding interests in Culross, where it was decided to preserve properties adjoining the Palace and other buildings. The Study was purchased together with a total of nine other properties in the vicinity of the Mercat Cross in the Square for the princely sum

of £318, which included a proportion for urgent necessary repairs! The Office of Works was closely involved in preparing plans and estimates for reconstruction of the properties acquired. By 1935 the Trust owned some 20 properties, costing a total of £1,537.16s 2d including purchase, repairs and legal expenses, all aimed at preserving the unique architecture and charm of this fascinating Royal Burgh. Two more properties were later acquired adjacent to the Study at the Mercat Cross.

OTHER EARLY PROJECTS

Sir John Stirling Maxwell alerted the Trust Council the need to save Provan Hall, a medieval house in Glasgow in danger of demolition. It was part of the Prebendary of Barlanark and originally used as the country house of the

[1] Quotations numbered in the text are assigned to their authors in Appendix 5 (page 298).

Provan Hall, Glasgow

owners of Provand's Lordship. A committee was set up to raise funds for its restoration. The Trust agreed to accept ownership when the final sum was realised. Sir John was also personally active in attempting to preserve the old portion of the keep of Stonebyres, Lanarkshire. From an exceptional 34 proposals for acquisition considered by the Executive Committee, six were ultimately acquired by the Trust. They were J M Barrie's Birthplace in Kirriemuir and Hamilton House, Prestonpans, in 1937; the Bachelors' Club, Tarbolton, part of the Roman or Antonine Wall and the Glenfinnan Monument in 1938;

and Abertarff House, Inverness, although not until 1963.

CONTINUING PROGRESS

In 1933, the Trust's Council took the view that 'since its inception rapid development would be dangerous and injudicious. We have therefore pursued a policy of considered caution.'[2] This was not because it was in possession of many properties or that it had rashly expended its meagre funds, but simply in recognition that it needed to gain more experience of running the charity. 'The Trust in Scotland was alert to any

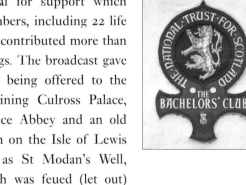

Far left: NTS Seal, designed by Sir D Y Cameron

Left: Trust staff, Neal Sharp and John Dymock, survey the Bachelors' Club, Tarbolton

Below: sign for the Bachelors' Club

offer, whether through government or by private generosity, of land to be administered for the public good.' Membership rose to 13 life members and 83 ordinary members. A new National Trust for Scotland bright red seal, used to authorise legal documents and designed by the King's Limner for Scotland, Sir David Young Cameron RA, was proudly displayed on the first page of Council's 1933 Report.

Appreciation was put on record of the advice freely given in its early years to The National Trust for Scotland by the National Trust. Unlike England, with its extensive enclosed farmland, two-thirds of Scotland was undeveloped land and the countryside was thus already more accessible to the public, without immediate need for Trust ownership.

In 1934, the Chairman, Sir Iain Colquhoun, broadcast a radio appeal for support which resulted in 385 new members, including 22 life members and many who contributed more than the obligatory ten shillings. The broadcast gave rise to further property being offered to the Trust. A building adjoining Culross Palace, glebe ground of Glenluce Abbey and an old Black House at Callanish on the Isle of Lewis were acquired, as well as St Modan's Well, Roseneath, Argyll, which was feued (let out) from the trustees of the late Duke of Argyll. Subjects under consideration were Sailor's Walk, 17th-century buildings in poor repair in Kirkcaldy; a section of the Antonine Wall; Hamilton House in Prestonpans; Souter Johnnie's Cottage, Kirkoswald; the Bachelors' Club, Tarbolton, Ayrshire with Burns associations; and Gladstone's Land in the Lawnmarket,

Balmerino Abbey, Fife

Opposite:
Gladstone's Land, the
Royal Mile, Edinburgh

Edinburgh, all acquired within four years. Such a variety of property illustrates well the range of the Trust's early ownership.

At this early juncture, the question of National Parks and National Forest Reserves in Scotland appears to have been largely in the hands of the APRS. It considered a memorandum produced by a member of the Trust's Council, Professor F G Baily. The matter appears several times in future major deliberations of Trust Committees.

There was optimism about plans discussed with the Royal Scottish Forestry Society for the preservation of remaining areas of the Old Caledonian Forest. Areas in Glen Loy near Fort William and possibilities for further areas of national forest in the Queen's Forest (Glen-

more), Glen Garry and Achnashellach were restored by the Society. Positive steps were taken by the Trust in collaboration with others to provide explanatory notices for these sites to promote the conservation of native pinewoods in Scotland. As a result of widespread publicity of the need for Nature Reserves, a Scottish Nature Reserve Committee was appointed by the Royal Zoological Society of Scotland.

The Trust was constantly seeking new members and requesting existing members to recruit their friends, or to give or bequeath property to the Trust. The Petition for a Royal Charter was refused on technical grounds and the Trust therefore pursued its original intention to apply for a Private Act of Parliament, as the National Trust had successfully done in

England. The Act, finally passed in December 1935, was known as The National Trust for Scotland Order Confirmation Act, 1935. It gave the Trust's constitution and aims a legal status.

The ruins of the Cistercian Abbey of Balmerino in Fife, founded in 1229, were gifted in 1935 to the Trust by Mr Scrymgeour Wedderburn, and admission charges were levied to pay for a part-time caretaker. This property was supervised by a strong local committee and apparently there was no requirement to request guardianship by H M Office of Works.

Stimulated by a conference called by the Cockburn Association in 1935, the Trust took an early interest in old Edinburgh property. A special committee was formed which resulted in the Trust's expertise being recognised and it being named the recipient of historic or characteristic architecture whether by purchase or gift. This interest in the Old Town was given practical impetus by the Trust and, through the generosity of Miss Helen Harrison, it was possible to save from demolition Gladstone's Land, a historic high-tenement building with a ground-floor arcade on the Royal Mile, bought by merchant Thomas Gledstanes in 1617. It was appropriate that the Saltire Society was the first occupant of this building, followed by the APRS.

On the initiative of Sir John Stirling Maxwell, Trust action was timely when it acquired the Caiy Stane, thought to be in danger on account of an adjacent building scheme. This well-known landmark, possibly commemorating an ancient battle, can be found at Fairmilehead, south Edinburgh.

The house in Ecclefechan where Thomas

Carlyle was born, together with his house in Cheyne Row, London, were offered by The Carlyle House Memorial Trust to the National Trust. The NT agreed to accept the house in London and suggested that the Ecclefechan house would more appropriately be held by the NTS. Council accepted the offer together with an endowment fund of £500.

There was now a further strong appeal for more members to promote the interests of the Trust, and local members were appointed to do so as widely as possible. It was also at this time that Sir John Stirling Maxwell made his apposite statement: 'The National Trust for Scotland serves the Nation as a cabinet into which it can put some of its valuable things, where they will be perfectly safe for all time, and where they are open to be seen and enjoyed by everyone',[3] a description as relevant today as it was then.

They were sentiments which caught the imagination, highlighting both The National Trust for Scotland and the National Trust's inalienable powers and the obligation to make properties in their ownership available to the nation. Inalienability is possibly the single most important factor in persuading the owner of heritage property to donate it to either Trust. The special approval of parliament is necessary before the compulsory purchase of any land or buildings which have been declared inalienable. NTS property is thus extremely secure. Coupled with their ability to draw up Conservation Agreements (known as Restrictive Covenants in the south), which variously depend on the terms established with individual owners, and to promote the preservation of land, build-

ings and chattels in any other way that they think fit, the Trusts are a formidable force in the land and are unique amongst kindred organisations. Some land and buildings of lesser significance are held alienably for a variety of reasons.

Membership remained stubbornly low with 47 life and 531 ordinary members but was still described as satisfactory, though this observation was coupled with the now usual exhortation of 'member make member'. Membership at 31 July 1938 exceeded 1,000 for the first time.

GLENCOE

In the summer of 1935, the historic and prime landscape of Glencoe came on the market. It is interesting to speculate whether the Trust's first introduction into this famous glen was planned or accidental! Arthur Russell, Law Agent to the Trust, was asked to travel to Glencoe to purchase Torren, Lot 33, which included the Signal Rock, for a price not exceeding £1,500. The Signal

Rock is believed to be the site of the signal which began the massacre of 13 February 1692. Arthur Russell travelled with his son George (who later succeeded him as Law Agent) and camped near the Clachaig Hotel on the night preceding the sale by Lord Strathcona of the Glencoe Estate, which was to be sold by public roup.

By coincidence they met a Dr Sutherland in the hotel that evening, who told them that if he was successful in his bid to buy Lot 33, Torren, as a residence for his family then The National Trust for Scotland could have the Signal Rock. Happily the bid succeeded and Dr Sutherland duly gave the Signal Rock to the Trust. Arthur Russell was thus in the fortunate position of being able to use the Trust's £1,500 as a bid for the Lot including the Clachaig Hotel (which was subsequently sold by the Trust) and the reputed site of the massacre. He was successful for just £1,350, and was also later able to negotiate for the Trust to buy the Aonach Eagach ridge for an

Opposite:
Thomas Carlyle's
Birthplace, Ecclefechan

Above left:
Glencoe: the Russells'
campsite in 1935

Above right:
Gearr Aonach (left)
and Aonach Dubh
across Glen Coe
Photo: R Matassa/
Scotland in Focus. This
picture also appears on
the front left of jacket

Culloden:
Achnacarry bungalow
during demolition

Opposite top: Hugh
Miller's Cottage, Cromarty

Opposite below:
Hugh Miller's Cottage:
presentation with double
life membership of the
National Trust for
Scotland to the Very
Reverend James Simpson,
Moderator of the Church of
Scotland, and his wife.
Left to right: Trust
Director Douglas Dow,
The Earl and Countess of
Wemyss, and Frieda
Gostwick, Manager of the
property. 1996

additional £750, contributed to by Lord Strathcona and members of the Scottish Mountaineering Club (SMC). Later in 1935, on the initiative of an 'anonymous donor' (only identified after his death as Percy Unna), and further generosity of the Scottish Mountaineering Club, additional land became Trust property, including the mountainous area south of Clachaig and the mountain Bidean nam Bian.

At the end of 1936, another exciting opportunity arose when Dalness Estate, adjacent to Glencoe, came on the market. Percy Unna, now President of the SMC, again approached the Trust and offered £5,000 anonymously towards the purchase price of the property, independently valued at £8,000. Lying between Glen Etive and Glencoe, it comprised 4,168 hectares (10,300 acres) of deer forest and 526 hectares (1,300 acres) of sheep grazing, as well as a mansion house and cottages. It was thought by

the Trust's Executive Committee to be ideal for its magnificent and representative scenery, worthy of being a National Forest Park as well as providing ready access from the cities of the central belt.

A circular sent out by the SMC to members of British mountaineering clubs and individuals yielded an immediate and generous response of £1,500. The Pilgrim Trust again contributed £1,500 towards purchase and the same amount towards upkeep. The total sum raised, £9,500, allowed the Trust to buy Dalness and retain a sum of £1,500 towards endowing the property. The mansion house and grazing ground were sold off to augment the endowment.

CULLODEN 1937–89

At Culloden, scene of the final defeat of Bonnie Prince Charlie's Jacobite army on 16 April 1746, Leanach Cottage, reputed to have been used by the Prince as his headquarters during the battle, was given by Alexander Munro of Leanach in 1937 and King's Stables, the Clan Graves, Memorial Cairn and Cumberland Stone were presented to the Trust by Hector Forbes of Culloden. In 1971, the Trust bought Achnacarry bungalow at Culloden. The unusual purpose was to demolish this inappropriate building on the battlefield site. Most importantly, in 1981, the Trust purchased 44 hectares (108 acres) from the Forestry Commission and was able to fell the trees and restore the 1746 appearance of the site. The Culloden local committee, headed by Sir Donald Cameron of Lochiel, charged with protecting the battlefield, was instrumental in having some unsightly petrol pumps in the vicinity of the Graves of the Clans removed to a less obvious site. The local authority diverted the road which had crossed the middle of the battlefield. The Field of the English was eventually purchased in 1989 with generous help from Ruth Berlin, the Glencoe Foundation and the Countryside Commission for Scotland.

HUGH MILLER'S COTTAGE 1937-95

In 1937, the Trust's willingness to take over a property once a local committee had raised the bulk of the sum required to put it in good repair, was again pursued over Hugh Miller's Cottage in Cromarty, and the Trust contributed the final £100. The local committee issued an appeal under the auspices of the Trust. The cottage was the birthplace of Hugh Miller (1802-56), stonemason, geologist and author of several books as well as editor of *The Witness*. For the first five years of his marriage he lived in Miller House next door to the cottage. In 1973, the house was substantially altered when it was the subject of a Little Houses Improvement Scheme (see Chapter Five). The Trust re-purchased the House in 1995 with a view to creating an interpretative display in 2002, the bicentenary of Miller's birth, thus enabling the birthplace cottage interior to revert to something akin to its original appearance when Miller lived there.

GIFTS AND CONSERVATION AGREEMENTS

In 1937, the Trust made its first connection with Mrs Elizabeth Murray Usher of Cally. At that time she gifted the Murray Isles in Wigtown Bay, off Carrick Point, to the Trust, with the

[19]

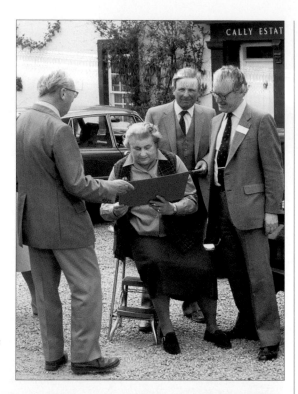

intention that the sale of houses would pay for the upkeep of this popular stretch of the Solway coast. Sadly, this source of funding was not realised and in 1959 the gifts were resumed by Mrs Murray Usher, but returned once more to the Trust's safekeeping in 1991. Mrs Murray Usher, who had inherited her father's estate in 1924 and became the superior of the Burgh of Gatehouse of Fleet, had strong opinions on the appearance of the Galloway countryside and was concerned to ensure that any new developments would blend with their surroundings.

As a life member of the Trust since 1936, she entered into discussions with the law agent, Arthur Russell, to determine how the Trust might become involved in long-term preservation *without* ownership. Sir John Stirling Maxwell, then President of the Trust, had similar ideas and as a result the Trust took legal steps in 1938 to enable it to enter into Restrictive Agreements, now Conservation Agreements. In 1943, Mrs Murray Usher entered into a series of such agreements with the Trust covering 4,452 hectares (11,000 acres) of Galloway coastline and countryside, specifically designed to prevent the construction of any buildings except for agricultural purposes, and then only under the control of the Trust. Venniehill lies just west of the town of Gatehouse of Fleet and is well known for its splendid view over the surrounding countryside. Mrs Murray Usher gave it to the Trust in 1981. The footpath to the top of the hill winds its way through ungrazed pasture with a colourful display of wild flowers which attract an abundance of butterflies.

Earlier however, under the newly confirmed

Order of Parliament of 1938, the outstanding event of 1939 was the first Restrictive Agreement, drawn up by Sir John Stirling Maxwell over 452 hectares (1,118 acres) of his Pollok Estate. This included areas and buildings covered by many leases benefiting organisations with Glasgow affiliations, three golf courses, a cricket ground, and two sets of allotments, as well as Pollok House together with offices and 23 cottages used in connection with the estate and Public Park. The aim of both Sir John and of the Trust was to preserve the rural character of the area. As the Estate was managed by Nether Pollok Ltd, no financial burden fell on the Trust. This pioneering arrangement received the full approval of the Council of the City of Glasgow.

ROCKCLIFFE 1937–90

Land near Rockcliffe on the Solway Firth, including the Mote of Mark and Rough Island, was donated in 1937 by Major John McLellan of Glenluffin in memory of his brother, the late Colonel William McLellan. The Mote of Mark had been the site of archaeological investigation in 1913 which revealed a prehistoric fort formed with a vitrified wall inside an earthen rampart. Brooches and ornaments from the 10th or 11th century AD were recovered and with other relics are now preserved by the National Museums of Scotland. Rough Island, which can only be reached at low tide, was declared a Bird Sanctuary. The Muckle Lands and the Jubilee Path were given in 1965 by Miss Hilda

Above left:
Pollok Estate, Glasgow,
viewed from the roof
of Pollok House

Above right:
Rough Island
near Rockcliffe

*The Linn of
Tummel, near
Killiecrankie,
Perthshire*

Longworth of Rockcliffe village.

The fine house of Auchenvin in Rockcliffe with 3 hectares (7 acres) of land were bequeathed in 1969 by Major J I A McDiarmid. In 1971 and 1990, more coastline near the Merse, Rockcliffe, was added to the Trust's ownership. The Trust's long-term protection has been important to this attractive region, so rich in flora and fauna and popular with visitors. A permanent ranger-naturalist lives in the village and the Rockcliffe advisory group of local residents has been the 'eyes and the ears' of the Trust in the locality for many years.

THE WAR YEARS

In 1939, the Chairman of Council, Sir Iain Colquhoun, wrote the Foreword to Robert Hurd's book *Scotland under Trust*, which told the Trust's story and did much to publicise its work.

The ruined Strome Castle, on a promontory projecting into Loch Carron, was a gift from Mr C W Murray of Couldoran, and the only property acquired in 1939, which was regarded as a year of consolidation. It was necessary, said J S Leadbetter, Acting Chairman of Council, 'to cut our coat according to our cloth'.[4]

The war years of 1939–45 might be

expected to have been characterised by a lack of activity, but this did not prove to be the case. During the war there were undoubtedly steps either forced upon or voluntarily taken by the Trust to reduce expenditure, and the annual reports were thin compared with previous years. Illustrations as well as the detailed list of ordinary members were omitted. Despite such cutbacks, eight new properties were added to the Trust's portfolio during 1944–45. The Secretary and Treasurer, Lieutenant-Colonel E D Stevenson, was called up for war service and Arthur Russell, the Trust Law Agent, became Interim Secretary and Treasurer. The Executive Committee temporarily took over the functions of the Property Committee.

A legacy of £6,000 from Mr Norman Percy Anderson for open space near Port Glasgow was received, but its use was deferred until after the war (see Parklea Farm in Chapter Two).

Amongst important properties gifted in this period were the dramatic 113-metre (370-foot) Falls of Glomach, 'a scenic feature of exceptional value' given by Mrs Douglas of Kilillan and Captain Portman of Inverinate; the Hermitage with its picturesque folly above the River Braan at Dunkeld, given by the Duchess in the name of the Trust's first President (1931–42), the Duke of Atholl, who had very recently died; the small islands of Ceardach and Bucinch in Loch Lomond given by Colonel Spencer of Warmanbie, Dumfries. The outstandingly fine estate of Kintail in Wester Ross, containing the Five Sisters and Beinn Fhada, came as a result of the personal interest of the then anonymous donor, Percy Unna, who put

£7,000 at the disposal of the Trust for the purchase of just such a mountainous property.

The Pilgrim Trust continued generously to make up the Trust's deficit on Dalness, the administration and infrastructure expenses associated with Burg, and the expenses in restoring the Hamilton Dower House.

Most notably, the Falls of Tummel were presented to the Trust by Dr G F Barbour of Bonskeid in 1944. The property includes the Linn which is the convergence of two splendid rivers, the Tummel and the Garry, and attractive woodland rich in flora and fauna. The property was destined to become the subject of the first Public Inquiry involving the Trust when a North of Scotland Hydro Electric Board scheme threatened both rivers. The Trust lost its case but gained much experience for the conduct of future inquiries.

SUMMARY

There is no doubt that the impact made by the Trust on the public before the war was sufficiently strong to leave a lasting impression. In just 14 years since its modest beginnings in 1931, the Trust firmly established itself in Scotland as the country's leading conservation charity. It acquired over 40 properties, was supported by 197 life and 1,295 ordinary members, and was integral in saving some of the finest Scottish landscape and buildings. An inspired and devoted voluntary leadership, ably supported by the permanent staff, was in a strong position to take up new challenges and responsibilities.

CHAPTER TWO
CHALLENGE
AND ACHIEVEMENT
1945–1950

'The Trust must remain independent and flexible,
for therein lies its strength.' [5]

THE EARL OF WEMYSS AND MARCH, 1950

FACING A DILEMMA

In 1945, emerging from the ravages and restrictions imposed by the Second World War, the Trust put a brake on any further development or expansion. Petrol rationing, which was to continue until well after cessation of hostilities, limited the ability of staff to visit Trust properties and building licences restricted the Trust's ability to undertake repairs. The Trust realised that in order to reinforce and strengthen its financial position, it might need to acquire some properties which did not fully conform to its objectives. This could produce much-needed revenue in order to allow it to take responsibility for other properties which could benefit the nation, but which could never be self-supporting.

The Trust publicly admitted to the real dilemma it faced in trying to decide which properties it should select from a bewildering variety. From its earliest days it had been regularly offered historic sites, examples of fine architecture, areas of countryside and a plethora of castles, most of which it had necessarily declined. Through practical experience it recognised not only the benefit of consultation with the Ancient Monuments Department of the Ministry of Works when considering the acquisition of ruinous buildings, but also the danger of conflict of interests. It began to realise that public access and the control of vermin could conflict with the preservation of wild fauna. The Trust could be said to be feeling its way at this time. The Trust was also dipping its toe into the murky waters of contentious public inquiries over the Hydro Board's proposals for the Rivers Tummel and Garry. The Tummel development

Chapter opening picture.
Ben Lawers in winter

would directly impact on the Trust's property at the Linn or Falls of Tummel which had been acquired in 1944 and declared inalienable. While the Trust was careful to establish its authority and purpose as trustee for the nation of such prime countryside, it also made clear that it did not object to hydro-electric development *per se*.

The Trust's objective was to assure the people of Scotland that property, once accepted and declared inalienable, was protected against compulsory acquisition by the government or local authorities. The National Trust was in consultation with the government over the matter and raised it through the Committee on the Acquisition of Land (Authorisation Procedure) Bill. Amendments to the Bill ensured that where objection was made to a Compulsory Purchase Order affecting inalienable land, the case would be subject to special parliamentary procedure, as with local authorities.

THE COUNTRY HOUSE SCHEME

In the first ten years of its existence, NTS had acquired a valuable and interesting variety of property, but no large country houses comparable with those owned by the National Trust in England. The National Trust operated a successful Country House Scheme, based on *Les Demeures Historiques* in France, a private organisation of owners of historic houses, which allowed public access on at least 30 days a year, pooling the entrance fees they charged. The proceeds contributed to the publicising and upkeep of houses which needed help. Most of the houses were *monuments classés* and the organisation acted as an intermediary between the owners and the State.

Increases in taxation and death duties as well as the cost of maintenance encouraged owners in England to take advantage of what must have been an increasingly attractive arrangement. Notable examples included Wightwick Manor, the 17th-century Wallington House, and Cliveden, an Italianate estate perched on cliffs above the Thames in Buckinghamshire.

In 1942, owing to the number of enquiries it was receiving, the Trust in Scotland set up its own Country House Scheme. In essence this allowed the owner to convey to the Trust his or her home, with or without policies or contents, but as a rule with an endowment fund sufficient to ensure its future maintenance. In return the owner, for taxation reasons, might remain in occupation purely under a 'gentleman's agreement' without any legal right. The Trust stipulated two conditions for taking over property. Firstly, it had to be satisfied that the building was worthy of preservation on historical, architectural or other nationally important criteria. Secondly, the public was to be admitted on stated days to parts of the building not occupied by the family.

There were clear benefits to the nation. Large country houses would be preserved which might otherwise become derelict or lose their links with the family. In the process the country would continue to be enriched by the possession of typical features of past life and history, and the public would be able to visit the buildings. In passing property to the Trust during his or her lifetime, the owner benefited not only by being allowed to carry on living there, but also from relief of death duties. Management of the property, if the donor wished, could remain in the hands of agents and solicitors, provided the Trust's responsibilities were duly carried out.

THE HOUSE OF THE BINNS

The pamphlet on the scheme produced by the Trust struck a chord with the Dalyell family at the House of the Binns in West Lothian. Colonel Dalyell's son Tam clearly remembers that, when he was 11, his father and mother asked to talk to him about something very serious. ' "We are thinking of giving the house which, in the normal course of events when we die would belong to you, to an organisation called The National Trust for Scotland" (which in effect for them was Scotland itself). My parents said they could not know what I would do in life, but they were very clear about the importance of the family in Scottish history.'[6]

After a favourable architect's report the Trust's Country House Committee recommended acceptance to the Executive. Tam recalls being sent for by his headmaster at Harecroft Hall, to come to his study, asked to sign a document, and being given his pen to do so. 'I became famous in the school for having been the only boy ever allowed to use the headmaster's fountain pen!'[7]

The extremely generous gift of the house, including valuable and historic contents and over 81 hectares (200 acres) of attractive parkland, was gratefully accepted by the Trust.

'Mrs Dalyell has been actuated by a desire to ensure, so far as she can do so, that the Binns

Right:
The House of the Binns
in springtime

Opposite top:
The House of the
Binns: the Blue Room

Opposite below:
The House of the
Binns: Colonel and Mrs
Dalyell with son Tam
and the Earl of
Wemyss and March
giving and receiving
sasine to signify the
transfer of the property
into the Trust's care

with its traditions and legends may be preserved for future generations and that her son Thomas Dalyell of the Binns may be able to reside there. In this she has been influenced by the pamphlet issued by the Trust entitled *Historic Country Houses in Scotland and their Preservation.*' wrote Sir Ernest Wedderburn, legal adviser to the Dalyells.

Although it was anticipated that the rental derived from the parks and the admission fees would prove sufficient endowment, Colonel Dalyell provided a further £4,000. It was agreed that, owing to staffing and other difficulties attributed to the war, the property would not open until hostilities ceased and then just for one day a week. The House of the Binns was transferred to the Trust by Charter in 1944 but it was not formally handed over by Mrs Eleanor Dalyell until 30 April 1946. The occasion was a colourful one, with the giving and taking of sasine by the two parties. Mrs Dalyell handed over the symbolic Binns earth and stone which

she had cut from the ground, to Lord Wemyss,
acting Chairman of the Trust. The sasine document is at the Binns for visitors to see.

HOUSES OF
NATIONAL IMPORTANCE

The House of the Binns was the first country
house handed over to the Trust, and before long
the Trust was approached concerning 'a number
of interesting proposals, under its Country
House Scheme.

The Trust's Council became steadily more
alarmed throughout the 1940s at the demolition
of old houses in places such as the Old Town of
Edinburgh, Linlithgow and Dunkeld. The principal difficulty was the lack of government
funds to preserve such structures, until the
Chancellor of the Exchequer set up a parliamentary committee on houses of national
importance, which made real progress.

The NTS, through the initiative and financial backing of the 4th Marquess of Bute, had in
1937 begun the important base-line study to list
all such buildings. It was not until after the war
that this enormous task was completed by architect Ian Lindsay. Official listing in Scotland
began in 1945 when the Scottish Office modified
the NTS lists and augmented them to produce
categories A, B and C. Although the Trust was
anxious to enlist government assistance, having
recently persuaded it to provide £20,000 towards
its work, it was only too well aware of losing its
independent role. This point was helpfully taken
up and emphasised by Sir Ernest Gowers, chairman of the parliamentary committee which
published his Report in June 1950.

*Leith Hall,
Huntly, Aberdeenshire:
aerial view*

The Report recommended that Historic Buildings Councils (HBCs) should be set up for England and Wales and for Scotland. Amongst their responsibilities the new Councils would supervise all houses of architectural or historic interest, including their contents. Acknowledging the Trusts' high standing and years of experience, the committee believed it was vital to retain the Trusts' flexibility, freedom of action and the positive relations they could engender with owners and other organisations. It was recognised that in Scotland the system of land tenure was historically and traditionally different from that in England; that there were exceptional problems in finding appropriate uses for houses in sparsely populated parts of the country; and that there were fewer houses with contents of outstanding value.

The Gowers Committee optimistically drew the attention of government to the wealthy state of the National Land Fund (NLF), which at that time stood at over £50m with yearly interest of £900,000. The Fund had been set up by Hugh Dalton, Chancellor of the Exchequer in 1946, to buy land or buildings as a memorial to all those who had given their lives in the Second World War. As has been indicated in the description of some properties in future chapters, the NLF has been a vital source of grant-aid for their purchase and preservation.

The House of the Binns was the first country house to be handed over to the Trust, and before long the Trust was approached concerning several further proposals under its Country House Scheme.

Leith Hall Garden:
the Moon Gate

LEITH HALL

Leith Hall, the Trust's first acquisition in Aberdeenshire, is a charming multi-period house set in pleasantly rolling countryside on the watershed between two rivers, the Don and the Deveron. It was handed over to the Trust in rather tragic circumstances. The laird, Charles Edward Norman Leith-Hay, had died in 1939. His only son, another Charles, joined the army shortly after his father's death and was serving in the Royal Artillery in Northumberland when, at the age of just 21, he was killed in a motorcycle accident. Fully aware of the value of her home and the long and distinguished pedigree of many of the family, Mrs Henrietta Leith-Hay was determined to ensure its future by giving it to the Trust in 1945. She included the Hall, a

Leith Hall:
military display

loan of £7,000 for alterations and improvements, heirlooms and relics of the family, many of whom had pursued a tradition of military service, and a garden and an estate consisting of 947 hectares (234 acres).

Mrs Leith-Hay continued to live in the house and in due course nominated her niece, the Hon Mary O'Neill, Mrs Gascoigne, to succeed her, so ensuring the connection with the family would not be lost. It was not until 1984 that all four wings of the house at first floor level were opened to the public. Previously only the west wing had been accessible. A further attraction for visitors to Leith Hall was added in 1994 when the Trust mounted a new exhibition entitled *For Crown and Country* bringing together the collection of militaria.

The garden, which slopes gently down to the avenue approach to the Hall, has a particularly delightful atmosphere; it was extended and designed much as it is seen today by Henrietta Leith-Hay and her husband. The series of small gardens, each with its own interest, as well as the redesigned rock garden, now attract visitors on a year-round basis. A circular 'moon gate' at the top of the garden leads on to the turnpike road, once the principal route to Aberdeen. Embedded in a tree close to the house is a horseshoe originally placed there by Sebastian Leith-Hay when the tree was a sapling. The horse cast its shoe as Sebastian left Leith Hall for the Crimean War, and he hung the shoe on the tree for luck. The horseshoe indeed brought good fortune as Sebastian returned safely to Leith Hall nearly 40 years later.

CULZEAN

If ever there was case of 'challenge yet achievement', Culzean in the prime example, for it almost sank the Trust's ship for good. As early as June 1944, the Trust had been aware that the Kennedys were having severe difficulties in sustaining the Cassillis and Culzean estates, close to Maybole in Ayrshire. Frances Lady Ailsa, a recent widow, had written to the Trust's Chairman, Sir Iain Colquhoun, asking him to make time to discuss a possible handover.

After the war, Culzean featured in discussions between the National Trusts of England and Scotland and the government over the problems of country houses. The secretary to the Gowers Committee asked the Trust to compile a possible list of such houses in Scotland. The Executive Committee, in June 1949, considered a first draft list including a separate category of houses of the 'highest importance'. Culzean did not appear on the select list. As a natural candidate, however, it became a test case for the Country House Scheme.

In the negotiations which ensued and were ultimately successful, the family was represented by Charles, the 5th Marquess of Ailsa. His elder brother, always known as 'Cassillis', had lived at Newhailes near Musselburgh for most of his life and had already died by this time. A famous photograph, reproduced here, was taken at Culzean when General Eisenhower was first invited there in recognition of his wartime role. The Kennedy family asked the General to accept the tenure of the specially created National Guest Flat in Culzean Castle, an invitation he warmly received.

General and Mrs Eisenhower and their son John during their first post-war visit to Culzean. Left to right: The 5th Marquess of Ailsa, Mrs Eisenhower, John Eisenhower, General Eisenhower, the Earl of Wemyss and March, later President of the NTS, the Marchioness of Ailsa, and the Dowager Marchioness of Ailsa.

There were other important links in this particular story. Teddy Stevenson, Secretary and Treasurer of the Trust, was married to the daughter of the General Officer Commanding Scotland who was a great friend of Brigadier Sir James (Jimmy) Gault. Jimmy, who was General Eisenhower's aide-de-camp from the moment he arrived in Africa, much admired Eisenhower and was subsequently the prime mover, along with Robin Prentice, Deputy Director of the Trust, when it came to establishing the Eisenhower Room in the Castle. In addition, the Kennedy Trustees included Sir John Milne Home, doyen of the Land Agency in Scotland and Head Factor of the Buccleuch Estates (and incidentally a cousin of 'Aunt Wee', wife of the 5th

Marquess of Ailsa), and Lord Kilmaine, nephew of the 3rd Marquess.

When the war was over, Lord Kilmaine became Secretary of the Pilgrim Trust (1945-67) which had supported the NTS from its beginnings in 1931 with grants towards administration costs. It continued to do so, providing grants for specific properties to the extent of nearly £8,000, before it assisted further work at Culzean.

Many preparations were made to welcome General Eisenhower and to make the Castle and grounds ready to receive visitors. The purposes of the Appeal launched in November 1945 included installation of central heating and electricity, and endowment of the National Guest

Culzean Castle and Fountain Court, Ayrshire

Flat, initially given for the use of General Eisenhower during his lifetime and later for other distinguished visitors. The appeal raised £20,000 within six months. The Prime Minister, Clement Attlee, wrote 'on behalf of His Majesty's Government' to thank the Trust for the 'generous action which well expressed the gratitude of Scotland to a great soldier, and a fine friend'.

Culzean would either make or break the Trust, for it was now spending more money than it was accumulating. It was characteristic of General Eisenhower that he insisted that the furnishing and refurbishment of the National Guest Flat should have a lower priority than more urgent matters. The Castle was finally opened on 1 May 1947 and attracted nearly 6,000 visitors in the first year. To the Trust's relief what might have been just a fleeting curiosity turned out to be solid and sustained support, and two years later the visitor numbers had jumped to 40,000. Deficits on the Trust's

Left:
Arthur Russell

Right:
Sir Iain Colquhoun

revenue account, however, still amounted to £13,000 during the years 1948 and 1949. These were chiefly attributable to Culzean.

Hoping to follow the National Trust's success in attracting £75,000 from government, the NTS appealed for £60,000. The response was disappointing – just £20,000 was made available, which was quickly swallowed up by capital expenditure and administration. At a meeting of the Executive in June 1948, the Chairman, Lord Wemyss, drew attention to the serious financial position of the Trust, and the Executive decided that the Law Agent, Arthur Russell, should ask counsel's opinion what would happen if the Trust were unable to carry on and required to be wound up. The consoling answer was that since the Trust had been incorporated by parliament, only parliament could bring it to an end.

Meanwhile Culzean struggled on: the biscuit-making and shipping industries came to its aid with substantial financial support from Sir Alexander McVitie-Grant and Sir James Lithgow respectively. As well as investment in facilities at the property, visitor numbers increased encouragingly and Culzean gradually recovered – by 1950 '... it is even possible that the accounts may break even in the current year and no longer show a deficit'.[8]

REORGANISATION

During this critical time the Trust was also undergoing fundamental changes in its leadership and administration, which were to have great influence on its development for many years to come. Sir Iain Colquhoun retired as Chairman in 1946, having held the post for the first 15 years of the Trust's life. The Trust was

The north side of Charlotte Square, Edinburgh

fortunate to be able to appoint as his successor the Earl of Wemyss and March, for Lord Wemyss already had some experience of being Chairman of the Executive and was a man of equal stature. Lieutenant Colonel Teddy Stevenson had taken over as Secretary from Arthur Russell and, apart from a brief period of war service, had also completed 15 years in this influential post. Jo Grimond, later destined for high political life, became Secretary for just two-and-a-half years, before handing over to the charismatic Jamie Stormonth Darling who was to lead the Trust first as Secretary from 1949 and then, between 1972 and 1983, as Director.

Expansion of Trust activities, as well as its staff, led it to offer to rent No 5 Charlotte Square, Edinburgh, when in December 1948 the Bute family intimated that it was going to lease it. The proprietors, Mountjoy Ltd, were asking a high rent which, together with anticipated running costs, made the Trust look seriously at the alternative of Gladstone's Land, its property in the Royal Mile, at that time leased to the Saltire Society. Wiser counsel prevailed, however, and the Trust entered into a lease for No 5 in July 1949.

The new Chairman and Secretary, in discussing the urgent state of the Trust's finances, agreed: 'The one thing to use is Culzean, and as the Americans say "major" on Culzean as our chief attraction, our flagship. That is the first thing to do to make the Trust popular and Culzean being our greatest burden, will be our greatest asset.' With Lord Wemyss now firmly in the driving seat, new, younger people were appointed to the Executive and enthusiastically took up leading roles on the finance and publicity committees. Eric Ivory and Ian Pitman did much between them to put the Trust on a sounder financial basis and to make it increasingly popular.

In addition to a ruling Council and Executive, administration settled into committees for finance, publicity and nature reserves, as well as 15 local committees to look after individual properties. The Nature Reserves Committee had as its prime objective the conservation of flora and fauna on Trust properties, but it proved too heavily biased towards ornithology. The committee was set up with 13 members, amongst whom were some eminent naturalists including Henry Douglas Home and the Misses Baxter and Rintoul, authorities in that field; Frank Fraser Darling; John Berry; and George Waterston. Perhaps because it increased its membership to an unwieldly 34 in four years, this committee did not survive, although its work to promote the Trust as a body concerned with nature conservation, albeit chiefly birds, was an early contribution to ornithology.

BALMACARA ESTATE, LOCHALSH HOUSE AND GARDEN

Balmacara Estate, which comprises most of this low-lying yet appealing peninsula in Wester Ross, was bequeathed to the Trust in 1946 by Lady Hamilton, widow of Sir Daniel Hamilton. Lochalsh House and Garden were acquired

Balmacara: the Lochalsh peninsula, with the Cuillins of Skye in the background

through National Land Fund procedures in 1954.

Daniel Hamilton began his career in the Glasgow office of the British India Steam Navigation Co, founded by a cousin of his grandparents. In 1881, aged 21, he travelled to Calcutta with the firm and there rose to be senior partner. Although primarily a businessman, Daniel was particularly interested in, and concerned for, the welfare of the rural community. He pioneered the 'co-operative credit' system to help Indian small farmers oppressed by village money-lenders. For such notable services, Sir Daniel received a knighthood in 1906. He returned to England in 1910 and eight years later he and Lady Hamilton bought the

*Duncraig Castle
from across the bay
at Plockton*

Balmacara Estate, including Balmacara House, residing there permanently from about 1925.

At Balmacara, the Hamiltons tried to emulate the successful formula they had established in India. Sir Daniel purchased Duncraig Castle Estate, contiguous with Balmacara and including Achnadarroch Farm. There he established a Rural Reconstruction Training Centre to train young girls in weaving and crafts and young men in crofting and small-scale farming. His motto on the outbuildings of the Castle was 'Fear God, work hard and be honest', the same as above the centre he had created in India.

Achnadarroch Farm proved rather small and had too few facilities for agricultural training, but, as Lady Hamilton's bequest to the Trust included Balmacara House and estate, the

opportunity arose for co-operation between the Education Authority, the North of Scotland College of Agriculture and the Trust. Balmacara House was subsequently used as a residential school of agricultural training for boys aged 14-17, developing a scheme parallel to that offered at Duncraig Castle School. The College withdrew its interest early on but the scheme flourished under the Education Authority, which also leased the buildings of the farm steading and fields at Balmacara and Kirkton.

By 1954-5 the farm scheme had become fully established, having shown a small credit balance in its first year. Balmacara House School closed at the end of the session in 1973, while Duncraig Castle School became Duncraig Castle College for Further Education in 1960, and

continued as such until 1989, when it also closed.

The woodland acquired with Lochalsh House in 1954 was primarily designed to provide shelter from the wind. During the late 1950s, Euan Cox, the well-known Scottish plant collector, became interested in developing a woodland garden at Lochalsh and carried out test plantings of a number of special rhododendrons, many of which flourished. Since 1978, the Trust has been engaged in realising the Woodland Garden, by reducing the rampant naturalised *Rhododendron ponticum*, and developing collections of plants which distinguish this garden from others on the west coast. Here are hardy ferns, fuchsias, hydrangeas, specimen trees and the National Collection of bamboos under the National Council for the Conservation of Plants and Gardens (NCCPG) scheme.

'We have a total commitment to Scotland – the whole of Scotland. In order to fulfil our purpose 100 per cent we must be able to act in concert with official agencies, central and local.' So wrote the Chairman of the Trust, Lord Bute, in the Annual Report for 1971. The property of Balmacara continues to be an excellent example of this principle in practice. Development of the area began with the Education Authority and the Forestry Commission, but in the early 1970s it crystallised round Drumbuie, one of eight townships on the Balmacara Estate. The discovery and exploitation of North Sea oil and gas were clearly recognised by the Trust as being of general benefit to the nation, but its immediate

Above left:
Drumbuie croftlands

Above right:
Lochalsh Woodland Garden

concern was that amenity and community well-being at Balmacara were at risk. Sloping sands with deep water immediately off shore offered ideal conditions, and two companies lost no time in submitting applications to develop 20 hectares (50 acres) at Port Cam opposite the township, to erect production platforms for towing to the oilfields.

Twenty-five crofters managing 15 crofts were united against the proposal, and as guardians of the inalienable land the Trust naturally resisted it, believing it unacceptable to the social structure and the environment. At the Annual General Meeting in 1973 an appeal to the membership for support resulted in agreement to make 'root and branch' objection to the applications, and the Trust published an informative leaflet entitled *Let It Be*. Over 5,000 members responded to the appeal, and £26,000 was raised towards a final expense of £36,000. A train was hired to take members to Drumbuie. The unusually long Public Inquiry proceedings, lasting 46 days, took place mainly in the Balmacara Hotel from November 1973 to May 1974. Neal Sharp, then the Trust's Area Representative, his late wife Dorothy and their family, deserve special mention for the way they accommodated and fed the inquiry team at Lochalsh House – an exemplary demonstration of 'the Trust spirit'.

The decision was favourable to the Trust and other objectors, thus protecting the croft lands of Drumbuie and the coastline to Kyle of Lochalsh and discouraging industrialisation of that part of Ross-shire. Neighbouring Kishorn was developed, to the detriment of its amenity,

although its isolation later led to its demise. It is intriguing to speculate what the attitude of the Trust would have been if all the crofters had been in favour of the development because of compensation and the jobs it would have provided, which were initially positively considered, but later rejected in the light of detailed examination of the issues.

More than 20 years later the Trust's second five-year management plan (1993-8) stressed issues such as nature conservation and crofting, including proposed action to bring into active use the buildings and land at Balmacara Square. Nature conservation has centred on the in-bye croft ground around Drumbuie, where in a system known as run-rig each small croft manages a strip of unfenced ground, restricting sheep and cattle to the common grazings in the summer. This practice allows the colourful local flora to flower and seed as well as attracting native bird life such as the corncrake. There are specially constructed enclosures to encourage this rare species. Such thriving integration of human and natural populations has been hailed an outstanding success, confirmed by Drumbuie winning the 1996 Crofting Township of the Year Award, established by the Scottish Crofters Union and Scottish Natural Heritage.

At Balmacara Square in 1996 the Trust, working closely with the local community, embarked on an ambitious programme costing £1.3m. The farm buildings which lie at the centre of the square have been restored to create accommodation and space for craft workers, a base for the ranger staff and a small interpretation room. Following old field patterns, eight

new crofts have been created by improving drainage and spreading lime, which will discourage rushes and make the in-bye land productive once more. The contract was begun and completed within 2000, arousing much immediate interest in both crafts and crofts, and the picturesque village will hopefully become a focus of interest for local people and visitors. An associated Millennium Forest project will improve footpaths in the surrounding woodland.

THREAVE

Amid the concerns for the Trust's future at this time, the proposition of a fully endowed property in a region of Scotland where it owned just a small island and a stretch of coastline, must have acted as a 'shot in the arm'. The estate of Threave, consisting of 607 hectares (1,500 acres) including Threave House, four let farms and a wildfowl refuge near Castle Douglas in

Kirkcudbrightshire, was offered to the Trust in 1948 by Major Alan Gordon. Major Gordon had bought the estate from his cousin in 1945 for £35,000 and continued to live in the house. While still living, he gave generous funds to be held in trust for the estate. In particular he was anxious that everything possible should be done to safeguard the future of the workmen and the estate. The 'Wages and Pensions Fund' was designed to pay and provide staff pensions, and the 'Repair and Improvement Fund' for general maintenance as required. Major Gordon also expressed a wish for the Trust to build more cottages and create a sanctuary for the bean geese and other bird species which in winter gathered to feed on the lower ground.

The Trust was deeply grateful to Major Gordon for the magnificent gift of Threave House and Estate, but the first report in 1947-8 contrasts interestingly with the way the property

Above left:
Balmacara Square
during development in
2000

Above right:
Balmacara Square
post-development

*Threave House and
Garden in summer*

is now described. The writer appears to be more intrigued by the historical and architectural merit of Threave Castle, already then under the guardianship of the Ministry of Works, and Kelton Mains, one of the four main farms gifted by Major Gordon, than the 'baronial style mansion house'. Even as late as 1990, Threave House was dismissed as being 'of no great architectural merit' in the Trust's guidebook to Threave. Since then, however, Professor David Walker, formerly of Historic Scotland, has rated

the house, designed by Charles George Hood Kinnear, as of exceptional interest. The designs were exhibited in the Royal Scottish Academy in 1872, a measure of the importance Kinnear himself attached to it. Kinnear was a pupil of David Bryce and one of the most important Scottish architects of mid-Victorian times. When the Trust originally accepted the property, the high garden wall seemed to be of more appeal than the garden itself. The policies are not large nor particularly striking, but very

[42]

Threave students in the year 2000. Left to right: Maeve Cunningham, Mairi Gordon, Robert McMeekin, Charley Mallalieu, Laura Kerr and Lauren Driskill

pleasant in spring, covered with daffodils. Mrs Alison Chandler, a relative of Major Alan Gordon, describes it as being 'a perfect walled garden kept up to a high standard, famous for its apples and visited by keen gardeners and garden societies from all over Britain'.[9]

The idea of creating a gardening school at Threave, which had already been discussed with Major Gordon before he died in 1957, made the Trust's case to the government's estate duty office that the *entire* bequest would be required as an endowment. The enterprise evolved as a two-year course for school leavers, master-minded and expertly supervised by Bill Hean for 36 years, and latterly as a one-year course for more mature students with some gardening experience, run by Trevor Jones. The garden now extends well into the attractive parkland, having been transformed through years of devoted work by members of staff and students, and provides an ever-changing scene for visitors.

The picturesque stable block, contemporary

*Threave Countryside
Centre*

with the house, has been converted into a Countryside Centre with Heritage Lottery, Historic Scotland and Scottish Natural Heritage funding. New interpretation of the garden and wider estate including the Wildfowl Refuge has been introduced. Part of the house is still used as accommodation for six residential students and part is now open to visitors seeking a glimpse of how the family lived.

HILL OF TARVIT

The Trust considered itself fortunate when it received from the Trustees of Miss E C Sharp the offer of the former Wemyss Hall in Fife, including policies and an estate, plus Scotstarvit Tower, which had been the home of Sir John Scott, founder of the Chair of Humanities at St Andrews University in 1620. Sir John wrote *The Staggering state of SCOTS Statesmen for 100 years, viz. from 1550 to 1650; by Sir JOHN SCOT of Scotstarvet, Director of the Chancery Now first published from an original manuscript 1754*, an often less than flattering view of the major Scottish political figures of the time. The house had been largely reconstructed in 1905 by Sir Robert Lorimer, and contained beautiful furniture and furnishings. There were also two let farms and some woodland. The house and contents were understood to be in good condition. Both before and after the Executive decision to accept the property, there were concerns about the future use of Hill of Tarvit and many avenues were explored. As Secretary and Treasurer, Jo Grimond consulted no fewer than

Hill of Tarvit Mansionhouse

13 organisations, ranging from eventide homes to the English Speaking Union, and even the Order of St John of Jerusalem.

With a promising and appropriate tenant on the horizon in the form of a St Andrews University research centre for postgraduate students, the Trust's Executive decided to recommend acceptance. Unfortunately, the University withdrew and the Trust had to look elsewhere for a suitable occupant. A possible link with the College of Art in Edinburgh also collapsed. It was not until 1951 that the Marie Curie Memorial Foundation (now Marie Curie Cancer Care), approached the Trust with a view to establishing its first convalescent home for cancer sufferers in the mansion house. It was later agreed that terminally ill patients could be

accommodated and the Foundation continued its good work at Hill of Tarvit until 1977. Then the Trust first opened part of the House to visitors, combining this with letting apartments, and next began to develop the garden and policies. The link continues: the Foundation invited Lord Wemyss to become Chairman of its Committee for Scotland, and he is still involved with its work today. He spoke of the historical background of the property when 50 years of Trust ownership were celebrated in 1999.

PARKLEA FARM

A small but important property, Parklea Farm in Inverclyde demonstrates how the Trust may be left a legacy, but may not immediately be able to meet the requirements of acceptance. In 1939,

Above:
Parklea recreation
area looking north-east
from Broadstone

Opposite top:
Ben Lawers from
south Loch Tay

Opposite below:
Percy Unna right with
pipe: climbing party in
Switzerland, July 1925

Norman Anderson, a butcher in Port Glasgow, left £6,000 to provide for the creation or enlargement of open spaces near Port Glasgow for the benefit of its citizens, 'without imposing any obligation on the Trust for that purpose'.

Enquiries were immediately made, but Port Glasgow, on a narrow congested site with the River Clyde to the north and a steep hillside to the south, appeared to have no suitable space or beauty spot to fulfil the condition of Anderson's bequest. War intervened. The matter was postponed until 1948 when the MacMillans of Finlaystone estate made available Parklea Farm, a thin strip of land between the river and the railway. Lengthy negotiations followed involving the Council, the Scottish Home Department, the Department of Agriculture and the Trust. The effects of war were certainly still being felt.

On 20 April 1948, Jo Grimond, then Trust Secretary, wrote to Harry MacRobert, principal inspiration for the Parklea project, about a possible meeting. 'Although the Trust has very few petrol coupons, I think it would be easier if I did bring my car.' Eventually, using part of Mr Anderson's bequest, the Trust bought the entire farm and feued it to the Burgh Council (now Inverclyde), for recreational use. Culzean's open space benefited from the remainder of the bequest.

Some 20 years later, when plans were being developed for a motorway through Port Glasgow and beyond, the Trust defensively declared the land as inalienable in advance of a public enquiry. Before then, it had seen no need to do so, as it appeared it would only ever be used for recreational purposes. By declaring it inalienable, the Trust obliged the Port Glasgow burgh roads department to accept a more expensive cutting through substantial cliffs to the south of the proposed line. Later, the Scottish Office privately thanked the Trust for making it adopt this alternative.

BEN LAWERS, BEINN GHLAS AND MORENISH

When in July 1950 Arthur Russell, the Trust's lawyer, first received notice of the sale of Ben Lawers and Beinn Ghlas and possibly the Tarmachans, he must have immediately communicated with the 'anonymous' donor Percy Unna, who was on holiday in Austria. Unna's reply was typically brief and to the point: 'Suggest stick to the policy of owning large areas; and this would be a very desirable one.

Suggest buy the lot if the price is reasonable – discount for quantity, and then be a good landlord to the farmers.

'Sheep. If farmers can buy and sell sheep without going broke, Trust can do so as well.

'Ski Club. They will not like not getting a ski-lift but will have to lump it.

'All has my blessing subject to reasonably sound finance, providing the area is a large one. Next it will be a case of getting the Glen Lyon side and owning the whole range, and a good one not too far north. That however is in the future.'[10]

Unna, still anonymously, funded the entire purchase price of £7,500 for Ben Lawers and Beinn Ghlas. The sale was subject to servitude rights of grazing, a condition which was to restrict the Trust's ability to control grazing on the hill for many years to come. Later that year, Unna gave permission to the Scottish Ski Club to introduce a seasonal ski lift from their hut on Beinn Ghlas, provided it was used only to help young people to ski. The Trust decided not to pursue the purchase of Morenish at this time, although it was on the market.

The Trust supported Dr John Berry's proposal that the area should be declared a National Nature Reserve (NNR). This was proposed as much as anything to forestall War Department enquiries regarding requisition of NTS land through the Land Services Agency. Although the NNR was not declared until 1975, the Nature Conservancy (NC) and the Trust agreed NTS would look after estate management, while NC would direct scientific work and pay £300 per annum towards a keeper employed by the Trust.

Ben Lawers: Scottish Conservation Projects team on footpath work, 1989

on Creag an Lochain, the summit nearest to the Lochan na Lairige dam, established that tall herbs and willow scrub can regenerate well if protected from grazing animals. Substantial European grants covering the period 1998-2001 have enabled the Trust to act on a plan to erect three larger exclosures on the east of the Tarmachan range using electric fencing. Their management and the monitoring of the results of such pioneering work at high level, and often in adverse weather conditions, are a considerable achievement.

Difficulties were also experienced in managing footpaths on the reserve. Erosion, developing over successive years, reached crisis point in 1985, when driving rain opened gullies and cut through the vegetation. A combination of fact-finding expeditions to other mountain areas,

persuasive argument, and 85 per cent grant-aid from the CCS enabled the Trust to replace the temporary wooden erosion barriers with stone. A substantial European grant funded a four-year programme in the late 1990s and this expensive programme is continuing, extending to less eroded but nonetheless worrying areas.

SCOTLAND'S GARDENS SCHEME

In the early 1930s, owners of gardens of modest size were often able to employ at least one full-time gardener. Great houses frequently supported larger numbers of experienced gardening staff. Owners and Botanic Gardens sponsored collectors to travel abroad to bring back a host of new species, nurserymen became more ambitious to meet increasing public demand, and literature on gardens was expanding in quantity and quality. Many Scottish gardens were already open to the public, if for no other reward than the pleasure of their owners in seeing them appreciated.

In these auspicious circumstances, Scotland's Gardens Scheme (SGS) came into being in 1931, the same year as NTS was created. The money raised on open days at private gardens went to the Queen's Nursing Institute of Scotland, to help pay pensions for retired nurses and to assist with the training of young nurses. In 1948, however, the National Health Service took over these functions. In view of the Trust's increasing responsibilities for gardens, the Scottish Gardens Committee held its first meeting in October 1950, when the Gardens Scheme agreed that there should be a permanent alliance between the Scheme and the Committee of the Trust.

Two years later the Trust became an equal beneficiary of SGS with the Queen's Nursing Institute of Scotland. This highly successful and happy partnership continues to the present day, and now involves 360 gardens of widely varying size. Entry fees and revenue derived from teas and plant sales go to support Trust gardens, the Gardeners' Royal Benevolent Society and the Royal Gardeners' Orphan Fund, as well as registered charities of the garden owners' choice which can receive up to 40 per cent of the gross takings. From a total in 1950 of nearly £12,000, the gardens opening under the Scheme in 1998 raised the truly magnificent sum of nearly a quarter of a million pounds. Since its inception the Scheme has raised some £4.5 m.

From the start, the Scheme has been organised and enthusiastically supported by a legion of volunteers and it is a marvellous example of what can be achieved in promoting so many worthy causes.

SUMMARY

There was certainly plenty in the five post-war years for the Trust to 'challenge and achieve'. It was integral to the creation in 1953 of the Historic Buildings Council for Scotland, which had an important advisory role on the relative merits of buildings. Throughout its existence the Trust has benefited from the grant-aid and skilled advice made available through the Ministry of Works inspectorate and architects. There was recognition at the highest level that Trust independence and flexibility were invaluable to its purpose. The Country House Scheme encouraged many owners of historic and archi-

Plant sale at Hill of Tarvit

tecturally important houses to enter into agreements with the Trust.

The Trust had taken a huge risk in accepting Culzean, becoming almost bankrupt in the process. Complete faith in the all-essential support being forthcoming, if the project was worthwhile, was to be a dominant characteristic of Jamie Stormonth Darling's 34 years as Secretary and Director. The Trust united with Scotland's Gardens Scheme to form the Scottish Gardens Committee, a unique partnership benefiting both organisations. The Trust added significant property to its ownership and this, together with the reorganisation of its staff, contributed to an increase in membership to 2,400 – more than double that in 1945. The cost of joining was still ten shillings (50p) for ordinary membership and £20 for life membership, remaining so until 1963.

CHAPTER THREE
PARTNERSHIP
AND PROGRESS
1951–1960

'… *not a private society but a*
live and personal force.'[11]

THE EARL OF WEMYSS AND MARCH, 1948

BUILDINGS GREAT AND SMALL

In the 1950s, support for the Trust and its work grew significantly. Increased publicity for a growing portfolio of properties led to a seven fold rise in membership between 1950 and 1960 to 17,500. In that year, the Trust income was more than five times that of 1957. It could be said that the Trust finances were on a more even keel than ever before. This stability was coupled with a developing respect outwith the organisation for the conservation work it was achieving.

The Trust has never been acquisitive. Properties have generally come to it as the result of approaches by generous and far-sighted owners and their families, or initially through their legal advisers. It is during these crucial transitions, often extending into years, that the Secretary of the Trust and the Trust Law Agent become involved in acquisition, whether by gift or through purchase. Fortunately, there has been notable continuity in both roles. Wise legal advice and negotiating skills have been available through the Edinburgh firm of Strathern and Blair, later Anderson Strathern, throughout the Trust's existence. Arthur Russell, one of the founding fathers of the Trust, was its Law Agent until 1950. His son, George, then took over the reins until 1982, when Robin Stimpson was appointed. There was also remarkable continuity in the Trust's auditors, Bryson and Craig, who served from 1931 to 1963. A G Bryson of that firm has the distinction of being the first member of the Trust.

The emphasis in acquisition, apart from the unusually empty years of 1955, 1956 and 1960, was on significant buildings, often with impor-

Chapter opening picture. Brodick Castle and Garden

tant gardens, but also gardens with their special qualities. Several notable islands were acquired, and also smaller houses, from which evolved the Little Houses Improvement Scheme, the principal subject of Chapter Five.

CRATHES CASTLE

The 20th anniversary of the Trust was aptly celebrated in 1951 by the gift, with generous endowment, of Crathes Castle and Estate, including its outstandingly beautiful gardens, from Major General Sir James Burnett of Leys and Lady Sybil Burnett. As well as the fine contents of this Aberdeenshire castle, the endowment comprised extensive woodlands and three farms and three crofts in the Brathens locality near Banchory. The Castle and policies were declared inalienable and the woodlands were dedicated by the Forestry Commission – a management agreement that enabled planting grants to be made to the Trust.

'In name and fame, in reputation and substance, it still remains and may it ever remain, their place, and they remain its lairds.' So said Lord Wemyss at the formal opening of the Castle on 24 May 1952. The Burnett family had had a long association with Deeside, Robert Bruce having granted a portion of the ancient lands of Leys to Alexander Burnard in 1323. Crathes Castle, built between 1533 and 1593, retains the traditional L-shaped keep form and, lacking ground-floor windows, reflects the former requirement for defence. A stairway within leads the visitor to the Tower Room, originally the great Hall of the Castle. The most striking object here is the famous Horn of Leys,

Crathes Castle,
Aberdeenshire

understood to have symbolised the original gift of lands by Bruce to the family.

On the third and fourth floors the rooms known as the 'Stair Chamber', 'Muses', 'Green Lady's' and 'Nine Nobles', are renowned for their painted ceilings, with remnants of an early vibrant colour scheme. The Stair Chamber illustrates an untouched example of the art whilst the ceilings in the other rooms were revealed and 'restored' in the 19th century.

After a great deal of discussion and consideration of options with Historic Scotland and with the Stenhouse Conservation Group, the Trust since the 1960s has chosen to carry out no further conservation work. The ceilings will be allowed to reflect change and decoration from later years, just as valuable in historic terms.

Crathes Castle:
the Horn of Leys

[55]

Fluctuating temperature and humidity, which are harmful to the paintings, are very difficult to control owing to the open nature of the rooms. It is also known that the cement harling on the Castle walls does not allow them to breathe and causes dampness to remain. This problem could only ultimately be solved at great expense by removing the cement mortar and replacing it with more traditional lime mortar.

The first features which strike the visitor on approaching the garden are the well-grown and carefully tended yew hedges and topiary dividing the four gardens at the higher level. On the lower level, formerly the vegetable and fruit garden, are four more gardens, each with a different theme and often with a stunningly colourful array of flowers and shrubs. The woodland surrounding the garden, much of it planted by Sir James, is also well worth exploring.

The great gale of January 1953 blew down much of the estate's woodland, which has subsequently been replanted. In January 1966, a fire destroyed the Queen Anne and late Victorian additions to the Castle. Destructive though the fire was, it gave the Trust and Jamie Burnett the opportunity, advised by the Historic Buildings Council for Scotland and the Royal Fine Art Commission for Scotland, to remove the Queen Anne storey from the original laigh building. Schomberg Scott was the architect. After three-and-a-half years' work, the former two-storey building, probably 17th-century, emerged with a roof in line with the original 'laigh biggins', or low buildings, formerly in association with the main structure, and in better proportion to the dominant medieval building of the Castle. The

Opposite:
Crathes Castle:
the Green Lady's Room

Top:
Crathes Garden:
trimming the yew hedges

Below:
Crathes Castle:
the Earl of Wemyss and
March at the opening
of the newly restored
Queen Anne wing

Falkland Palace:
aerial view

Opposite left:
Major and Mrs
Michael Crichton
Stuart with their
children and HM
Queen Elizabeth
The Queen Mother

Opposite right:
Falkland Palace:
the Queen's Room

Opposite below:
Falkland Palace:
the Chapel Royal

opportunity was also taken to create a new entrance for visitors and accommodation for the property manager, and to build a separate house for the family.

FALKLAND PALACE AND GARDEN

John Slezer's illustration of Falkland Palace with its garden in *Theatrum Scotiae* (1693) emphasises the dominance of this fine Renaissance building. The Palace and the Royal Burgh were the first Conservation Area designated in Scotland (1970). The Royal Burgh has inevitably lost many of its older buildings, most seriously in the Cross Wynd in the 1940s, but enough remain to form an appropriate context for the Palace. It is due to the enlightened attitudes of

the 3rd Marquess of Bute, his grandson Major Michael Crichton Stuart and the Trust itself, that so much of interest does remain here.

The 3rd Marquess of Bute, who acquired the onerous office of Hereditary Constable, Captain and Keeper of the Palace of Falkland in 1887, renovated the rooms of the south range and the gatehouse, and restored the Royal Tennis Court, the second oldest in Britain, the stables and the Cross House. Not wishing to deceive the onlooker, he made a point of distinguishing his new building from the old, by inserting a course of red brick at the junction between them.

Michael Crichton Stuart took up residence in the Palace with his wife and family in 1947.

[58]

He had a number of priorities to achieve, one being the conversion of the Palace Garden, which had provided a source of much-needed vegetables during the war, to a new design by Percy Cane. The garden certainly complements and enhances the building with its sweeping lawns and broad herbaceous borders, trees and shrubs. Cane also incorporated the remains of the early Falkland Castle in his garden design, although the Trust archaeologist has since removed the vegetation to preserve the remaining structure.

The Major's interest in building conservation led him naturally to develop a partnership with the Trust, which he appointed in 1952 as Deputy Keeper. He also provided the contents

wife May, became the Trust's representatives at Inverewe as well as advisers on gardens to the Trust, beginning a tradition of knowledgeable and authoritative staff. The Cowans anticipated that very large numbers of visitors would come to the garden, and replaced the narrow peat paths, metallising the surfaces with material derived from blasting the rock. The garden at Inverewe continues to attract hundreds of thousands of visitors, despite its remote location in the north-west Highlands.

CRUISING

Its acquisition of several west coast gardens, including Inverewe, stimulated the Trust to demonstrate its new horticultural interest to the membership and beyond. Bus tours were popular but some of the most interesting gardens were accessible only by boat. Dr Cowan was the inspiration and mainstay behind the first Gardens Cruise in 1953, on the *Lady Killarney*, a significant feature of which was the occasion of the handover of Inverewe Garden.

The innovation of cruising, with distinguished and well-informed leaders and specialist speakers, was immediately successful. It was commented upon in the 1953 Trust Newsletter No 8 as, 'fairly setting the *Erica cinerea* of the gardening world alight!'

In 1958, the *Meteor,* a ship with capacity for 150 passengers, took the regular Trust Gardens Cruise, continuing the tradition of visiting far-flung gardens but adding islands and castles to the itinerary. In 1961 and 1962, the *Meteor* shared honours with the first big Trust cruise ship *Dunera*, which ran appropriately named

Top:
Dunera cruise: left to right: Donald Erskine, Lord Wemyss and Jamie Stormonth Darling during the excursion to the Torridon Hills

Below:
Black Prince with Rum in the background

adventure cruises for 750 passengers. In 1968, the large 'schools ship' *Uganda* was chartered and began a long association with enthusiastic passengers willing to share dormitory accommodation. In the early 1970s, *Regina Maris* undertook the islands and castles and gardens cruises, whilst *Uganda* sailed the 'adventure' run.

By 1982, *Uganda* had been requisitioned for duties in the Falklands War but the cruise department soon secured a suitable alternative in *Black Prince*, of the Fred Olsen line. This ship is smaller and more expensive than the big ships, but has served the Trust very well indeed over 16

Major James and Mrs Keith in Pitmedden Garden pre-NTS involvement

years, travelling to a wide variety of destinations.

Cruising has undoubtedly been a highly successful NTS initiative, giving great satisfaction to a large number of people. Scottish Heritage USA, the Trust's supporting organisation in North America, actually began to evolve on board an early cruise ship! The 'big ship' cruises in particular introduced the Trust to new people, many of whom became members. Indeed, a number of future members of staff and even of Council were first introduced to the Trust through the enthusiasm and spirit of cruising. Much goodwill towards the Trust has grown out of the comradeship and mutual interest amongst passengers, as well as a useful income for Trust projects.

PITMEDDEN GARDEN

When Major James Keith decided to offer Pitmedden Garden in Aberdeenshire together with £50,000 and two of his farms as endowment, it contained a flourishing market garden filled with flowers, vegetables and fruit trees. As both Major and Mrs Keith sadly died within a few months of the gift being made, the endowment was considerably enhanced through their

Pitmedden Garden:
parterres

wills. The Trust was therefore in the unusual position of having sufficient resources to adopt a bold and creative approach to the restoration of the 17th-century garden.

The inspiration came with the appointment, as consultant, of the retired Principal Inspector of Ancient Monuments, Dr Jimmy Richardson, an architect by training and a former pupil of Sir Robert Lorimer. He researched the early layout and suggested that the Palace of Holyroodhouse in Edinburgh might provide the historical basis for replanting a parterre garden at Pitmedden. Dr Richardson was a pragmatic man: his remedy for the ailing but historically valuable yew trees in the garden was to 'give 'em bullocks' blood!'

It was no mean achievement to transform the market garden to the glory that is the Great Garden of Pitmedden today. George Barron, the gardener, visited comparable gardens at Vaux-le-Vicomte and Versailles in France, as well as Scottish gardens such as Balcaskie and Kinross, to get practical help to assist the interpretation.

Restoration of all the stonework was a priority, followed by raising enough boxwood trees to complete 2.5 km (4 miles) of hedging, designed to contain 40,000 annual plants raised in the glasshouses and frames, and planted out every year. Major Keith's description of Pitmedden as 'a very complete and unaltered example of a late 17th-century garden with raised terrace at one end, unique in north-east Scotland', was at last realised.

The Great Garden is naturally the first feature which attracts the visitor, but Pitmedden also houses a diverse collection of agricultural and domestic implements, the property of the late William Cook, or 'Auld Cookie'. Living nearby at Little Meldrum, Tarves, William was a squirrel of the first order, attending every local farm sale and accumulating a vast collection of items, which filled his house and outbuildings, spilling into his garden. This treasure has gradually developed into the Museum of Farming Life, including a furnished bothy, and an implement shed containing interpretation of the farming year, providing an unusual insight into north-east farming life. Such presentation is appropriate to Pitmedden as Major Keith was an experienced and knowledgeable farmer, significantly adding to improvements in agricultural techniques of his day by writing his scholarly book *Fifty Years of Farming*.

PROVOST ROSS'S HOUSE

'An occasional growl from a trusty watchdog has a salutary effect in keeping people from straying from the right path.' This statement was made in November 1954 by the Rt Hon James Stewart, Secretary of State for Scotland, commenting on the way the Trust had recently opposed some development proposals.

Battles in which the Trust was embroiled, usually in the person of Jamie Stormonth Darling, included those over Provost Ross's

Above left:
The Cook Collection
at Pitmedden

Above right:
Pitmedden:
the farm bothy

Above left:
Provost Ross's House

Above right:
Plewlands House

House, Aberdeen, and Plewlands House, South Queensferry.

Provost Ross's House was in danger of falling down when Aberdeen Town Council asked the Trust to become involved in the restoration of the house and adjacent property, offering the sum of £13,000. The Aberdeen building contractors Alex Hall unexpectedly came to the Trust's rescue by generously offering to conduct the contract on a non-profit-making basis, for a maximum of £13,800. There was help from the Pilgrim Trust, and the British Council took a long lease of the building. So a fine house dating from 1593 was saved; apart from Provost Skene's House (formerly Cumberland's Lodging) and the Wallace Tower, now relocated to Old Aberdeen, it is the only one left in the city built before the 18th century. Provost Ross's House now contains part of the Aberdeen Maritime Museum run by Aberdeen City Council.

PLEWLANDS HOUSE

In order for road alignment to proceed, South Queensferry Town Council proposed that Plewlands House should be demolished. The Trust, recognising the importance of this historic 1643 building, with its key position on a corner of the High Street, entered the lists with a letter to the press by the President, Lord Wemyss. Lord Home, the Minister of State, made a personal visit to the house and a campaign was launched to save the building. Perhaps the most persuasive factor in the discussions was the Pilgrim Trust's decision to give a grant of £4,000, nearly half the costs of restoration. Provost Miller of South Queensferry also offered that his firm would undertake the work on the same basis as Alex Hall for Provost Ross's House.

This 'test case', in which the Trust challenged the original intentions of the local authority, fuelled the idea that if the Trust set up

Left:
George Waterston, centre,
on board ship off Fair Isle

Below:
Fair Isle Bird Observatory

its own housing association, restoration of houses of historic and architectural merit could benefit from favourable grants under the Housing Acts. The association was established in 1953, financed from the Trust's own funds, but eligible for government grants.

FAIR ISLE

Dr George Waterston's name will forever be synonymous with Fair Isle. His enthusiasm was kindled during several visits there, prior to the Second World War. Then, while he was a prisoner-of-war with his friend and Edinburgh lawyer Ian Pitman, his ideas for the organised study of bird migration had time to evolve.

In 1948, Waterston was able to buy the island from Robert Bruce of Sumburgh and establish the Bird Observatory there – one of the earliest in Scotland. This purchase was warmly supported by the friends of Fair Isle, the Nature Conservancy, and once again the Pilgrim Trust.

Above left:
Puffin on Fair Isle

Above right:
Fair Isle Marine
Partnership launch in
1999: left to right:
Professor Ian
Cunningham
(Chairman, NTS),
Fiona Mitchell, and
Lord Sewell, Minister
of Agriculture, the
Environment and
Fisheries at The
Scottish Office

menting that created by more conventional generators, is a true reflection of Fair Isle's firm position in the modern world. Computers, too, have been in use for many years and the island's schoolchildren now delight in their use.

The children here are fortunate that members of the community willingly visit the school to teach special subjects, for example Art, German, Physical Education and – Weather. Yes, Weather! This is a subject of great importance to Fair Isle, and the island is particularly lucky in having an enthusiastic and knowledgeable Meteorological Officer in David Wheeler. With an eye always on the weather David and his wife Jane can predict whether ship or plane will leave either Fair Isle or Lerwick. Nursing services well qualified to deal with most problems are resident on the island, a doctor calls regularly, and Loganair runs an air

ambulance emergency service, using the renovated old war-time air strip.

Accommodation for visitors is provided at the Bird Observatory. Company is congenial, and there is encouragement to take part in the activities of the enterprise and contribute to and learn about the intriguing subject of bird migration. In addition, you can explore the island from botanical, geological, archaeological and other points of view. It is not surprising, therefore, that the success of Fair Isle and its community has been recognised both individually and collectively. In 1955, by the light of a Tilley lamp, three islanders scaled down 61 metres (200ft) to reach an injured colleague, George Stout, who had fallen trying to retrieve a ewe with its lamb. The Islanders evacuated the patient without delay on the *Good Shepherd*. The highest award of the

Fair Isle. the Museum

Carnegie Hero Fund, the bronze medallion, was later given to the 12 Fair Islanders involved in their daring and brave rescue.

In 1969 Stewart Thomson of Shirva was appointed as the NTS Representative on Fair Isle and served for many years, working closely with the Factorial Department and later with the Highland Regional Office of the Trust. Stewart and Annie Thomson were awarded the George Waterston Memorial Award in 1983 for their special contribution beyond the normal call of duty. They have been the mainstays of support both to their island colleagues and to the Trust ever since they set up their home on Fair Isle. The highly coveted Council for Europe Diploma was awarded in 1985 to mark Fair Isle's outstandingly well-balanced social and natural history. In 1995, the island community was nominated Crofting Township of the Year for similar reasons. The Fair Isle Marine Partnership was launched in 1999 to protect the seas around the island, complementing similar action round St Kilda.

Walking over the island it is noticeable and most enjoyable that there is complete freedom to go anywhere without restriction. This may well have developed out of the community's early tolerance of the bird watchers or 'twitchers' who annually invade and are apt to wander where rare birds fly. Thus for ease of access, the boundaries between crofts are abundantly provided with simple wooden stiles over the low fences.

George Waterston would have been delighted to see how his initial involvement, fostered through birds, could develop the harmonious relationship between Bird

Top:
St Kilda puffins

Middle:
St Kilda fieldmouse

Bottom:
St Kilda wren

of the island's remoteness, the Trust's willingness to relinquish custodianship to the NC, or the consequent financial liabilities. There was a growing movement in Scotland in support of the Trust's acceptance of the bequest.

At the Trust's Executive meeting on 13 December 1956, it was decided to recommend to Council that St Kilda should be accepted, subject to an appeal fund being launched. A special meeting convened on 8 January 1957 decided to recommend immediate acceptance.

The scene then shifted to London where on 24 January 1957 Lord Wemyss and Jamie met the head of S.13 which dealt with all matters to do with land at the Air Ministry. As a result of this meeting the Trust won many of its points. The Secretary of State laid down conditions for the Air Ministry that it would:

a) not demolish any houses or walls within the perimeter of the village unless it were necessary to demolish part of the wall to allow the road through

b) construct the road outside the village wall if practicable

c) accept the advice of the Ministry of Works' representative and the NC Warden as to cleits and field walls which could be used as material for the road

d) make a photographic record of any cleits, walls and other archaeological interest which were demolished, and supply copies

e) make accommodation available for the NC's warden

f) contact the Trust, the Ministry of Works and the NC regarding transport arrangements to the island.

The ensuing agreement between the Air Ministry, and later with the army, was crucial in forming the basis of the longer-term co-operation which has characterised their relationship with the Trust. The NC sub-leased certain small areas to the Ministry of Defence, on which they built their constructions. The road and installation of the technical radar equipment was completed by 1959 when the first missiles were fired from the South Uist range. Over the next 40 years, military installations have been added to, upgraded and finally replaced in the early 1990s, but not before the latter proposals were referred to the Secretary of State for Scotland for the final decision.

FLORA AND FAUNA

What makes St Kilda so special? To put it simply, nearly everything. From the maritime grassland heath and peatland to its outstanding birdlife, including the largest colony of gannets in Britain and Europe breeding on Boreray, the largest colony of puffins in Britain, and a field mouse and wren which are peculiar to St Kilda, its flora and fauna are exceptional. As if that were not enough, Soay sheep, the most primitive breed in Europe, are present on the island of Soay, and on Hirta to which they were introduced shortly after the evacuation. The Trust leased the entire archipelago as a National Nature Reserve to the NC, which later became the Nature Conservancy Council and finally Scottish Natural Heritage (SNH). SNH now has the duty to conserve all flora and fauna of the islands. In addition to the unusual terrestrial life, the offshore waters are very clear and support a rich marine flora and fauna. SNH, in declaring St Kilda a Marine Consultation Area, stated that: 'Coupled with the cave and tunnel systems and the oceanic water type, the archipelago is unique in the British Isles and probably in the North Atlantic, and is of the highest conservation importance.' [14]

THE ST KILDA CLUB

Fruitful collaboration with the army has enabled the Trust to organise volunteer work parties every year to carry out a prodigious amount of restoration and maintenance of Hirta's historic and archaeological structures. Six of the 1860 cottages as well as the Church/Schoolroom and Store House have been reconstructed. Numerous black houses, cleits, dykes and drains have also been successfully repaired.

The enthusiasm generated by the original group members under the leadership of Alec Warwick and Allan Aitken led in 1958 to the formation of the St Kilda Club, membership of which is exclusive to those spending at least 24 hours on St Kilda. The Club, probably one of the most successful in the Trust, also raises considerable finance for restoration and conservation on the islands and for young people on the work parties.

DESIGNATIONS

Not surprisingly, the unrivalled nature of the St Kilda archipelago has led to a large number of designations highlighting its superlative natural qualities. The importance of the islands' geology was recognised by their inclusion as a Geological Review Site in 1984. The cultural and historical

past of St Kilda is partly recognised by the Scheduled Monument status conferred in 1986 to extensive areas of Hirta. Surprisingly, even the World Heritage Site (WHS) status does not refer to the cultural and archaeological history for which St Kilda is justifiably famous although it is hoped that this will soon be rectified. UNESCO (United Nations Educational, Scientific and Cultural Organisation) has invited the Trust to extend its application to recognise the cultural significance of the islands, enabling St Kilda to attain this additional recognition by 2003. In January 2001, the Trust launched its first website (www.kilda.org.uk), dedicated to these emotive islands, providing a definitive resource for information about the past, present and future of St Kilda.

OIL DEVELOPMENTS

Since St Kilda's nomination as a natural WHS in 1986, additional blocks or tranches of the seas, as near as 70 km (114 miles) to the islands, have been targeted for oil exploration. In October 1999, the Trust's Council supported a policy to stress publicly the urgent need to provide a zone of protection permanently free of tanker traffic in the vicinity of St Kilda. It called for any oil produced in the area to be transported by pipeline, and an overall plan to be developed, providing permanent tugs and clean-up equipment close to the area. The use of deep-water reefs to the west of the islands by deep-water cetaceans was recognised as worthy of special protection. Finally, lest the spotlight for marine conservation should fall only on St Kilda, the Trust called for inclusion of its other islands such as Fair Isle and Canna, at risk from oil exploration and tanker traffic, in any protection measures being adopted.

St Kilda's marine environment is protected as a Special Area of Conservation (SAC) under the European Union Habitats Directive, but this incorporates only the reefs and submerged caves up to 1 km (1½ miles) offshore. The WHS designation currently extends only to Low Water Mean Spring level although it is the intention to increase the designation to the SAC boundary. There is currently no protection for the sea birds in the waters around St Kilda.

THE ANGUS FOLK MUSEUM

Jean, Lady Maitland's marvellous collection of artefacts reflecting life in the County of Angus always merited appreciation by a larger public, but simply lacked adequate accommodation. Through generous donation by the Earl of Strathmore and Kinghorne, six 18th-century cottages near Glamis Castle became available, but required £6,000 to put them into serviceable order. The enthusiasm particularly of the Lord Lieutenant of Angus, Lord Airlie, and the Lord Provost and Town Clerk, an anonymous local donation, and grants once more from the Pilgrim and Russell Trusts of £1,500 and £750 respectively, finally achieved the required endowment. The collection, later known as the Angus Folk Museum, opened to visitors in 1958.

This fascinating collection, arranged by theme throughout the charming stone-roofed cottages, has been added to through the years. A horse-drawn hearse, originating from Glenisla, appropriately occupies the building which once

housed the hearse for the parish of Glamis. When Strathmore Estates, with continuing generosity, allowed a cartshed and granary to be resited from Knockenny to house larger implements and equipment, a new exhibition entitled *Life on the Land* was introduced. The Trust is indeed fortunate to have this, one of the finest folk collections in Scotland, in its ownership.

Opposite top: St Kilda: work-party, June 1983

Opposite below: St Kilda: Boreray and Stac an Armin

Above: Angus Folk Museum: Madge's Room

BRODICK CASTLE

From the ferry to Brodick on a clear day the castle stands out as a prominent red sandstone building set amidst mixed deciduous woodland with more regimented plantations behind, and dominated by the highest mountain on Arran, Goatfell, rising to 874 metres (2,867 feet). The impressive castle was principally a Hamilton house – it was the 10th Duke of Hamilton who commissioned its enlargement and transformation from 1844. James Gillespie Graham was responsible for the handsome additions to the west of the original building, including the lavish neo-Jacobean remodelling of the interiors, in which A W N Pugin was involved.

As early as November 1953, NTS had been approached with a preliminary offer of Brodick Castle and its gardens. The Trust's Architectural and Artistic Advisory Committee and Scottish Gardens Committee visited the estate and reported very favourably on it. The Historic Buildings Council (HBC) visited in 1954 and thought every effort should be made to save this property.

Executive and Council confirmed the Trust's enthusiastic interest and it was suggested to the Arran Trustees that the woodlands and hills, including Goatfell, might also be considered. The Pilgrim Trust was approached for £10,000. The Mountainous Country Fund, set up in 1943 by Percy Unna to endow mountainous property belonging to the Trust and to acquire further similar ground, agreed to contribute £4,000, if Goatfell could be acquired for £8,000. Lady Jean Fforde, daughter of the Duke and Duchess of Montrose, made a dona-

tion of Goatfell, in exchange for £10,000 which she credited to the Brodick fund.

In 1957, the Duchess of Montrose died. Jamie Stormonth Darling was successful in persuading Committee members that the Trust should acquire Brodick subject to a public appeal for £10,000. His proposal to set up a 'caretaker government' during the summer of 1958 while the appeal was running was also accepted. Wide-ranging and carefully targeted publicity generated over 70,000 visitors to the property that season. A successful appeal chaired by Lord Bilsland, and confirmation that all other sources of funding would be realised, led to the Trust finally accepting responsibility for Brodick Castle, its contents, the gardens and woodlands

Opposite:
Aerial view of Brodick Castle, Goatfell and the Country Park

Above:
Brodick Castle and Garden

Brodick Castle:
the Drawing Room

and Goatfell, on 23 October 1958, five years after it was first considered.

The Trust entered into an agreement in 1980 with Cunninghame District Council, later North Ayrshire Council, to establish Brodick Country Park. A permanent ranger was appointed a year later and a purpose-built reception centre was created, with a countryside centre constructed in 1992. As well as managing the Park the ranger service is also closely involved with restoration of the footpath system on Goatfell, supervising and working with groups of Trust Conservation Volunteers and Thistle Camps, as well as other groups of willing helpers.

SUMMARY

The 1950s were outstanding for a number of reasons, perhaps most importantly through the charismatic leadership of the Chairman, Lord Wemyss, and the Secretary and Treasurer, Jamie Stormonth Darling, and their single-minded, active and personal promotion of the Trust and its aims. Amidst the acceptance of responsibility for major and not-so-major property into the Trust's care, they spread interest in and knowledge of the Trust far and wide. Lord Wemyss, as well as wisely presiding over the Trust Council and Executive Committee, represented the Trust's interests in the House of Lords and visited Canada and the United States to develop new support there. Jamie's grasp of the Trust's ramifications as well as its finances and his singular belief that if the project was right then the money would be found, contributed greatly to his successful leadership of the growing charity. These two gifted visionaries made the Trust a 'live and personal force'.

The increasing panoply of properties coupled with improved publicity and enthusiastic communication through Trust publications must have contributed to the large increase in membership. Numbers of visitors to properties such as Culzean, Inverewe and Culloden positively rocketed, confirming the interest of members and the public at large. The death in 1956 of the Trust's enormously-respected President, Sir John Stirling Maxwell, had been a blow, but a President's Fund was set up in his memory to advance Trust support in Glasgow and the south-west.

The Historic Buildings Council for Scotland (HBCS) began to wield important influence in the conservation of the best of Scotland's buildings, and the Trust continued to benefit from its advice and financial support. The success of HBCS persuaded the Trust and others that the time was right for an equivalent body to be set up in Scotland, for the countryside. Yet it did not support the Scottish Council for National Parks continuing its operations, despite the existence of a similar body in England, because it believed

Brodick Country Park: pond-dipping

that the situation in the two countries was quite different.

Possibly due to the high profile of the Trust's activity in the conservation of Scottish vernacular architecture, and prominent public figures taking a personal role in promoting the modern use of historic buildings, several local groups established their own preservation societies. The Trust had been active in the field since the earliest years of its existence, for example in Culross and Dunkeld, and in 1957 its now famous Little Houses Improvement Scheme was born.

CHAPTER FOUR
CONSERVATION AND ACCESS
1961–1970

'a force of nature'

'an idealist in a self-propelled fighting vehicle' [15]

THE EARL OF WEMYSS AND MARCH, 1969
QUOTING FROM TWO CONTEMPORARIES
OF JAMIE STORMONTH DARLING

SETTING THE SCENE

The established purposes of The National Trust for Scotland are both to preserve the heritage of the country, in whatever form, and to make it available for access by and enjoyment of the public. In order to achieve these goals, parliament has given the Trust power to own and manage land and buildings, flora and fauna, and to declare any heritable property inalienable, thus giving the Trust the right to invoke special parliamentary proceedings in the event of any attempt at compulsory acquisition. It also gave powers to the Trust to enter into Restrictive Agreements (later called Conservation Agreements) with owners of land, whereby they and their successors could not carry out any improvements or alterations without prior Trust approval (see Gifts and Conservation Agreements, page 19).

In the earlier decades, little, if any, serious thought was given to the ultimate effect of combining an aim to conserve with an aim to encourage access. The young Trust was more concerned with positively attracting visitors, certainly to enjoy the experience, and importantly to increase public support for its work.

In the 1940s and 1950s, the conservation sights of the Trust were firmly focused on the built heritage. Such countryside and mountain properties as were owned had complete freedom of access, all sporting rights having been waived in favour of the public. This was the case not only over Trust land but also that of the Forestry Commission and some Nature Conservancy property. The fact that the law of trespass was far less proscriptive in Scotland than in England

also caused the Trust to recommend in 1956 that the Scottish Council for National Parks was unnecessary and should be wound up. By 1958, however, the Trust's Executive felt that Scotland was falling behind in legislation for its countryside and that there should be a new government body set up as a constructive alternative to a National Parks body, comparable with the Historic Buildings Councils (HBCs), to co-ordinate management and access.

THE COUNTRYSIDE IN FOCUS

At the Trust's 1960 AGM the Chairman, Lord Wemyss, made a speech which marks the beginning of a period during which the Trust made strenuous efforts to have a 'Council for Places of Natural Beauty' set up in Scotland. The trigger for this action was a proposal by the North of Scotland Hydro Electric Board to flood Glen Nevis in order to generate electricity. Lord Wemyss' speech attacked the procedure governing development in Scotland, but he also offered practical advice:

'The democratic process works most happily where persons and communities take charge of their own affairs and when an issue arises, observe a few simple rules. The first of these is to go immediately to the promoters of the scheme and to one's elected representatives in local government and in parliament. In every case the primary object ought to be to get discussions started before proposals and personal attitudes have become hard-set.'

The 1960 AGM endorsed his three recommendations: that there should be an immediate government review of the whole question before

Chapter opening picture: The Painting, September, of Kellie Castle and Garden, by John Henry Lorimer © Richard Green Gallery, London

Opposite: Glen Nevis and the Steall Waterfall

any further schemes were proceeded with by the Board and economic factors should be considered; to assist in preservation a 'Council for Places of Natural Beauty' should be established to help preserve the landscape; that the Secretary of State's attention should be drawn to the imperative need to ensure that responsible objectors be heard at the expense of the developer, and that the onus to prove the case should lie with the developer.

At the unanimous request of Trust members at the AGM on 30 April 1960, Lord Wemyss wrote to the Secretary of State urging the need for high-level consultations on the subject of hydro-electric schemes in relation to conservation of natural beauty in the North of Scotland. This representation had no effect and the Glen Nevis scheme was published on 7 October 1960. Meetings were held with the Board and with the Secretary of State's Amenity Committee. The Trust, however, was not satisfied that sufficient weight was being given to amenity considerations. Consequently, an objection was lodged by the Trust, seeking more broadly-based talks than purely the question of the Nevis proposals.

Although Glen Nevis was not in Trust ownership, naturally, the Trust had made it quite clear that it was in sympathy with the objects of the Board. After all, it already owned property inhabited by local communities which were, or would be, benefiting from improved power supplies. Largely as a result of the Trust's lobbying and persistence, the Hydro Board finally dropped its plans for Glen Nevis.

The Nevis experience alerted the Trust to

the need for a definitive and impartial landscape survey. W H Murray, already well-known and respected as a mountaineer and author, was the natural choice to assist in the process of assessment. He was appointed as the Trust's Mountainous Country Properties Adviser and commissioned to write his enlightened survey *Highland Landscape*, which was published in 1962.

This slim volume proved to be a classic. It was written in the unpretentious but knowledgeable language of one who had taken the trouble to survey and appreciate each of 52 areas in Scotland 'from the lowest ground to the highest mountain tops'. From his knowledge based on 30 years' experience, he selected 21 out of the 52 as outstanding. The Trust has come to own or be closely associated with more than half of these magnificent landscapes.

Murray provided a description and critical commentary on cases where damage had already occurred, for example the 'approach to Loch Maree from the east down Glen Docherty marred by both pylons and telegraph poles, and the new road up Cairngorm into Coire Cas forming an ugly scar on what was till recently the fairest scene on the north side of the range'.[16] Although he recognised the benefits brought to the country by both the Hydro Board and the Forestry Commission, he reinforced the urgent need for 'a body created for the purpose to be granted powers by government so that checks and safeguards might be instituted'. He predicted that 'the Scottish people will lose by neglect what remains of their heritage' if such a step were not taken.

The stimulus for further action came with HRH the Duke of Edinburgh's initiative in establishing the *Countryside in 1970* conferences of 1963, 1965 and 1970. The first conference had stemmed from the establishment of the Council for Nature in 1958 which led to National Nature Week in 1963 of which the conference was a natural sequel. The question posed was 'What sort of countryside do we want to see in 1970?'[17] In the Duke's own words, 'It is simply intended to help you [the 200 delegates] to see more clearly what needs to be done.'[18]

In the conservation working party set up by the 1963 conference, Jamie Stormonth Darling supported the view that knowledgeable reception, while fully extending facilities for open-air recreation, would be the only hope of safeguarding the countryside. He also took the opportunity of continuing to promote the idea of a Countryside Council similar to the HBC and financed by a grant of £20m from the National Land Fund. The Trust participants resolved that the initiatives taken in London should not falter, and proceeded to organise Scotland's own Countryside Conference in April 1964 in Inverness. The general theme was 'the urgent need to reconcile and co-ordinate policy for economic growth and for the conservation of landscape, with particular reference to areas of outstanding natural beauty to which even larger numbers of visitors will be attracted in the future, and the services which are required in such localities to provide for seemly reception, information and guidance'.

The second *Countryside in 1970* conference was scheduled for November 1965. Professor

Robert Grieve was asked to chair the deliberations of study group 9, charged with co-ordinating the Scottish contribution to the conference. The group discussed two main themes: preservation of landscape and buildings and information on the countryside. The Trust was also asked to submit a paper on whether an overall countryside authority was necessary and, if so, what form it should take.

Study group 9's conclusion was: 'Unanimous support for a central body, possibly with the title the 'Countryside Commission for Scotland', to have adequate powers and finance to ensure conservation in the countryside and the promotion of development of recreational resources within it.'[19] The recommendation was adopted by the 1965 conference and went forward to be considered by government.

The Trust had supported the view that the main provisions of the National Parks and Access to Countryside Act 1949 should not apply to Scotland. By the 1960s, the Trust's view had not changed. Instead it recommended increased expenditure by local authorities to enable them to exercise appropriate powers. Its insistence that different needs necessitated different legislation was realised by the announcement of Willie Ross, then Secretary of State for Scotland, that the government proposed to set up separate Countryside Commissions for Scotland and for England.

The Countryside (Scotland) Bill (1967) followed and the new Countryside Commission for Scotland (CCS) was determined that the process of establishing Country Parks in Scotland, provided for in the Act, should not be delayed. There was an urgent need to improve facilities in the countryside for the increasing number of townspeople seeking recreation. Particularly attractive to the Trust was the CCS offer of 75 per cent grant-aid plus support of ranger services, which became integral to the Trust's mountain and other countryside properties. Debates in the 1960s culminated in European Conservation Year 1970, when the theme in Scotland was 'Information and Interpretation in the Scottish Countryside'. As its contribution the Trust, with other agencies, published a calendar of events and played a prominent role in more than 100 of these events taking place all over Scotland.

The need for a training course for rangers had become evident. Generous grants in 1971 from the MacRobert Trusts made it possible for the Trust to organise a course in consultation with other organisations. The course was repeated in 1972 and 1973 before the CCS took over responsibility for training rangers, nationally.

THE COUNTRY PARK AT CULZEAN

The Trust was quick to grasp the opportunity of obtaining financial and other support for Culzean, itself then the subject of a national appeal for £100,000. This had been stimulated by urgent conservation requirements, not least because the HBC had been insistent that the Trust raise sufficient investment capital to ensure a regular income for Culzean. This project was associated with the buildings, principally the Castle which was to be excluded from the formula worked out for the Country Park, and remains wholly the responsibility of the Trust.

Left:

The Marquess of Bute with William Paterson, Convener of Ayrshire County Council, at the anniversary of the Home Farm, now the Park Centre at Culzean

Right:

Left to right: Elisabeth Beazley, Consultant Architect for Culzean Country Park, with Eric Robson, Head of Gardens, and Murdo Mackay, Head Forester at Culzean, in Happy Valley

In order to promote a proposal to have Culzean declared as Scotland's first Country Park, it was necessary to obtain the support of Ayr County Council, Kilmarnock and Ayr Town Councils and the Countryside Commission for Scotland. With the Trust Secretary's energetic enthusiasm, agreement was quickly reached and the declaration made the following year. David Watson, the Trust's Representative in the south-west, who had carefully steered Culzean through difficult times, was about to retire. This vacancy and the requirement to staff the new Country Park led to the appointment of John Mott as Representative and myself as Principal and Chief Ranger (thus satisfying the criteria for grant-aid from CCS). I admit to having been a little doubtful about transferring from 1,300 feet up in the Pennines and seeing 1,600 students a year through a Field Centre, to a castle and estate on the west coast of Scotland visited by over 100,000 people! My interview was held in the grand round drawing-room of the Castle and so began an 'affair of the heart' with Scotland's leading conservation organisation which has lasted over 30 years.

Jamie Stormonth Darling had the knack of

bringing together the right people at the right time, and this was especially true of Culzean. The first was Elisabeth Beazley, who originally wrote to Jamie asking for information on the Trust's work in providing picnic places and information centres and in the anti-litter campaign. From this initial contact grew a constructive relationship which benefited the Trust in a great many spheres. Elisabeth went on to become the Consultant Architect for Culzean Country Park.

Geoffrey Jarvis, the Glasgow-based architect, was another good choice. His special sympathy for the use and treatment of old buildings was particularly appropriate for the Robert Adam Home Farm, set around a wide courtyard and perched, as Culzean Castle, on top of the sea cliff.

The CCS, already fully supportive of the Trust's initiative in establishing Scotland's first Country Park, was also generous in offering a grant of £177,000 towards the conversion of the Home Farm to a Countryside Centre, which was opened in 1973. Agreement with three local authorities provided the remaining 25 per cent of the Park's operating costs. Without their contin-

Culzean: aerial view of the Park Centre

uing and heartfelt support through periods of local government reorganisation, the Country Park at Culzean would have failed.

GREY MARE'S TAIL

The Grey Mare's Tail, a spectacular 61-metre (200-ft) waterfall near Moffat, came to the Trust's attention through Sandy Harrison, founding member and Treasurer of the Association for the Preservation of Rural Scotland, set up in 1926. His forthright advice to the Trust was to buy it. Appropriately, the Trust's Mountainous Country Fund, of which Sandy was a Trustee, was used in 1962 to acquire over 809 hectares (2,000 acres) of the unplantable land of Polmoodie Farm (White Coomb, Loch Skeen and the Grey Mare's Tail)

from the Forestry Commission. The cost of purchase was £3,500. Jamie Stormonth Darling had already earmarked an area at the foot of the Tail next to the road for an information point and car park.

The principal interests of the Tail property are its Arctic flora and geological and geomorphological characteristics. Together with the 52 hectares (128 acres) of Dob's Linn acquired in 1972 with CCS grant-aid, the Nature Conservancy designated these areas as a Site of Special Scientific Interest (SSSI). Upland bird species include the peregrine falcon, ring ouzel and wheatear. The peregrine was the target for bird and egg thieves in earlier years but a systematic voluntary wardening scheme, co-ordinated through the Trust's ranger service, has

ensured more consistent breeding success. This has been reliable enough to enable the Trust to upgrade interpretation of the peregrines in 1999. The Trust is at pains to inform visitors of the inherent dangers at this property where there have been fatalities, exhorting walkers to be properly shod, keep to paths and avoid treacherously steep grass slopes.

Since Loch Skeen was thought to be a likely environment in which the vendace, extinct since the 1960s, had formerly lived, a project to reintroduce the fish was undertaken by SNH in cooperation with the Trust. Dob's Linn, the nearby gorge, became well-known following the investigations of amateur geologist Charles Lapworth (1842-1920). He used the fossilised marine animals he found, called graptolites, as a key to understanding the adjacent sequence of rocks.

TORRIDON

'Glen Torridon, its loch, and the mountains on either side, exhibit more of mountain beauty than any other district of Scotland including Skye.'

So wrote Bill Murray in *Highland Landscape*, published in 1962, and anyone who has visited this magical area will agree. Torridon first came to the Trust's attention that same year. At the time ownership of Liathach and Beinn Alligin, together with a substantial access agreement along the corridors with Beinn Eighe, were being actively negotiated with Lord Lovelace, the owner of the Torridon Estate, the Nature Conservancy and the Scottish Youth Hostels Association. They 'agreed that there

Opposite:
Grey Mare's Tail:
the waterfall

Above left:
Grey Mare's Tail:
cloudberry

Above right:
Grey Mare's Tail:
Loch Skeen

Left:
The village of Inveralligin
and Beinn Alligin

ought to be a man of the mountains on the spot'. This was later to be realised by the appointment of Lea MacNally, the Trust's first ranger, who remained at Torridon for 21 years. Jamie Stormonth Darling confessed to a passing doubt: 'that by going to such pains to make maps, stick in arrows, and open a way over the hills, we would be departing from Mr Unna's Principles. I reckon in this case it would be wholly justified because it seems to be the only solution (the number of accidents is increasing and in Torridon is becoming serious), and we are now beset with a problem far beyond anything envisaged ten years ago.'[20] The scheme discussed with the ailing Lord Lovelace and his nephew was to allow visitors to Torridon 'to enjoy these glorious hills while doing the minimum damage to themselves, sport and stock, and to consider how roadside development might be organised and co-ordinated with the question of zoned access to the hills.'[21]

Negotiations appeared to be going well but, sadly, a serious illness for Lady Lovelace put the project on hold until February 1965. When Lord Lovelace died, his trustees offered the whole estate to the Trust except the mansion house and its associated fishing and shooting rights. Ben Damph was retained by the family.

This offer was immediately taken up by Jamie Stormonth Darling and his team who put a 'consortium' idea to the Lovelace solicitor. At the same time enquiries were being made as to whether Torridon Estate could be offered to the Inland Revenue towards estate duty.

Eventually, the original estate of 5,706 hectares (14,100 acres) was accepted by the

Commissioners of Inland Revenue in part satisfaction of death duties. In May 1967, the property was transferred to the Trust through the National Land Fund procedures. The Mountainous Country Trust, originally formed by agreement between Percy Unna and Arthur Russell in 1950, handed over all its funds, a sum of £17,000, to form the Unna Mountainous Country Fund for Wester Ross and, in particular, Torridon.

Alongside the negotiations over the Estate, Jamie's initiative to form a consortium of benefactors developed with others into a desire to formulate a plan for an area beyond Torridon. In January 1967, he enlisted the help of the recently formed Highlands and Islands Development Board by bringing into the discussion its experienced Chairman, Professor (later Sir) Robert Grieve, and Ross and Cromarty County Council. The Board was asked to initiate a study of the area with a view to formulating a national plan for appropriate development for recreation and public enjoyment, consistent with the welfare of the local community. Although the report was useful in bringing all interested parties together, its recommendations could not receive general agreement and the Trust proceeded to develop its own visitor facilities at Torridon and Inverewe.

The long thin estate of Alligin Shuas, small in comparison with the rest of Torridon, begins in the hill ground west of Beinn Alligin and drops to the shore of the loch following the Abhainn Alligin gorge on its eastern side. Initial enquiries of the owner, the Gordon family who resided in Canada, were disappointing. It was a marvellous surprise for the Trust, which was expecting to buy the land, when, late in 1967, the sons of Sir Charles Blair Gordon and Lady Gordon gave it in memory of their parents. The

Opposite:
Torridon: red deer
hinds in winter

Above left:
Torridon :
yellow saxifrage

Above right:
Torridon: Liathach
from Loch Clair

gift was warmly accepted by the Trust in January 1968. Since then the geological and botanical richness of the Abhainn Alligin gorge have been highlighted as nationally important, adding further significance to this property.

The realisation of the existing current master plan for Torridon will extend well into the millennium. It includes a bold initiative to restore the native tree cover and to increase the diversity of wildlife at the head of Loch Torridon. Present woodlands will be targeted for regeneration and planting, using native species including locally derived seed from Shieldaig. In the vicinity of the Mains Farm and the Trust's Visitor Centre, existing plantations will be enlarged, former grazing will be transformed into species-rich grassland, and freshwater will also be managed for wildlife.

The wider community will be encouraged to take part in this enterprise and come to appreciate why the Torridon area appears as it does. On the north edge of Loch Torridon runs a most attractive footpath which it is planned to repair and connect to the new road linking the scattered houses of Inveralligin with Rechullin.

CRAIGIEVAR CASTLE

One of the most renowned 17th-century castles in Scotland, and one of the Midmar group of castles (Crathes, Midmar, Castle Fraser and Fyvie), Craigievar is a tower house of outstanding architectural achievement. The ancient family of Mortimer began the construction of the Castle, but financial difficulties forced a sale to William Forbes of Menie (1566-1627). Known as 'Danzig Willie' because he made his fortune by trading in the Baltic, William could afford to employ skilled masons and craftsmen to create both a comfortable and defensible home. Sadly, he died just a year after the Castle was completed. The family name later changed to Forbes Sempill.

This tall and slim tower house with its turreted and corbelled upper floors stands proudly in wooded parkland amongst beautiful rolling Aberdeenshire hills. It must have been hard for the family whose forebears had lived in the area since the 15th century to decide they could no longer do so. In the early 1960s, the health of Lord Sempill was giving cause for concern and clearly the future must have looked very uncertain. During a visit in the summer of 1962, Lady Sempill made her first direct approach to the Trust on the future of the estate. Matters moved comparatively rapidly, beginning with a number of meetings between the trustees, who included both Lord and Lady Sempill, and, naturally, their lawyer with representatives of NTS.

Lord Cawdor, Chairman of the HBCS, was kept fully informed of developments. The future of Craigievar would depend on the recommendation given by the Council to the Ministry of Public Buildings, and Works. Lord Cawdor expressed the keenest interest in the future of the property, and once the trustees had obtained Senior Counsel's opinion that they had the power to sell any of the estate, the way was clear for real negotiations to begin.

Sir Edward Muir, Permanent Secretary to the Ministry, had alternative proposals. His view was that as there was no immediate threat, the

Opposite:
Craigievar Castle

Craigievar Castle:
the Blue Room

future could be secured simply by means of Building and Tree Preservation Orders. The Trust could see serious risks in this course, as it provided no security for the contents, which could be dispersed in the event of the death of Lord Sempill. It would have had to be proved that the Castle was not being properly cared for, before the Order could be implemented, and there was no guarantee that an Order would keep it in repair. In the spring of 1963, the Trust decided to proceed with a plan of its own to secure the future of the property. The plan ensured that, after the death of Lord Sempill,

his widow might continue to live in the Castle during her lifetime. Such a plan followed the established policy that whenever possible a family should continue to be associated with property acquired by the Trust.

Thanks to the generosity of individuals and of the Pilgrim and Russell Trusts among others, substantial headway was made to achieve both purchase and endowment funds by the end of 1963. Financial help was provided by the Aberdeenshire building firm of William Tawse, and Lawson's of Dyce. Tawse was already note-worthy for its support of the Trust at Inverewe and contributions towards the Trust's General Funds. Support from Lawson's the butchers was also welcome: while there was still some doubt about that contribution, Jamie had commented 'the sausages haven't joined up in any way yet!'

On the strength of the response to the appeal for benefactors, the Trust was able to make a formal offer to the trustees in mid-September 1963. The Castle and policies of Craigievar, together with a majority of its contents, were purchased for £12,000. A Conservation Agreement was made over an area round the property and an additional 24 hectares (60 acres) of farmland was later acquired to safeguard the vicinity of the Castle.

A public announcement on the acquisition of Craigievar, the combination of a series of intensive negotiations, was made on 9 October 1963. Lord and Lady Sempill must have been both pleased and relieved that their initial generosity had played such a vital role in the successful outcome.

More recently, the increasing popularity of this distinctive castle led the Trust, in the interests of preserving the delicate fabric of the interiors, to control the visitor numbers.

KELLIE CASTLE

Kellie Castle is first mentioned in a charter of David I in 1150. It has had a number of distinguished owners, including the Oliphant and Erskine families, and finally the Lorimers who rented the property from the 1870s until they bought it in 1957–8. Shortly before they did so, the Earl of Mar and Kellie tried to interest both the Trust and the Historic Buildings Council for

Scotland in buying the property. The NTS was prepared to accept Kellie on the condition that it was fully repaired, as both the Castle and Kellie Cottage needed modernising. Consultation with the Lorimers determined that the family should remain as tenants on at least a ten-year lease and that the Earl of Mar and Kellie should be asked to contribute £5,000 towards a reserve fund.

The NTS believed that it would not be possible for Kellie to be both readily accessible to the public and lived in as a family home and, as the latter was of prime importance, proposed that opening should be limited to one day a

Kellie Castle and Garden

Kellie Castle:
the Great Hall

week, with the possibility of the garden opening more frequently.

It soon became apparent that the Earl of Mar and Kellie could not contribute to any form of endowment. The plan for HBCS to acquire Kellie and later transfer it to Trust ownership, became an impossibility as the conditions on which the Trust would accept the transfer could not be fulfilled. Hew Lorimer and his wife,

Mary, then considered buying the property, which they achieved in 1957–8.

The negotiations over Kellie were in abeyance until 1969 when Mrs Gore-Browne Henderson of Malleny gave the Trust £50,000 towards its purchase. Support was expressed in many quarters for the Trust to take responsibility for this great house and its attractive Lorimer contents. It seems inappropriate to call it a castle for within it, and its walled organic garden, there is a warmth and a gentle character which is immediately appealing.

Again the Pilgrim and Russell Trusts rallied to the NTS cause. The Marquess of Bute, Chairman of the Trust, sent out a personal appeal. It was not going to be easy to raise the necessary funds until the Treasury, advised by the HBCS of the case for Kellie, suddenly made a most welcome offer of £15,000 towards purchase of the Castle, grounds and cottage, and £10,000 towards the contents.

With such a positive move on the part of government and a substantial donation by an anonymous benefactor, the Trust was finally able to raise the remaining finance. On 16 November 1970 the announcement was made that Kellie Castle, its contents and wonderful garden, had been acquired by the Trust for the nation.

BRANKLYN

Branklyn Garden on the Dundee road out of Perth is a gem, perhaps best known as a garden specialising in rhododendrons, alpines, herbaceous and peat-garden plants, but also for its rather special autumn colour. It was lovingly created by John Renton and his wife to become 'the finest two acres of private garden in the country' and was bequeathed by them to the Trust in 1967.

The three-month deadline on acceptance was fortunately extended to enable the Trust to raise funds to manage and endow the garden. The Rentons had generously bequeathed £10,000 in their will and the garden had been left in good condition. The garden was known

Branklyn Garden: visitors by the pool

and appreciated by the City of Perth, so the first move was to enlist the City's practical help through Provost David Thompson. This was forthcoming in the offer of staff to assist in running the garden, as well as co-operation over car parking. The Trust, however, still had to raise some £30,000 to ensure its future success. The appeal was partially successful largely due to £5,000 given by Mrs Gore-Browne Henderson of Malleny and the same amount offered by Sir

George Taylor, Director of Kew, in the expectancy that he might become Trust Representative and tenant of Branklyn, providing his expert advice in return for a minimal rent. Ultimately, this arrangement could not be agreed and, instead, the recently formed CCS occupied the house at Branklyn for three years before moving to its new headquarters at Battleby, just north of Perth.

MALLENY

Malleny House and Garden lie close to the village of Balerno on the south-west side of Edinburgh, a location that was part of the reason why the Gore-Browne Hendersons left the property to the Trust. They were concerned that expansion of Balerno might impinge on Malleny, and in particular on the garden, to which they and previous owners had devoted much attention.

The present building is thought to have been built by Sir James Murray of Kilbaberton, prior to 1647. In 1656, the first of six families of Scotts of Malleny bought the estate and it is believed that early generations of this family planted 12 yew trees. Between 1910 and 1939 the house was tenanted by Sir Thomas Gibson Carmichael and then by Mr K M Gourlay, both devoted gardeners who considerably influenced the garden. The property was acquired by Commander and Mrs Gore-Browne Henderson in 1961. They completely replanted the garden, increasing the collection of shrub roses, other shrubs and ground cover. The 'Twelve Apostle' yew trees, which must have become too dominant, as well as being most difficult and time-

consuming to prune, were reduced to four and renamed 'the Four Evangelists'. The present Head Gardener, Philip Deacon, uses a hydraulic lift to prune the trees and, along with other Trust gardens, makes good use of the yew cuttings by sending them for the extraction of a substance used in the manufacture of Taxol, a drug successfully used in fighting breast, ovarian and lung cancer.

Commander Gore-Browne Henderson died in 1968 leaving his half-share in Malleny to the Trust. In the same year, his wife gifted the remaining share of the property, along with £40,000 as endowment and the residue of the estate. She remained as tenant until 1970 when she moved into Edinburgh.

CHARLOTTE SQUARE, EDINBURGH

In 1791, Robert Adam produced his designs for the Square, in which the concept of terrace houses designed as a palace-fronted block achieved a perfection which has never been surpassed. Adam died in the following year and it was left to the City of Edinburgh to insist that the private owners or speculators who built the houses conformed to the original plan.

As tenant of 5 Charlotte Square since 1949, the Trust was first notified in 1958 that Nos 5-8 had been offered by the Commissioners of Inland Revenue in satisfaction of death duty, payable in connection with the death of the 5th Marquess of Bute two years earlier. The Treasury, however, were prepared to negotiate

Opposite:
Malleny: the 'Four Evangelist' yew trees

Above:
Charlotte Square: an aerial view

Charlotte Square:
Bute House

tion were both accepted. The properties were transferred to the Trust's care in 1966.

At the same time, the City Council Engineer proposed the construction of a three storey car park for 300 cars in the overgrown garden areas belonging to the private owners on the north side of the Square. Rather than allowing individuals to propose alternatives that would possibly detract from the area's appearance and be more costly to achieve, the Trust took the initiative to co-ordinate responses. This encouraged agreement of all the proprietors to use the upper part of the site for a shared ground-level car park, landscaping the remainder.

The Trust developed No 7 as The Georgian House, a property open to visitors, to complement its Old Town property of Gladstone's Land. Subsequently, the top floor of No 7, converted with a substantial grant from the Baird Trust in celebration of its centenary, became the official residence for the Moderator of the General Assembly of the Church of Scotland, until they bought a house of their own in 1999. No 6 became the official residence of the Secretary of State for Scotland and was known as Bute House. It is now the official residence of the First Minister (see pages 251-2) for acquisition of Nos 26-31 Charlotte Square).

POLLOK ESTATE

As soon as the legislation provided for it in 1939, Sir John Stirling Maxwell established the first Restrictive Agreement (later known as Conservation Agreements) with the Trust over Pollok. This extraordinary foresight was the basis of the Trust's long and fruitful involve-

acceptance of just Nos 5 and 6 with a view to transfer to the Trust. After not a little negotiation as well as timely intervention by a number of helpful individuals, No 7 was added, providing the Trust declared all three properties inalienable and devoted any surplus on them to the opening of No 6 to the public. The 6th Marquess of Bute intervened in 1965, stating that he was only prepared to transfer his properties if No 6 was preserved as a home. He also made the suggestion that No 7 might be used as the space for an exhibition centre and to display the work of the Trust. His condition and sugges-

Pollok House across the golf course

ment with this splendid stretch of countryside lying within the City of Glasgow. The Conservation Agreement had the necessary correcting influence to ensure management was sympathetic to the long-term aims of the family and the Trust. The City intended to make a Compulsory Purchase Order for the estate as housing land which, in the 1960s, would certainly have succeeded. Sir John's daughter, Mrs Anne Maxwell Macdonald, knew the value of the Agreement and in 1966 offered the House, as well as the estate, to the Trust. Only pre-emption in favour of the City and the enor-

mous running costs, with lack of endowment, precluded the Trust from accepting such an extremely generous offer. Thus the City became the owners but with future development restricted by the Conservation Agreement.

In 1971, the plan for the new motorway link for the City – the Ayr motorway – which was to connect the Renfrew motorway (M8) to the south-west, was going to impinge on the western boundary of Pollok's parkland and woodland. The Trust commissioned the eminent landscape consultant, Miss (later Dame) Sylvia Crowe to advise on the effects of this development, and

Above:
Glenfinnan:
the Visitor Centre
under construction 1966

Opposite:
Bannockburn: statue of
King Robert the Bruce

increasing awareness of the opportunity to inter-pret the history of properties and their signifi-cance to a wider audience, and to demonstrate how an agricultural estate worked   an early attempt to bridge the gap between town and country was an important aim.

'History on the Spot' pilot schemes, financed initially from interest-free loans from Scottish banks, were launched at essential road-side halts and picnic sites in Glencoe, on the A87, on the Trust's estate at Kintail and on the A837 Gairloch-Braemore road in Wester Ross, close to Inverewe. As early as 1956, it was decided that illustrative plans and maps should be displayed at the Trust's historic sites, 'intelli-gence centres and collecting points for litter', evolving in succeeding years into more sophisti-cated interpretation, such as weather-proofed illustrated panels, maps and guidebooks. The first information centre, grafted on to an existing tearoom at Glenfinnan, heralded the beginnings of a successful policy for site interpretation. The NTS was therefore in the vanguard of organisa-tions that recognised the importance of commu-nicating the significance of a place to its visitors through the most appropriate media.

Derived from the 'History on the Spot' enterprise, interpretation was conceived for the crucially important property of Bannockburn, site of the Scots' great victory in 1314 and confirmation of their nationhood. Sir Robert Matthew, Chair of Architecture at Edinburgh University, was commissioned to design the overall scheme. The battle plan, knowledge of which had only recently been updated with new evidence brought forward by General Sir Philip

entered into discussions with the Corporation. Sir Robert Russell, whose logical approach and acute knowledge of planning were invaluable, undertook to investigate the plans. Modifications of the original proposals made it possible, ultimately, for the Trust to accept the alignment of the route and the interchanges.

The Trust was a member of the working party established to examine the plans for the motorway. It made available the findings of Sylvia Crowe, who had emphasised the sensitiv-ities of the route in such a location, and although her suggestion of a bridge was accepted by both the Trust and the Highway Authority, it was not adopted at the design stage.

SPREADING THE WORD

In parallel with consideration of conservation and access to the countryside and acquisition of important   properties,   this   period   saw   an

Christison, was housed within an open-air rotunda encircling the flagstaff and known as the borestone site. The rotunda was orientated to focus the visitor's attention on views – to the south, along what was probably the line of King Edward II's advance, and to the north, towards his military objective of Stirling Castle – and to conceal the nearby housing estate. It was agreed that the sculptor Pilkington Jackson would design an equestrian statue representing Robert the Bruce. This was the first of several improvement schemes for the property, and was one of the most ambitious of its kind in Scotland in the 20th century. The Heritage Centre was opened by HM The Queen in 1964.

Knowing the value of staff experienced in the fields of journalism and press relations, Jamie Stormonth Darling recruited Robin Prentice, an accomplished and knowledgeable feature writer for the *Glasgow Herald*, who in turn recommended Phil Sked, another conscientious and talented newspaper man. Shortly afterwards, the *Herald* lost a further member of its team when Findlay McQuarrie's long and varied career with the Trust began as Publicity Assistant in 1961. Artist-designer Jim Nicholson was appointed and began to develop in-house illustration and design for guidebooks, the Year Book and, initially, small-scale exhibits.

Robin provided an experienced link with the Scottish Office. It was said of him 'you could mistake him for the Minister at meetings, he spoke with so much knowledge and quiet authority'. As Jamie's deputy from 1960 to 1973 he was able to write effective policy for the Trust and was well versed in political, social,

Grandfather Mountain Highland Games, North Carolina, USA: Parade of Tartans

Melville had left Scotland as a young man of humble circumstances, but through his enterprising shoe business, had made a great deal of money in America. With very strong Scottish ties, he firmly believed that Scots and Americans would benefit from experiencing each other's countries.

During a visit to Brodick Castle, Jamie Stormonth Darling and Robin Prentice met Ian Robinson and his American wife, Anne, who were on holiday in the Castle flat. Anne often visited her mother, who lived just outside New York, where Wallace (Wally) Jones practised and was Ward Melville's tax lawyer. Ian agreed to meet Wally and together they conjured up an organisation which they called Scottish American Heritage Inc (SAH Inc), later renamed Scottish Heritage USA Inc (SHUSA).

In the early days, SHUSA financially supported the Eisenhower Flat in Culzean Castle. Robin Prentice was an important Trust link with SHUSA, especially in connection with the room devoted to Eisenhower memorabilia. And true to Ward Melville's ambition, it is in the exchange of people across the Atlantic that SHUSA has excelled. A gardener exchange between the Trust Garden at Threave and Longwood Gardens, Pennsylvania, continues to the present day. Many Trust staff have benefited from an exchange between the United States National Park Service and the Trust's ranger service, and from arrangements involving other disciplines.

Most recently, the Trust has established an office and a member of staff in Cambridge, Massachusetts, and it is to be hoped that

and architectural areas of Trust interest. He was responsible for many of the increasing family of Trust publications, editing the first *Guide to The National Trust for Scotland* and providing the text for the very informative booklet *Conserve and Provide*. He was integral to the establishment of the Trust across the Atlantic when Scottish American Heritage Inc was set up. Phil and Findlay had the all-important personal contact with the press and made sure that news of the activities and influence of the Trust were spread countrywide.

The Scottish-American link was forged through a friendship which developed between a Scottish and an American family on an early Trust cruise. Sir Angus Cunninghame-Graham was a Vice-President of the Trust, while Ward

through the recently established North American Foundation he will rekindle the enthusiasm and the support which was originally generated. To quote from Anne Robinson: 'We all believed it was personal connections which made it so successful.'[22]

This view of the importance of putting a face to a public Trust was shared by SHUSA who financed the annual visit of Donald and Catherine Erskine to the Grandfather Mountain Highland Games in North Carolina for 15 years, where they represented both organisations. They also acted throughout those years as the liaison between the two bodies, reporting to SHUSA on the Trust's major activities and on the projects which SHUSA had elected to support.

The Trust became a founder member of Europa Nostra when Margaret Mackay, the Trust's London representative, attended the inaugural meeting in Paris in November 1963. The purpose of Europa Nostra is to promote the protection of Europe's architectural and national heritage, and to encourage high standards of modern architecture and of town and country planning. The Trust maintains close links with Europa Nostra, from which it has received several prestigious awards for its work to conserve and manage the Scottish heritage. Lester Borley, after his period as Director for the Trust, became Secretary General for Europa Nostra and remains a Council member to this day.

SUMMARY

By the end of the 1960s, the Trust had made significant advances. The addition of experi-enced staff to promote its aims and activities had had a positive effect on membership, which more than doubled, to over 34,000. Site interpretation of an expanding number of properties was adding to public knowledge and appreciation of the organisation, providing additional incentive for visitors to support the Trust. It now had a prominent and an appropriate location for its Head Office in No 5 Charlotte Square, Edinburgh, as well as control of Nos 6 and 7.

Successful pressure on government to create a Countryside Commission for Scotland in parallel with the Historic Buildings Council for Scotland had added to the Trust's national status. These two statutory bodies, for which the Trust could justifiably claim to have been the catalyst, would continue to be most important sources of advice and future grant-aid for the Trust's work.

The contacts made with North America through SHUSA and with Europe through Europa Nostra were integrated into the Trust's operations and proved to be no small contribution in promoting productive and harmonious relations with people in both continents.

With ownership and practical management experience of more than 100 properties, most of which were held inalienably for the benefit of the nation, the Trust could look forward to the 1970s with confidence.

CHAPTER FIVE

THE LITTLE HOUSES
1931–2001

'… *all old houses have an architectural*
value and there must be few which have
not equally a domestic value.'

THE FOURTH MARQUESS OF BUTE, 1936

FIRST INITIATIVES

The Trust's international reputation for the preservation of the vernacular architecture of Scotland is very much bound up with the earliest years of its development. The Trust had been formed during a severe depression. Housing had been neglected and was sub-standard: overcrowding and poor health were in evidence. Both central and local government realised they had to clear away run-down dwellings to make way for new housing. The Scottish Board of Health, later the Department of Health, took the initiative and local authorities were obliged to upgrade the building stock in their areas. Age and historic provenance were ignored in the drive to build anew. The Housing (Scotland) Act of 1935 had unwittingly put a premium on the destruction of the country's 16th- and 18th-century domestic architecture.

Following the purchase in 1932 of Culross Palace in Fife, the Trust's attention was largely centred, for several years thereafter, on the buildings surrounding it. Virtually all these smaller 16th- and 17th-century buildings in the heart of the Royal Burgh merited preservation and most were in poor condition. As the Trust's financial position was, to say the least, fragile, it was fortunate that two anonymous donors came forward with £150 to buy the Study at the Mercat Cross, the third most important building in the community after the Palace and the Town House. Nine further properties were also purchased.

In securing a long-term future for the Palace and the Study, and in particular for their superb painted ceilings, the Trust had immediately sought the expert help of HM Office of Works.

This government agency relieved the Trust of future liabilities, at least for the Palace, by accepting it into guardianship. (In 1991 the Trust assumed management responsibility for the Palace which was reopened in 1994 following major restoration and new presentation.) The urgent need to protect the unusually complete historical core of the Burgh had been officially recognised. By the end of 1935, the Trust had increased its ownership of property in Culross to 20 buildings.

That same year, the Trust was either offered or had brought to its notice over 30 properties of historic and architectural value spread across the country. In Edinburgh, Gladstone's Land in the Lawnmarket had been condemned, but in 1934 thanks to the generosity of a life member, Miss Helen Harrison, the Trust was able to accept the

property. Plans for improved living accommodation within it were approved and implemented. The Saltire Society became the Trust's first tenants, using the lower floors of the building as their headquarters. In 1933, the Trust had obtained an option to purchase Sailor's Walk, the old custom house in Kirkcaldy. This was in danger of demolition when, with Trust co-operation, a local committee was established to purchase and restore the property. Restoration was completed in 1935 and the building was handed on to the Trust.

The 4th Marquess of Bute was personally involved in acquiring and preserving Acheson House in the Canongate, Edinburgh and Lamb's House in Leith, both in danger of demolition. Lamb's House had been drawn to Lord Bute's attention in 1937 through a paragraph in *The*

Chapter opening picture.
The Gyles: Pittenweem
harbour

Opposite top:
Culross Palace 1971

Opposite below:
Culross Palace 1990

Above left:
Sailor's Walk,
Kirkcaldy

Above right:
Lamb's House

Aberdeen and Menstrie Castle near Alloa, at all of which restoration was carried out.

The Trust's AGM in 1953 was devoted to the theme of Scotland's domestic architecture, and the Earl of Dundee, Chairman of the recently formed Historic Buildings Council for Scotland (HBCS), spoke appreciatively of the work the Trust was doing. He also appealed for the Scottish people to turn away from the 'patchwork of grey ghastliness amid Victorian ribbon development of mud-coloured monotony', and recommended that the Trust, working in co-operation with a local authority, should 'equally help one another, not only in restoring and preserving a little of our past loveliness but in creating a new loveliness for the future of Scotland'.[23]

Established in 1953, the Trust's Architectural and Artistic Advisory Panel took responsibility for the architectural treatment of all buildings in Trust ownership. The same year the Trust was to embark upon a village restoration scheme that was to be a model of its kind.

To prevent the heart of old Dunkeld suffering the slow indignity of crumbling decay, the Trust accepted the gift in 1953 from Atholl Estates of two groups of 'little houses', on the north side of Cathedral Street and the Cross, or market place, of the town, considered to be one of the finest and best preserved of its kind in Scotland. The north side of Cathedral Street had been rebuilt in the early 18th century following destruction in 1689 during the Battle of Dunkeld. The Trust's project received one of the first grants from the HBCS. Trust members, together with the Atholl Amenity Trust, also contributed to the imaginative scheme.

Perthshire County Council handed over 6 Cathedral Street, which was beyond all hope of restoration. The Trust decided to reconstruct the entire house, incorporating the arched pend that gives access to the garden at the rear of the building. The Council also undertook to restore the south side of Cathedral Street. Reharling and light colour-washing of both the Trust's and the Council's restored buildings, as well as those in private ownership, helped to revive the design and feeling of unity in the community. The charming approach to Dunkeld Cathedral, set amongst fine trees by the fast-flowing River Tay, makes an outstanding contribution to the local scene. In 1958, the redevelopment and construction work by both the Council and the Trust won an award from the Saltire Society and later from the Scottish Civic Trust.

Where work could be classified as 'improvement' the Trust was able to claim a grant from the Department of Health under the Housing Act of 1950. grant-aid for the restoration of smaller historic properties at that date consisted of an additional subsidy under the Housing Acts. Some special grants were available to the Trust and whenever practical it took advantage of these. The purchase of even a small proportion of buildings in danger and which ought to be preserved was still out of the question and in the immediate post-war years securing adequate building licences made the Trust's task more difficult.

The incentive for a change of attitude was given fresh impetus at the 1954 AGM when the Secretary of State for Scotland, James Stewart, was invited to give the address. He thought that the people of Scotland were at last awakening to a new appreciation of their heritage. Lord Wemyss stressed that the Trust was in favour of encouraging local authorities, who until that point had had little motivation from government, to work with other bodies and individuals to help to preserve the best of Scotland's architecture.

In reviewing the state of building preservation in Scotland, the Trust's own Newsletter for 1956 was full of the subject of the state of building preservation in Scotland. Furthermore, 18 years after Lord Bute and Ian Lindsay's first endeavours, full-time staff had finally been engaged to categorise buildings of architectural or historic interest in Scotland.

Along with HBCS the Trust pushed for action to complete the survey and make the lists statutory rather than provisional, so that they had legal effect. Progress was hindered by the need to register the listing in the Sasines, which was slow and time-consuming work, a situation not revised until 1968. So long as the lists remained non-statutory the planning authorities were not obliged to heed them – although the majority did. Implementation of the first statutory lists by category did not take place until 1957. The official definition of the categories in 1948 may be abridged as follows:

A – Buildings of national importance;

B – Buildings of lesser importance the alteration or destruction of which should be allowed only in the face of more important public interest;

C – Buildings of lesser importance which may be good examples of their period, or in some cases, group well together with others in A and B.

Opposite top:
Cathedral Street,
Dunkeld: pre-restoration

Opposite below:
Cathedral Street,
Dunkeld: post-restoration

Preservation work in Culross continued on the Sandhaven between the Palace and the Town House. The Trust's aim was to have these derelict houses lived in once more and so return life to the Royal Burgh. The four tenancies that were created helped to provide much improved domestic accommodation. The exteriors were given new harling and a colour-wash to protect the old stone from the ravages of salt-laden winds.

To publicise the benefits of restoring old buildings, and following the example of the building industry, the Trust began the annual practice of opening a show house to demonstrate how attractive such old houses could be to live in. The first was in Dunkeld, at No 3 Cathedral Street. It attracted over 10,000 people, and in the process a few hundred of them signed up as new members of the Trust.

Nos 44-48 High Street, Linlithgow, had been given to the Trust in 1938, but it was not until 1958 that these 16th- and 17th-century properties were restored. Here one four-apartment and one five-apartment house were created and, as in Culross and Dunkeld, the allocation of tenancies was arranged in close consultation with the local authority. On Fair Isle, where restoration of the islanders' homes was a high priority for the Trust, and on St Kilda, where under skilled leadership the volunteers' enthusiastic repair and improvement of the houses on Village Street on the island of Hirta was carried out, the Trust made a major contribution to the preservation of vernacular Scottish architecture.

Following the earlier example set by St Andrews, a Preservation Society was formed in

Inveresk, Musselburgh, in 1957. The primary object of the Society was to preserve the row of small houses opposite Halkerston Lodge. It acquired two of these. A donation of £100 from the Trust made possible the acquisition of another, as well as the superiority of the ground on which the remaining cottages stood, and the cost of architect's plans for a comprehensive restoration scheme. The intention was to attract a restoring purchaser but, if one was not forthcoming, the Society would proceed with the restoration itself, selling or letting the houses later. In any event the superiorities of the group were to remain in the hands of both the Society and the Trust, the external appearance of the houses being governed by the conditions of the feu charters. Such an arrangement might be seen as the first example of the 'Little Houses Improvement Scheme', which the Trust later developed.

Gable End Cottage at the harbour in Kirkcudbright is another example of the Trust's willingness to be involved in the preservation of buildings not in its ownership. It was David Watson, former secretary of the HBCS and the Trust's representative in south-west Scotland, who offered advice and encouragement to the local committee, presided over by artist Charles Oppenheimer.

By 1960, the number of local preservation societies was growing apace. In the special case of Eaglesham, the Trust was closely involved with the Joint Restoration Committee which consisted of the County Council of Renfrew, the District Council, the Tree Lovers' Society and no fewer than three village associations. The Committee devoted itself to creating a favourable

Opposite top:
The Sandhaven,
Culross: pre-restoration

Opposite below:
The Sandhaven,
Culross: post-restoration

Above:
Eaglesham:
Montgomerie Street

climate of opinion and conditions to foster interest inside and outside the village in preserving its original plan, laid out in 1760 by Alexander, 10th Earl of Eglinton. Many of the individual houses were in very poor condition and immediate action was vital if the village was to be saved. Following these endeavours, on 27 June 1960 Eaglesham became the first village in Scotland to be statutorily listed as a place of special architectural or historic interest under Section 28 of the Town and Country Planning Act of 1947.

THE LITTLE HOUSES IMPROVEMENT SCHEME (LHIS)

The idea of this innovative Scheme was first raised in an address by the Chairman, Lord Wemyss, to the AGM in 1957: 'I seem to have concentrated mainly on two things – the personal touch and small houses; two very important things I hope you will agree. The great pity is that in the work on small houses we wish we could do more, much more … If all the properties that we restore have to be held inalienably, we obviously cannot save and preserve a very large number, but if we could restore and resell, possibly even at a profit in some cases, the money would obviously go much further. The main snag is that the £400 per house granted under the Housing Act (1950) would not be available unless the owner lives in the house after restoration.'

The 1950 Act had made part or all of the improvement grant repayable if the property was sold within 20 years. The Trust's scheme was therefore delayed until 1959, when the period was reduced to three years. The net result was that the Trust could purchase an architecturally worthwhile house and restore it with the aid of an improvement grant. It could then sell it with entry in three years' time.

The concept had been developed by Jamie Stormonth Darling. The idea was to purchase, restore and then sell under feu disposition, later under a Conservation Agreement as well. While the Lands Tribunal had power to vary the terms of feu charters if they were thought to be onerous or against public interest, though never tested, Trust Counsel advised that it did not have power to amend Conservation Agreements. This advice allowed the Trust to insist on such agreements as well as on feu charters.

The Trust Council approved an allocation of £10,000 to a special fund to inaugurate the LHIS. Jamie, realising its potential as a revolving fund, called for the appointment of new staff in Fife, in order to stimulate preservation activity.

Hew Lorimer was appointed to look after building restoration in the Kingdom of Fife and in the late 1950s Colin McWilliam took on responsibility for continuing restoration at Culross. Jamie's approach to the Pilgrim Trust for support was successful and a matching sum of £10,000 was received. The Trust also promoted a system of interest-free loans for LHIS. The fund attracted individual donations, notably that of Sir Steven Runciman who came forward with the first gift and later £1,000 in support of the Scheme. Sir Steven was over many years a wise and generous friend to the Trust, as a member of its Council, Executive and finally as a Councillor Emeritus.

The first houses to be restored under LHIS were Nos 5 and 6 Rumford, Crail, two 17th-century cottages restored as one house in 1961. Shortly afterwards they were opened as a show house and, with the Trust's new publicity team now operating, received 10,552 visitors during the period June to September. It had been decided to concentrate the Trust's effort on the coastal villages of Fife, particularly in their harbour and adjacent areas, since they were attractive places in which to live.

In the initial years of the Scheme, thanks to the enthusiasm of Hew Lorimer and others, properties were acquired and restored in Crail, Anstruther Easter and Wester, Pittenweem and St Monans. Hew had trained as an architect before becoming a sculptor: he also had valuable local connections and was able to persuade people with derelict property to sell. Hew and Ronald Cant, Reader in Scottish History at St Andrews University, gave encouragement to the

Crail: Rumford cottages

formation of local preservation societies, spreading the influence of those already formed in St Andrews and Crail to the whole of central and eastern Fife.

The concentration of LHIS within the coastal burghs had minimised direct contact with the County authorities. By restoring Mason's Lodge in the village of Ceres the Trust hoped to stimulate a favourable reaction from the County Council with a view to obtaining a direct financial contribution towards the Scheme. Fife County Council contributed £1,000 per year for five years, on condition that the Trust contributed in like manner. This was believed to be the first time any County Council in Britain had responded in such a positive manner towards preserving its ratepayers' cultural heritage.

Fife County Council later offered the Trust an interest-free loan of £2,500, repayable in five years, and another loan of this nature for £20,000 was offered anonymously as a result of an appeal in the Trust's Newsletter. Such assistance was of crucial importance in keeping the revolving fund of the Trust solvent and active.

Hew Lorimer, writing on 'New life for old burghs' in *Country Life* for August 1963, describes James VI and I's 'golden fringe on a beggar's mantle' thus: 'The local sandstones, when left unpainted, are of warm browns, yellows and greys; the gables are characteristically crow-stepped; there is a preponderance, still, of red pantiled roofs, with here and there one of grey slates; and the occasional flourish of sycamores or fruit trees completes the ingredients of this simple vernacular tradition ...'

Touring the East Neuk of Fife on a fine

Top left:
Perth: the Old Granary:
before restoration

Top right:
Perth: the Old Granary:
after restoration

Opposite top:
Tollcross Mansion House,
Glasgow: before restoration

Opposite below:
Tollcross Mansion House,
Glasgow: after restoration

in 1987 with the generous sum of £300,000 being made available to NTS for sheltered housing. It was first used in 1988, together with funds from other bodies, to make possible the purchase and conversion of the Old Granary, City Mills, Perth. This provided seven retirement flats on the upper floors and until summer 2000 accommodated the Trust's Central, Tayside and Fife Office. In 1993, the Agreement was amended to allow occupation of sheltered homes by those with special needs, not only elderly people.

The NTS Mackay Fund for Galloway began to be used in constructive ways by offering interest-free loans. These included a loan of £50,000 to the Camphill Village Trust to restore their garden cottage at Loch Arthur for the villagers' use, £50,000 to a former Methodist Church in Dumfries, and the same sum to Kirkcudbright District Council for the conversion of the tolbooth in Kirkcudbright for a variety of artistic and other uses. From the early 1990s, priorities for future use of the Mackay Fund were more specifically directed towards protection of

coastline and mountain property, as well as using part of the capital to buy and restore buildings much larger than any previously tackled. In 1990, a new JRF with North East Fife District Council was set up to match a Trust investment of £50,000 and the following year a small JRF was established with Central Region for the same purpose, although this fund was never large enough to be viable.

By the 30th birthday of LHIS in 1991, 200 properties had been restored, and compared with the 'acorn' cost of £10,000 to start the Scheme, £193,000 was spent in that year. However, the acquisition of properties suitable for restoration had become more difficult because of the increased interest in this sector of the market by estate agents, surveyors and property speculators. Meanwhile, the capital invested under the LHIS banner was either being revolved or was realising interest to be used as suitable properties came on the market. If any of the JRFs had to be terminated, the capital provided was to be repayable to the local authority.

LARGER PROJECTS

The 1990s were characterised by fewer small projects but included some very much larger and time-consuming restorations. A total of 14 projects was tackled, compared with over 50 during the 1980s.

The first was Tollcross Mansion House, designed by David Bryce, a mid-19th-century A-listed country house in what had become a public park in the east end of Glasgow. Here the Trust's involvement brought an end to a long-standing impasse which greatly aggravated the eventual costs. It had been a children's museum, and was to have been passed to the property developer Nicholas Groves Raines Stenhus, but Councillors, reacting to local feeling, would not agree to privatising property in a public park. The house was eventually acquired using the CMHCT revolving fund rather than the Strathclyde Region JRF. The plan was to restore the building to provide 13 sheltered housing flats at a cost of £2.4m. The Trust was fortunate that a single owner could be found for the property in the Shettleston Housing Association, who finally leased it to the Church of Scotland for accommodation of the frail and the elderly, many of whom are local residents. Conversion of the interior to its new uses has retained much of the original layout and provides spacious rooms of character. Restoration was completed in 1993.

Myrtle Cottage in the Border village of Yetholm was first brought to the Trust's notice in 1991 and identified as a future project under LHIS. It became clear that Borders Regional Council intended to demolish this thatched domestic property. The proposal went to Public

unanimously accepted by the Executive. The Dumfries and Galloway, North East Fife and Kirkcaldy JRFs were duly dissolved and the Borders fund was dissolved with the capital being divided between the LHIS fund and Scottish Borders Council.

St Margaret's Gatehouse in Restalrig, Edinburgh, a small A-listed house, was restored with support from Historic Scotland and Edinburgh District Council's Planning and Housing Departments. It was bought from the Church of Scotland Trustees, previously having been a vesting-house, school, domestic dwelling and clubhouse for the Lothian and Borders Miniature Railway Society. The Turret House, Kelso, had been in Trust ownership for over 20 years when it became redundant as a public building on the non-renewal of the tenancy by the local authority. It had been variously a church centre, tourist information centre and town museum. The B-listed house was restored as a single domestic dwelling.

A STORY OF INITIATIVE AND ENTERPRISE

As a result of the early vision of the founders of the Trust there has been, beyond doubt, a 'national awakening' as to the historic merit of Scotland's vernacular architecture. The act of faith by the original donors, private charitable trusts and later the crucial role of government agencies and local authorities have been vital to the success of the Little Houses Improvement Scheme.

Little houses restoration projects carried out in its first 30 years, followed by the LHIS Revolving Fund of the 1960s and 1970s and the JRFs with local authorities of the 1980s and 1990s, tell a remarkable story of initiative and enterprise. The various projects undertaken have given the Trust a unique opportunity to co-operate with a wide variety of agencies and individuals in joint endeavours, which have done a great deal to restore and maintain over 300 buildings. Together, they retain an important part of the special character of Scotlands vernacular architecture and have helped both to consolidate and sustain the life of the historic centres of these old Scottish burghs. Practical and attractive accommodation has been provided for residents, in the process doing much to raise the national and international profile of Scotland's architectural heritage.

The evolution of the Trust's LHIS has not always been easy or straightforward. It has had to face criticism as well as praise. It has had to adapt to changing circumstances in legislation and in local government. Most recently, the Abolition of Feudal Tenure (Scotland) Bill 1999, later passed by the Scottish Parliament, recognised the importance of conservation bodies such as the Trust, and introduced non-feudal real burdens or 'conservation burdens'. The Trust will require to examine all 1,200 of its existing feus, including over 200 'Little Houses', to judge whether, in the national interest and at considerable cost, they should be converted into 'conservation burdens'. As part of the government's wider land reform agenda, a Title Conditions Bill will be considered in the next session of parliament, when it will be become clearer just what effect these changes in legislation will have

Previous pages: Culross: features of the Royal Burgh

[138]

The ancient settlement of Dunkeld, from above the town

on the protection of the Trust's 'Little Houses'.

In recent years, the Trust has restored comparatively few properties under the LHIS. Those it finally selected are of the highest architectural or historical quality, requiring the most measured approach, in close consultation as to their final treatment and use, with Historic Scotland, the Heritage Lottery Fund, local authorities and others. The work of the Trust's restoration under LHIS has not only saved individual houses, but has also been an example and an encouragement to others including local authorities and housing associations who have themselves saved much of our vernacular heritage.

The Trust has promoted the value of such buildings by practical conservation throughout Scotland and has amply demonstrated the 4th Marquess of Bute's general proposition that 'all old houses have an architectural value and there must be few which have not equally a domestic value'.[24]

CHAPTER SIX
THE HOLISTIC APPROACH
1971–1980

'The Trust now leads the world

in the wholeness of its approach to

environmental management.'

SIR FRANK FRASER DARLING, 1969

THE FIFTH DECADE

The eminent conservationist and naturalist Sir Frank Fraser Darling included the statement which heads this chapter during a BBC Reith Lecture in a series entitled *Wilderness and Plenty*, broadcast in 1969. In the 1970s, the Trust was particularly concerned with trying to live up to such an accolade. Readers may judge by the end of this chapter whether or not it succeeded in doing so.

In 1971, the Trust celebrated its 40th anniversary and the year began with ominous signs in the financial firmament. General expenses were anticipated to exceed £200,000. Convener of the Investment Committee, Ian Pitman, was asked to look into the financial health of the Trust. The situation at the time was influenced by a countrywide crisis, including a pay freeze, a three-day working week and a petrol shortage, all of which combined to make it difficult for visitors to reach Trust properties.

Major developments took place at a number of properties. Site interpretation as well as shops sprang up to attract interest and raise funds for conservation from an ever-increasing number of visitors. The Trust took more seriously its responsibilities for educating the young and appointed Marista Leishman as its first full-time Education Secretary.

The second half of the decade was taken up with negotiations over new properties, mostly offered to the Trust but occasionally bought. These included Castle Fraser, Drum Castle and Haddo House in Aberdeenshire, the Island of Iona, Brodie Castle in Morayshire and the House of Dun in Angus, together with the natural history-rich headland of St Abb's Head in Berwickshire. The acquisition of 1 North Charlotte Street relieved pressure on Trust Head Office at 5 Charlotte Square. It is worth mentioning that significant properties often appear in Trust discussion many years before they finally come into Trust care. Good examples first discussed in the 1970s were the island of Canna (1981), The Hill House (1982) in Helensburgh and Fyvie Castle (1984) in Aberdeenshire.

The Trust was also greatly concerned about oil-related developments. Protection of inalienable property against the construction of offshore platforms on its Balmacara Estate at Drumbuie was coupled with a genuine anxiety for the preservation of the social fabric of the community living there, and extended to the rest of the western seaboard. This campaign is described in Chapter Two. Trust resources were severely stretched, although the support for the cause, which was won, led to a surge in membership.

Battling its corner for appropriate new legislation on a variety of subjects is a continuing theme throughout the 1970s, and again the Trust was fortunate to be able to call on its leadership and the legal skills of George Russell (Law Agent), in concert with Jeremy Benson of the National Trust in England, to promote the cause of conservation.

PRIORWOOD AND HARMONY GARDEN

Mrs Jill Currie, who owned Priorwood House and Garden in Melrose, wrote to the Trust in the early 1970s to enlist help. There was a proposal

Chapter opening picture. St Abb's Head: guillemots, razorbills and a pair of kittiwakes

Priorwood Garden: gathering dried flowers for display

for a road through her walled garden, adjacent to Melrose Abbey, to relieve the pressure of traffic in the town centre, and only one councillor on the Roads Committee – Haig Douglas – was speaking out against the decision. Fortunately, when he presented his views to the Secretary of State for Scotland, the by-pass scheme was vetoed. Following Jill's death in 1974, Peggy Douglas, Haig's wife, a former member of the Trust's Council, first drew the Trust's attention to the impending sale of Jill's property. Although engrossed in the Drumbuie Inquiry at the time, Jamie Stormonth Darling quickly recognised the value to the Trust of acquiring such a strategic position in the town as well as owning more property in the Borders. The Trust

had been left a legacy by Mrs McMillan of St John's, Melrose, and was thus able to buy the property in 1974.

Through the inspiration and dedication of Bettina, Lady Thomson, and her band of willing and enthusiastic volunteers, Priorwood was successfully developed as a garden to grow plant material suitable for drying and subsequently for sale. She was also responsible for creating a display in the orchard illustrating 'Apples through the Ages'. At the same time, under the leadership of Peggy Douglas and her friends, a Trust Centre for the Borders was established to raise support and funds for the Trust. This was the forerunner of the Borders Members' Centre.

The Centre also planned and funded the

Above:
Harmony Garden:
fritillaries and daffodils

Opposite:
Harmony Garden
and Melrose Abbey

attractive dove sculpture, designed by David Annan and set on a large stone provided by Haig Douglas, in memory of Jill Currie. For her outstanding voluntary contribution to the enterprise, Bettina, Lady Thomson was awarded the Trust's George Waterston Memorial Award in 1984 (see Chapter Seven for more details of this coveted prize). New flower-drying and arranging facilities, together with an expanded dried flower shop, were built in 1995 to cope with Priorwood's increasing popularity.

Jack Pitman and his wife, Christian, first approached the Trust in 1977 concerning the future of Harmony, their lovely home and garden in Melrose. Christian Pitman's family, who had lived in the property for five generations, had carried out pioneering excavations between 1905 and 1910 of the Trimontium Roman Fort, at Newstead close to Melrose. Her father, Dr James Curle, a Melrose solicitor, was responsible for the first investigations of the fort, objects from which are permanently exhibited in the Museum of Scotland.

The Pitmans had the generosity and foresight in 1977 to make an interest-free loan of £50,000 to the Trust in the anticipation, but not the assumption, that when Christian died, she would bequeath Harmony to the Trust. This she did and in the interim the £50,000, with interest, had grown to £450,000. The Trust was thus able to accept the property in 1996. A condition of the bequest was that in Trust hands it would benefit the people and visitors to Melrose. Although the house and a small piece of the

garden is privately tenanted, accommodation in the basement is used by the Trust's Borders Members' Centre, the Trimontium Trust and the Melrose Historical Association.

Open to visitors in spring and summer, Harmony Garden is at its most appealing in spring, exhibiting a wide range of colour with nodding snake's-head fritillaries, some unusual daffodils and dog's-tooth violets, all purposefully and happily naturalised in long grass. One of the attractive views is over the bulb field to the Eildon Hills. In the summer, mixed borders on either side of a 'crazy-paved' path lead the visitor's eye to Melrose Abbey, with the well-tended vegetable and fruit garden in the foreground. It was therefore the active determination of Christian Pitman at Harmony and of Jill Currie, the former owner of Priorwood Garden, which first prevented inappropriate and harmful developments taking place in this historic and popular Borders town.

PLANNING ISSUES

Although the Trust cannot devote time and expertise to every case which may come before it, a number of issues have proceeded to Public Inquiry, whenever the Trust believed there was a just cause. Perhaps the classic cases of Glen Nevis and Drumbuie, already described in Chapter Two, demonstrate the inevitability of a leading conservation body becoming regularly involved in such cases. The staff now included a member singularly well equipped to reason that the Trust case was a sound one. Assistant Director Findlay McQuarrie was charged with dealing with all planning proposals, and the co-

ordination of a well-reasoned conservation cause linking the various voluntary organisations and central statutory agencies.

Amongst causes championed in the 1970s by the Trust were opposition to two proposals for caravan sites, one on Seil Island south of Oban, and the other on land adjacent to the beach at Croy Bay, Ayrshire. The first affected non-Trust property, and the second was adjacent to the Trust's recently declared Country Park at Culzean.

In 1972, the Trust, the Association for the Protection of Rural Scotland (APRS) and five local residents appealed against the decision of Argyll County Council to allow a caravan park for up to 60 caravans on Seil Island, in full view of the A-listed Clachan Bridge, or 'Bridge over the Atlantic'. The Trust had the support of two expert witnesses it had commissioned to produce reports on the requirement for caravan sites in this part of Scotland, and on the impact of the proposed development on the surrounding landscape. The developer had already received outline and detailed planning approval. The Secretary of State, making an exceptional intervention in the planning authority's decision, upheld the Reporter's recommendation against the proposal. He believed it was contrary to good planning practice and was impressed by the number and the quality of the representations against the Council's decision.

At Croy Bay there had been a history of proposals for caravan sites on this attractive part of the Ayrshire coastline as well as a long tradition of local people parking their cars on the beach. The development in 1973 of the Culzean

*Clachan Bridge or
'The Bridge over
the Atlantic'*

*Culzean Country Park:
NTS car park at
Croy Bay*

Country Park Centre on the top of the cliff nearest to Croy meant that even more people would have both caravans and cars in their view north along the coastline. The farmer's proposal for 78 caravans on the thin strip of land adjacent to the beach contravened road safety via the Croy road exit, and was in direct view of Culzean Castle. It was strongly opposed on aesthetic and safety grounds by the Trust, the Royal Fine Art Commission for Scotland, Ayrshire County Council and the police, and was turned down. Much more recently, in the year 2000, the Trust took the positive step of shielding car parks in landscaped areas behind the beach, which is now free of vehicles. This initiative has encouraged responsible use of the area by visitors.

A major planning proposal which fortunately did not go to Public Inquiry, but which certainly took up a great deal of time, was the scheme from the North of Scotland Hydro Electric Board (NSHEB) for a pump storage station on the north flank of Ben Lomond at Craigroyston. The extraordinary strength of the public response is a measure of the significance of this great landscape. Local resistance to the proposal grew rapidly with the formation of the Friends of Loch Lomond, a potent force led by Hannah Stirling. The two regional councils and two district councils with interest in the land were also active in its protection.

The Trust gathered together a knowledgeable committee and other experts and arranged several fact-finding reconnaissance visits to the site, to Loch Sloy and to Dinorwig Power Station near Llanberis in North Wales, to compare and learn about the environmental and other impacts of these existing operations. Findlay McQuarrie, now Deputy Director of the Trust and its Glasgow Representative, led the Trust's enquiry, arranging meetings with the Hydro Board and giving informed lectures to keenly interested groups such as the Conservation Society. To the relief of all, NSHEB announced on 28 May 1980 that it had withdrawn its £3m plan for Ben Lomond, 'because of recent reductions in forward load estimates'.

CASTLE FRASER

In January 1975, Mrs Lavinia Smiley, a member of the Trust's Executive Committee, wrote to Jamie Stormonth Darling to intimate that she and her husband, Michael, were thinking of offering Castle Fraser to the Trust, with contents and, at a later date, muniments, together with an endowment. The Director's reaction was tempered by the Trust's recent experience of owning such property. Already in its ownership in Aberdeenshire were Leith Hall, Pitmedden House and Garden, Crathes and Craigievar Castles. The Trust was also committed on the death of Henry Quentin Irvine to accepting Drum Castle, and the transfer of Haddo House was under active discussion. The visitor and revenue earning potential of Castle Fraser was not seen as very large.

Nonetheless, the castle had been described as 'the most spectacular of the Midmar (or Castles of Mar) Group' by Oliver Hill, the well-known English architect. A traditional Scots castle, Fraser is unusual in retaining its 'laigh biggins', the essential practical accompaniments

Opposite:
Castle Fraser,
Aberdeenshire

Castle Fraser:
the Worked Room

as well as servants' quarters which emphasise the scale and grandeur of the main structure.

Jamie Stormonth Darling believed that to respond negatively would be both ungracious and ungrateful in view of the generosity being shown by the Smileys. Negotiations were entered into on the basis of an endowment, which would enable acceptance of the property without calling on the General Funds of the Trust. In order to raise the endowment, it was necessary for the family to sell farms on the estate. The anticipated sale raised approximately £200,000 and this, together with £15,000 from Mrs Smiley, was thought to be sufficient. The

property was accepted with a date for opening to visitors fixed for 9 September 1977.

David Learmont, the Trust's Curator, described the outside of the Castle as an 'architectural gem' but the inside as 'bleak indeed'. He produced a plan phasing the opening of rooms to show how the house developed over time. The High Hall, Peacock Parlour, Worked Room and the rest of the Michael Tower including the kitchen would open in the first year, with the Library or Victorian rooms at the top of the castle the following year. The Michael Tower Rooms would be furnished in the 17th-century manner, the Dining Room late Georgian, the

Castle Fraser:
the Library

Worked Room and the Victorian Rooms at the top of the Castle to emphasise what was done in the 19th century.

On the deaths of both Smileys in 1991, the stables became available for development as the regional office for the Trust. In 1996, the Trust commissioned a Historic Landscape Survey to provide the basis for future management of the gardens, policies and woodlands. This survey made strong recommendations for restoration of the landscape to something akin to the original concept of Miss Elyza Fraser during her long life of 80 years (1734-1814). Her companion, Miss Bristow, whose name is given to the wood-

land in the south of the property and to a cottage, is believed to have influenced her in the plan. Since 1996, a major thinning programme has been introduced in Miss Bristow's Wood, favouring broadleaf trees such as oak, beech, birch and sycamore, ultimately to create an oak-dominant wood. Planting individual trees is restoring the 18th-century parkland layout. It is exciting to see the historical landscape taking shape once more.

DRUM CASTLE

In 1960, when Henry Quentin Irvine first called at the Trust offices in Edinburgh, it was to offer

Drum Castle,
Aberdeenshire

Drum Castle with its estate and an endowment. Jamie Stormonth Darling, while discouraging new commitments 'until we can consolidate', thought the property would relate particularly well to and complement Crathes Castle. Jamie sought the advice of the Librarian-Historian of Aberdeen University, Dr Douglas Simpson, who was in no doubt whatever that the Trust should accept. He cited several cogent reasons: 'It is late 13th-century and the Tower is the third earliest known Scottish tower house with the mansion added in 1615. Altogether a choice specimen …

of the Indian summer of Scottish Gothic. It has been continuously occupied by the Irvine family since 1333, a family notable in north-east history for six centuries.'

The suggested endowment of £65,000 was thought to be an obstacle as Quentin Irvine could not see his way to raising it, but negotiations were continued. The lawyers on both sides explored the possibility of the owner giving the Trust £30,000 whilst he was still living, as an endowment fund which would be applied to Drum on his death, when the property would come to the

Drum Castle:
the Drawing Room

Trust as an inalienable bequest. The gift would include the Castle, and the original Drum Charter with other muniments, the policies, gardens, woodlands and the Old Forest of Drum, together with associated smaller estate buildings. When Quentin Irvine died in November 1975, he bequeathed an additional £25,000. The Trust assumed ownership in May 1976.

It is always difficult to continue the horticultural use for walled gardens, which were features of large, amply staffed estates. The walled garden at Drum was no exception – until 1988, when the Trust conceived the innovative idea of creating a Garden of Historic Roses planted in period settings. The garden, which opened in 1991, following a public appeal, contains a specially commissioned sundial dedicated to Scotland's Gardens Scheme which, like the Trust, celebrated its Diamond Jubilee that year.

HADDO HOUSE

Lord Aberdeen (the 4th Marquess) died on 13 September 1974, before he had concluded discussions with the Secretary of State for Scotland, the

Above:
Haddo House,
Aberdeenshire

Right:
Haddo House:
the Dining Room

Opposite:
Lord Haddo by
Pompeo Batoni

NTS and Aberdeenshire County Council, about the handover of his estate of Haddo to the nation. Lady Aberdeen was determined that her late husband's wishes would be carried out. It had been Lord Aberdeen's intention that part of the designed landscape at Haddo, containing a lake designed by the artist James Giles for the 4th Earl of Haddo in the early 19th century, should be declared a Country Park.

Complicated negotiations followed involving the Trust and the Scottish Office, the National Land Fund, the local authority, the Haddo House Estate Trustees, the executors to the late Marquess and legal staff. On 18 May 1974, Jamie Stormonth Darling and other senior staff had conducted a crucial meeting with Lord and Lady Aberdeen and their solicitors. This meeting proved to be the basis of the agreement which eventually enabled the Trust to accept the William Adam designed house and ancillary buildings with the immediate policies, while other land became a Country Park under Grampian Regional Council, the relevant local authority following reorganisation in 1975. In addition to gifting the property and most of its contents to the Trust, Lord Aberdeen had envisaged provision through National Land Fund procedures, for sale of certain contents not vital to the presentation of the house. He would then provide part of the endowment through the proceeds.

The financial arrangement involved the sale by the Haddo House Estate Trustees of two farms to the sitting tenants at £260,000 and the sale of a Caracci painting which, after deduction of Christie's commission, realised £234,000

Cammo in 1896

towards endowment and capital works of £494,000. The property first welcomed visitors in July 1979. After their first visit to Canada in 1890, the 4th Marquess and his wife, June, had created the specially constructed Hall with its splendid acoustics, venue for performances by the highly successful Haddo House Choral Society (known since 1988 as the Haddo House Hall Arts Trust). June Aberdeen ably directed this body for 50 years. The Hall and adjacent peat yards were refurbished in the early 1990s. The Hall itself was reroofed in 2000.

CAMMO

Although perhaps on the fringe of Trust activity, Cammo, near Cramond, Edinburgh, merits inclusion if only because 'it was quite the most complicated will and situation from all taxation angles in the life of the Trust'. So said George Russell when notice of the bequest was first received in 1975. Taxation was to prove far from the only complication. Of 30 dogs, which roamed the main house for 20 years, 16 remained in residence. The owner, Percival Louis Maitland-Tennent, lived in a caravan nearby. Members of the Executive Committee on their first visit were warned that 'the building is flea-ridden and it is strongly recommended to bring gumboots or other foot-wear which can be washed after your visit'.[25]

While the Executive Committee was by no means unanimous regarding acceptance, discussions were opened with the City of Edinburgh District Council (CEDC) and the Leisure and

Left to right: The Earl of Wemyss and March, George Russell and Provost Kenneth Borthwick giving and receiving sasine, 25 April 1980

Recreation Department of Lothian Regional Council. Both showed interest and offered co-operation. While not of great nature conservation importance, Jamie likened Cammo to Parklea in Renfrewshire, recognising the value of such undeveloped land on the perimeter of the City of Edinburgh as recreational and educational space.

Following continued theft of its contents, vandalism increased at the house and in March and May of 1977 two destructive fires rendered the building beyond restoration. A short time later, CEDC's Director of Building Control advised the Trust that demolition would proceed without delay because the building had become a danger to the public. The action began without further notification to the Trust who threatened an interdict, whereupon work ceased on condition that the building be made safe and future policy for it be decided within the week.

It was agreed that the Trust would accept Cammo House and Estate, engaging a contractor to demolish all but the shell of the former building. By the old Scottish procedure of symbolic deliverance of a feu or taking sasine, earth and stone from the estate were handed over by Lord Wemyss to the Provost of Edinburgh, Kenneth Borthwick, on 25 April 1980. After reimbursement of its expenses from the bequest, the Trust established the Edinburgh Fund to benefit Cammo and other Trust properties within the City.

One of the conditions of the agreement with CEDC was that a Joint Advisory Committee

consisting of Trust and local authority representatives, with a Trust Chairman, should be set up.
This duly met, with Roger Wheater as
Chairman, for a number of years. The two
organisations produced a five-year Prescriptive
Management Plan. This was directed chiefly at
improving the derelict estate, in particular the
tree cover. Footpaths would be provided for visitors and the artificial waterway restored, leaving
much of the 38-hectare (94-acre) estate in its
natural state to encourage wildlife and provide
opportunities for recreation within the City. The
overgrown walled garden has a marvellous
display of snowdrops in spring.

A proposal in 1982 for housing development
in fields adjacent to Cammo was successfully
resisted on the grounds that it would generate
unwelcome and noisy traffic, diminish the rural
character of the land close to the park, and
encourage development along the quiet country
road known as Cammo Walk. The Trust was
represented in a Public Inquiry over a further
application on the same area in 1987. The
proposal, by Cala Homes, for residential development was contrary to Green Belt and Local
Plan policy as well as detracting from the
amenity of Cammo. Objections from NTS,
CEDC, Lothian Region and the Cockburn
Association, also representing the Cramond
Association, together with 80 private objectors,
ensured that both a planning appeal and outline
planning permission were refused.

A Woodland Management Plan was
prepared by CEDC: as a result, diseased elm
trees were felled and a thinning and planting
programme undertaken throughout the wood-

lands. The comprehensive Historic Landscape
Survey by the Paul Hogarth Company produced
in 1999 stated: 'Cammo Estate is important for
its veteran trees and lowland park habitat, for its
rich and diverse fauna, particularly badgers and
birds, for a number of plant species of restricted
distribution, and for its ecological interest.' Also,
one might add, for its considerable recreational
and educational values.

IONA

'A man is little to be envied whose piety would
not grow warmer among the ruins of Iona.' So
wrote Dr Samuel Johnson in his *Journey to the
Western Isles of Scotland* (1775), and anyone who
has been to this beautiful island must agree that
it is a very special place with a unique atmosphere.

Dr David Russell, head of the paper-manu-
facturing firm of Tullis Russell in Fife, who
helped the Trust in its acquisition of Burg in
1935, had visited Iona as a boy and developed a
warm affection for the island. It was he who first
had the idea of providing a retreat there for
divinity students and, in co-operation with the
Church of Scotland, arranged the first retreats
of a week's duration for students from Scottish
universities. These gatherings focused David
Russell's attention on the need for residential
accommodation, and on the restoration of the
ruins of the Abbey as the means to achieve this.

Close association with Dr George MacLeod,
later Lord MacLeod of Fuinary, who had similar
ideas about training ministers to equip them for
work in deprived areas, led to the adoption of
Iona as the spiritual home of the Iona

Opposite:
Iona from the air

Iona: coastal communities

Opposite: Iona: the Abbey

Community. Dr MacLeod became deeply involved in the restoration and practical use of the church buildings, developing a close liaison between the Community and the Iona Cathedral Trust (ICT), which had owned several buildings since 1900.

In 1973, David Russell wrote to Jamie Stormonth Darling, to express his 'pipe-dream' for the island. He envisaged the handover of Iona by the Duke of Argyll to NTS as well as an appeal for its maintenance and sought Jamie's personal ideas prior to an imminent meeting of the Iona Cathedral Trustees. Inveraray Castle, seat of the Argylls, had suffered a disastrous fire and was apparently underinsured. The 12th Duke realised he could raise urgently required

resources by marketing most of the island. When the sale was publicly announced in May 1979, there was a public outcry that such a sacred island should be sold. The asking price was somewhat inflated at £2m. The Trust's acquisition of Iona was a classic case of Jamie's implicit faith that if the proposal was right, then the necessary finance would follow. The fact that Iona was one of the best known Scottish islands undoubtedly helped.

There was extreme pressure on NTS to act quickly to energise the necessary support. It was vital to secure the confidence and encouragement of the Church of Scotland, which had such a crucial role to play in protecting the religious buildings, including the Abbey. As it happened, that year the Moderator of the General Assembly of the Church of Scotland was the Rt Rev Professor Robin Barbour, a good friend of Donald Erskine, a Deputy Director of the Trust. Both Jamie and Donald, with Donald's uncle Colonel David Baird, a member of the Trust's Executive, were present at the 1979 General Assembly of the Church of Scotland to make a heartfelt appeal for Iona on behalf of all its people and the nation. Support was also forthcoming from Strathclyde Regional Council, Argyll and Bute District Council and the Countryside Commission for Scotland.

The Secretary of State, while in favour of ownership ultimately being invested in the Trust, was unable to contribute more than £2-300,000 to the purchase and encouraged the NTS to take the initiative during the negotiations. The Trust offered £600,000 before the island went on the open market. The intention was to provide an endowment to benefit not only ICT, but also the resident community of whom there were about 130 living in 13 crofts or farms and in a number of houses in the Village, which included two hotels. The anticipated rejection of the offer of £600,000 by the Argyll trustees did not deter the Trust and while leaving that sum 'on the table' until 31 July 1979, an appeal for £1m was prepared. On 25 May 1979, the trustees announced that an offer from the Fraser Foundation of £1.5m had been accepted to ensure the island's long-term future in suitable ownership for the benefit of the nation. It was Sir Hugh's initiative to buy the island and give it to the nation in memory of his father, Lord Fraser of Allander.

With such an unexpected but most welcome development, the Trust could combine its appeal, now for £500,000, with the ICT's own Abbey Appeal. This was to provide a capital reserve as well as an endowment for the island. The Secretary of State agreed that NTS should be invited to accept ownership of Iona, a decision approved by the Fraser Foundation Trustees who offered an additional £150,000 as a contribution to the endowment.

The appeal generated £700,000, of which £400,000 was given to the ICT as an endowment for the Abbey, on condition that a Management Board be set up representing the interests of the ICT, NTS, local residents and the Iona Community, tenants of the Abbey. The Board continued in operation until 1993. In the following year, Iona Abbey Ltd was established as the administrative and management arm of ICT, with significant financial and manpower commitment from Historic Scotland. The company produced a business plan based on which a substantial conservation and repair programme was achieved. The plan continued until the year 2000 when, in order to ensure the long-term conservation of all the religious buildings, Historic Scotland took over responsibility for their administration and upkeep, and appointed a resident manager for these properties.

GREENBANK GARDEN

Greenbank House, Clarkston, Glasgow, was built in 1764 by an unknown architect for Robert Allason, a Glasgow merchant. Bill Blyth, an enthusiastic and knowledgeable gardener, bought the house in 1961 and first wrote to the Gardens Advisory Service of the Trust in December 1962, in order to seek advice on the design and layout of the walled garden. Eric Robson, then an Assistant Secretary of the Trust and later its Gardens Adviser, replied, and in due course visited the property, making suggestions and establishing a friendship with Bill Blyth.

In 1973, the Blyths offered the Trust the house, walled garden and the policies with the intention that the garden should be developed as an advice centre for owners of small gardens, similar to the one at Suntrap in Edinburgh. There was no endowment, but the Trust, anticipating that an appeal might raise sufficient funds, was interested in the proposition as ownership would provide it with a 'foothold' in Greater Glasgow.

An appeal for £100,000 was launched in March 1976. By April £60,000 had been received from local authority, charitable trusts, industry, banks and generous individuals. The Trust's Council meeting that month agreed to accept the property. The appeal finally reached £77,000. Jim May was appointed as head gardener and now combines that appointment with property management. He has two full-time garden assistants and regular help from the Friends of Greenbank, a support group established in 1981. The Friends are integral to the success of Greenbank. As well as working in the garden they provide cheerful voluntary help by organising fund-raising events, plant sales, dried flowers and floral art, a sewing group whose projects benefit many Trust properties, plus guiding in part of the house on Sunday afternoons and catering for occasional visiting

Greenbank House and Garden, Clarkston, Glasgow

parties. Their chairwoman, Kathy Rice, was presented with the George Waterston Memorial Award in 1995.

The garden lends itself to easy access and has been enhanced with less able visitors in mind. The structure remains to a large extent as it was in the Blyths' day with a series of well-grown hedges dividing it into compartments, but now enclosing an intriguing variety of layouts and plants. These include a garden for the less able with raised beds, a plant trial area run in association with *Gardening Which?*, and the pool garden with its striking bronze statue of a water nymph entitled 'Foam' by Pilkington

Greenbank Garden: statue of 'Foam'

Brodie Castle

Jackson, cast originally for the Glasgow Empire Exhibition in 1938 and gifted to Greenbank in 1986. The rich mixture of planting, always evolving in Greenbank, is designed both to advise the amateur gardener and to give constant pleasure to all who take the trouble to find this delightful garden, still bounded by farmland and close to residential Glasgow.

Greenbank House has made an ideal office for the Trust's West Region. There was no furniture available when the Blyths left, but the Trust's Curatorial Department has furnished the rooms seen by visitors in an interesting and appropriate manner, retaining the family atmosphere.

BRODIE CASTLE

'We are horribly stretched at the moment in every field and especially over the future of certain other great Family Houses in Scotland.'[26] Such was Jamie Stormonth Darling's early reaction to the initial approach by Brodie of Brodie in 1972 to interest the Trust in becoming owners of Brodie Castle in Moray. But Jamie also said that the Trust would do everything possible to help over the future of Brodie and its priceless contents, and this he proceeded to do. Brodie and his wife, Helena, were concerned for the future of what had belonged to his family for more than 800 years. Mrs Brodie was seriously ill in hospital, their son Alastair was apparently permanently settled in Australia, and their grandchildren were minors.

The Trust Curator, David Learmont, was initially less than enthusiastic, but a second look and a 13-page list of contents which it was thought essential to keep within the Castle convinced him. He recommended full Trust involvement. The hope was that the Secretary of State would purchase both Castle and contents through the National Land Fund, so that the property and contents might then be held by the Trust for the nation. The gap which existed in that part of Scotland for a property of the standing of Brodie was also recognised.

Brodie's offer was public-spirited and in consultation with the Trust he composed a personal letter to the Secretary of State, Gordon Campbell, seeking his co-operation in finding a financial solution using the National Land Fund. The support was sought of the Department of the Environment and, in particular, the expert view of Stewart Cruden, the Inspector of Ancient Monuments. He emphasised that what the building lacked in architectural terms it more than made up for in its good furniture and paintings. The negotiations for this complex acquisition, begun in 1973, were finally concluded in 1978 when Bruce Millan, as Secretary of State for Scotland, announced that he had purchased the Castle along with certain contents for £405,000. The National Land Fund reimbursed the Secretary of State and the property came to the Trust in September that year.

Although there is no formal or other garden as such in the flat, rather uninspiring landscape

that characterises Brodie, there are two very interesting features. One is the shrubbery laid out originally in the 1830s and attributed to William (1799-1873), 22nd Brodie of Brodie, and developed by Major Ian Brodie (1868-1943), 24th Brodie of Brodie. This contains an attractive arrangement of flowering shrubs with ground cover of wild flowers, which is being encouraged by the current gardener, David Wheeler. The other is the collection of daffodils created by Ian Brodie. One of the three greatest breeders of daffodils of his day, he produced over 400 varieties which the Trust has been at pains to locate and re-establish at Brodie. These

Brodie Castle:
Ninian Brodie of Brodie

*Brodie Castle Drawing
Room: daffodil display*

provide a unique additional attraction for visitors who may buy a 'Brodie' daffodil when they visit this delightful property. The Trust has laid out a woodland walk round the 2-hectare (4-acre) pond for the enjoyment and interest of visitors.

Ninian Brodie, the 25th Laird, has been a joy for the Trust to negotiate with. He has continued to help the Trust in innumerable ways, including acting as a congenial host to thousands of astonished and delighted visitors. He and his wife's generous and public-spirited action in making their home – it still feels like a home – available to everyone, is remarkable. Ninian was awarded the George Waterston Memorial Award in 1993 for his exceptional voluntary service. (See Chapter Seven for more details of this coveted prize.)

THE NATIONAL HERITAGE BILL

Both National Trusts are indebted to successive governments for introducing legislation to grant-aid heritage and conservation subjects. As early as 1894 there had been special exemption introduced for national heritage objects when they were retained by the family and passed on from one generation to the next. The following year, 1895, total tax exemption for historic buildings was given to the newly formed National Trust, and in 1931 this privilege had been extended to The National Trust for Scotland.

The National Land Fund was created in 1946 as a memorial to the dead of two world wars by Hugh Dalton, then Chancellor of the Exchequer, in order that 'through this Fund we should make some of the loveliest parts of this land dedicated to the memory of those who died in order that we might live in comfort'. It was endowed with £50m.

Following all-party agreement in 1950, the government established the Historic Buildings Councils in 1953 and provided funds for purchase and grants for the upkeep of heritage buildings, including those privately owned, subject to reasonable public access.

In addition there had been special provision for the government to acquire and transfer property to the National Trusts when offered in payment of capital taxes. Listing of heritage buildings became the yardstick for grant eligibility and special protection under the Planning Acts. Support and help grew from government agencies such as the Countryside Commissions, the tourist boards and local authorities following realisation of the importance of countryside for conservation and recreation and of national heritage for tourism. Capital Gains Tax was introduced (1965) and income taxes rose. There was a threat of a wealth tax and the impending introduction of Capital Transfer Tax. Estate owners made increasing demands on the two National Trusts to help to preserve their homes.

The National Land Fund was controlled by the Treasury but was so little used that a large part of its funds was diverted for other purposes. In 1977, however, the sale of Mentmore, the Earl of Rosebery's Buckinghamshire mansion, together with its contents, caused a public outcry after a proposal that the collections should be taken over by the Victoria and Albert Museum had been discouraged at ministerial level. There was strong criticism that the Land Fund had not been used to keep the house and contents for the benefit of the public. An inquiry into the workings of the Fund was set up. A White Paper published in 1979 recommended that the National Land Fund should be wound up and a new body created outside the control of government. That autumn, the National Heritage Bill was introduced in parliament. The Bill enjoyed all-party support, evidence of the wide political backing for the main recommendations, one of which was the establishment of the National Heritage Memorial Fund. It was due to a Trust initiative and Tam Dalyell of the Binns, MP for West Lothian, that the 'memorial' aspect was importantly added to the new Fund at a crucial stage in the Bill's passage through Parliament.

Both Trusts had played significant roles in achieving this highly important piece of legislation. Congratulating Maurice Lindsay, Director of the Scottish Civic Trust, on his appointment in 1980 as the trustee with special interest in Scottish heritage matters, Jamie Stormonth Darling wrote, 'I do not think anything has absorbed so much of our time as the Bill, from last November until Easter (except Drumbuie!)'. The major part of the money remaining from the National Land Fund was handed over for administration by a body of 11 independent trustees. This amounted to £12.4m, the remaining sum going to the Department of the Environment and the Office of Arts and Libraries to finance the acceptance of items of importance to the national heritage, in lieu of capital taxation. In addition the government was committed to paying an annual grant to the new Fund.

HOUSE OF DUN

When Mrs Millicent Lovett, née Erskine, the last of her line and 21st Laird of Dun, offered her property to the Trust in 1976, Jamie Stormonth Darling was on the Council of the Scottish Wildlife Trust (SWT). He had been instrumental in directing £5,000 of a bequest to SWT for bird sanctuaries, towards its purchase of the adjacent Montrose Basin as a nature reserve. SWT had acquired Mrs Lovett's rights in the Basin and on the foreshore adjoining the Mains of Dun. Jamie's enthusiasm encouraged the NTS because of the potential for partnership with SWT over the Reserve. He must also have had a shrewd idea of the importance of the William Adam designed A–listed House of Dun, immediately calling on architectural adviser Schomberg Scott to provide the necessary expert opinion. Schomberg was in no doubt whatsoever as to the high quality of craftsmanship both inside and outside the house, especially in the saloon with its singularly fine plasterwork, designed and executed by Joseph Enzer in 1742, and particularly the unique quality of the great Roman triumphal arch which sheltered the front door.

As the house had been used as a hotel since 1947, the Trust could not obtain vacant possession until 1985, when the tenant acquired another house, Mrs Lovett's Broomley, nearby. After several visits, a will by Mrs Lovett in favour of the Trust was drawn up which included two farms, the Leys of Dun and the Mains of Dun, as well as the House, policies and woodlands. Mrs Lovett died in June 1980 and the Trust had just three months in which to make up its mind

House of Dun, Angus

whether or not to accept the bequest. With the previous consent of Mrs Lovett the Trust decided it would need to sell Leys of Dun and part of a collection of porcelain not crucial to the presentation of the House to help to fund the extensive repair and restoration which was Mrs Lovett's wish. The Trust also launched an appeal, which raised over £500,000 towards the capital works and endowment required. The Trust finally accepted the property and declared it inalienable on 14 August 1980.

Initially, it was hoped to open at least the ground floor and locate a suitable tenant for the upper floors. As the full potential was realised of the various rooms, much of whose original furniture was discovered languishing amid the soggy splendour of the 'new' kitchen or the ruinous stable buildings, or the basement and attics of the House, it became clear that here was another 'gem', which deserved full and sympathetic restoration for presentation to the public.

The Trust's restoration of the estate, the courtyard, the House and garden is a remarkable story of determination with meticulous attention to historical detail, carried out with help from a wide variety of sources over a period of five years. The dual purpose was to restore the property to its original 18th-century condition, but to reflect early 19th-century adaptations. The first phase of restoration was carried out in the surrounding parkland and woodland, consisting of 346 hectares (856 acres). Very little management had been carried out prior to the Trust's acquisition and many trees – too badly

damaged, or simply over-mature and dangerous – were removed. The former landscape is being recreated for future generations to enjoy, by replanting the avenues of beech and lime as well as clearing and resurfacing woodland walks.

The second phase of restoration was concerned with complete renovation of the ruined courtyard buildings including the central green, in the centre of which stands an intriguing wooden game larder raised on a central stilt. In the past, wagon and potting sheds, a bothy, hen houses and a late 18th-century kitchen were among House of Dun's outbuildings. Today there is the bothy complete with the model figure of a gamekeeper, a potting shed, shop and toilets for visitors. Ian Dale, the last handloom linen weaver in Scotland, is accommodated here and produces an attractive range of linen goods of traditional design. A tearoom has been created in the north stable and carriage house.

The House itself had to be entirely reslated and releaded, chimneystacks rebuilt and the south elevation refaced with rusticated masonry which had been removed early in the 20th century. The other major alteration was the replacement of the plate glass windows installed in 1857 with glazing bars conforming to the style of the 1730s. It was fortunate that one internal window remained to be copied. The intended balustrades on the north and south fronts of the house have been created by the Trust from William Adam designs, but funding still has to be found to provide the stone urn finials.

The careful rehabilitation and restoration of the interior of the House matches the standards of the outside work. Original colour schemes

Opposite:
House of Dun:
the Saloon

Left:
House of Dun: East
Walled Garden c 1890s

have been reinstated as far as possible using scrapes of the historic wallpapers. Furniture and paintings were recovered from various corners of the house and gently restored where necessary. The Saloon, which had been blue and white since the early 19th century, was painted sage green with white plasterwork and oak-grained doors. In this, the first room the visitor enters, Joseph Enzer's intricate decoration makes a lasting impression. It contains emblems referring to the 'Auld Alliance' between Scotland and France.

There has been some criticism in recent years that House of Dun was over-restored and that more of the existing decoration should have been kept. This latter approach is being

House of Dun: the restored Rose Garden

*House of Dun:
the official opening by
HM Queen Elizabeth
The Queen Mother,
28 April 1989*

porated to reflect her original design. Among the great glories of the gardens, policies and woodland are the snowdrops, which carpet the ground extensively in February, often coinciding with the spectacle of thousands of greylag geese winging their way over Montrose Basin.

ST ABB'S HEAD

The Head has a large and varied colony of around 70,000 nesting seabirds with spectacular coastal cliffs and stacks, and a freshwater loch created along a former glacial overflow channel, highlighting a geological fault between the volcanic rocks of the Head with older marine sediments inland. An offshore marine environment with unusually clear water supports colourful animals and plants, and on the cliffs there are arresting displays of spring flowers. All contribute to this stretch of dramatic unspoilt Berwickshire coast.

It is not surprising that the coast, from the village of St Abb's in the south to Fast Castle in the north, has been designated as a Grade 1 Site of Special Scientific Interest (SSSI). With the agreement of the landowner, farmer Tom McCrow of Northfield Farm, the Scottish Wildlife Trust (SWT) managed its natural resources, including seabirds and the Mire Dean, which provides cover and a food supply for migrating birds. This agreement was in place for three years prior to Northfield Farm being placed on the market.

The NTS realised the possibility of conferring permanent protection on the site and of working in close co-operation with SWT. George Russell, the Trust lawyer, persuaded Tom

followed at Newhailes. House of Dun was in keeping with Trust views and should perhaps be seen as a proposal of its time, then much praised, but from which we can learn for the future.

Finally, a Rose Garden created in the East Walled Garden by Lady Augusta, who was the natural daughter of the Duke of Clarence, later William IV, and the actress Dorothy Jordan, had disappeared altogether. The Scottish Gardens Committee decided in 1987 to recreate Lady Augusta's garden, based on a surviving photograph. The principal horticultural and architectural features, the petal-shaped and circular beds and the central rose arbour have all been incor-

McCrow to divide the farm into lots and began negotiations with him to purchase Lot 3. It was agreed that the Trust would buy 78 hectares (192 acres) of the Head, principally the coast as far as Pettico Wick harbour and including the Kirk Hill, the Mire Loch with its important fringe vegetation and associated scrub woodland, and a building suitable for the ranger's accommodation. The purchase price of £76,000 was met from a Trust legacy specifically to benefit bird life, the Coastline and Islands Fund and a purchase grant from the Countryside Commission for Scotland (CCS) of £20,000.

Peter Gordon, who had been farming in

Above:
St Abb's Head:
aerial view

Left:
St Abb's Head:
razorbills

Galloway, bought the remaining part of Northfield Farm. To the Trust's delight he also had an enthusiasm for natural history, especially birds! A Joint Management Committee comprising NTS, SWT, NCC, CCS, Borders Regional Council and Peter Gordon an adjacent farmer and tenant grazier, was established in 1981. The idea of joint responsibility for the reserve was consistent with Tom McCrow's wishes in selling the property, and maintained SWT's interest in and identification with the reserve. Inalienability, conferred by the NTS, assured the reserve's long-term future. In 1983, the area between Northfield House in the south and Pettico Wick in the north was designated a National Nature Reserve. In an effort to conserve the unusual quality and importance of the offshore environment, consultations were held with local fishermen and divers. As a result, Scotland's first Voluntary Marine Reserve, based on St Abb's and Eyemouth and extending to a depth of 50 metres (164 feet) – the limit of light penetration – was established in 1983.

Agreement in 1986 with Peter Gordon enabled a variety of uses to be made of the attractive range of low pantile-roofed farm buildings and space for a car park on the southern edge of the reserve. This has been crucial in helping to confine visitors' cars to the perimeter and encouraging access on foot via an attractive path from the farm to Starney Bay and beyond. Cars carrying disabled or infirm visitors can still park near the lighthouse buildings. In 1994, the adjacent farm of Blackpotts came on the market. Scottish Natural Heritage, having replaced NCC and CCS in 1992, came to the Trust's aid,

providing 50 per cent of the purchase price of £82,000 for 50 hectares (123 acres). It is written into the grazing lease with this farmland that there will be surplus grazing capacity at all times for the stock on St Abb's Head, thus ensuring relief of pressure on that more sensitive ground.

As far as the seabirds are concerned, management is confined to regular monitoring and recording changes in population levels, which may give a guide to their response to natural or man-made influences. Land birds are also annually counted during a Common Bird Census and migrant species are recorded. Such long-term observations on one site are invaluable in contributing to our overall appreciation of the health of birds at St Abb's.

The flowering success and therefore the future of the flora is much affected by the vagaries of the weather, coupled with the level of grazing pressure and the numbers of visitors. The drifts of thrift or sea-pink, splashed with golden bird's-foot trefoil and purple milk vetch can be spectacularly beautiful in a favourable year. Close liaison between the ranger, Kevin Rideout, and the tenant grazier, coupled with controlled Trust publicity for the property, is achieving a sensitive ecological balance. The Voluntary Marine Reserve is managed by SWT and, with education and interpretation of the resource, the appeal to sub-aqua clubs to help in conserving the riches of the sea has had a favourable effect.

A revised management plan was completed in 1992 followed by a full descriptive and prescriptive plan with project register and five-year work plan for 1997–2002. New work on the

Opposite:
St Abb's Head:
guided walk to see the
profusion of sea-pinks
after reduction in
sheep grazing

social and economic context of the property will follow, based on detailed consultation with the local community. The joint management committee for St Abb's has been replaced by a liaison group involving the local community and a management committee monitoring progress in meeting the objectives of the management plan. In 1999, the SWT decided to withdraw from its management role at St Abb's.

In spite of, or perhaps because of, the multiplicity of the designations and close attention to management involving numerous organisations and individuals over 21 years, St Abb's remains one of the most attractive properties belonging to the Trust. It still feels a truly wild place – long may it remain so.

COUNTRYSIDE DEVELOPMENTS

The Countryside Commission for Scotland (CCS) published its *Park System for Scotland* in 1975. The report proposed the establishment of urban, country, regional and special parks, with specific measures for nationally significant landscapes. The Trust supported much of the report, in particular the proposals on regional and country parks, and agreed with the Commission about Areas of Special Planning Control and the desirability of 'special parks', although it thought that the term 'special' was not explicit enough. The Trust's Council and Executive were also concerned that the report failed to recognise the part played by the voluntary sector in recreation and conservation in Scotland.

CCS with a selection of 40 areas of outstanding scenic beauty, which the Commission hoped local authorities would actively conserve, published *Scotland's Scenic Heritage* in April 1978. As with *Highland Landscape,* commissioned by the Trust and written by Bill Murray in 1962, nearly half the areas described included land either owned by the Trust and/or under Conservation Agreements: for example, Torridon, Kintail, Glencoe, St Kilda, Ben Lomond, the Island of Canna, Ben Lawers, and the River Tay (Dunkeld).

In response to the increase in visitors to the Scottish countryside, and to mountains in particular, Nigel Hawkins and Dr Denis Mollison, both elected members of Council, wrote a paper entitled *The Management of the Mountain Properties of The National Trust for Scotland.* Published in 1980, it certainly achieved its primary aim of stimulating discussion on the critical balance between preservation and 'welcome reception' at the Trust's mountain properties. As well as making positive comment and constructive recommendations on practical management, the authors proposed the creation of a Mountains Advisory Group to report regularly to Council. This was duly formed and remained active until its scope was broadened to become the Trust's Countryside Advisory Panel (1986–91). The report was seen by some as critical of the Trust and to address this, discussions were also held with the representative members on Council directly concerned with the Trust's mountainous and countryside properties – the Scottish Mountaineering Club, the Mountaineering Council of Scotland and the Scottish Countryside Activities Council.

In an effort to come to a common understanding over the criticisms levelled at the Trust and to improve communication, the two latter bodies were subsequently elected to the Trust's Council. Bill Myles, as the first representative member for the Mountaineering Council of Scotland, was important in 'pouring oil on troubled waters'. The Trust began to seek more financial support and advice for its programme of repair and maintenance of mountain footpaths and enlisted the expert services of Dr Bob Aitken on techniques and repair. As an independent consultant, Bob conducted a reconnaissance review of mountain footpaths in 1984 for CCS and was involved in trial work on Trust and other properties in Scotland.

The Trust had also long been concerned at the lack of statutory protection and grants for historic gardens and still more importantly designed landscapes, which had been ravaged since the war, by timber merchants and inability of most country-house owners to maintain them adequately. Although HBCS had been given powers to grant-aid gardens and historic landscapes, the expectation of the Scottish Office and the Treasury had been that such grants would be met out of the building repair grant vote which was already overstretched. Protracted negotiations on the subject having proved fruitless, with the Trust's encouragement the Royal Botanic Garden, the CCS and the HBCS initiated a joint pilot study of selected gardens undertaken by two very experienced garden historians employed by Land Use Consultants. This was published in 1982.

In 1984, a wider ranging assessment of 275 designed landscapes was carried out, a five-volume *Inventory of Gardens and Designed Landscapes in Scotland* being published in 1988

Opposite:
Glencoe: drain construction

by Historic Scotland and the successor body to CCS, Scottish Natural Heritage. The inventory became the key to statutory protection of the landscapes in it, under article 15 of the Town and Country Planning (General Development Procedure) (Scotland) Order 1992. In 1993, work began on the more important sites not included in the 1988 Inventory. It cannot be said, however, that the issue of the long-term maintenance of historic landscapes still in private hands has been resolved. The Inventory can only ensure that they are not actively eroded.

NEW WAYS AND MEANS

During this decade, membership of the Trust almost trebled, reaching over 100,000. The appeal of the increasing variety of properties, now consisting of over 40,470 hectares (100,000 acres), was clearly reaching a discerning and wider public. Commercial developments in the Trust, through 11 shops, were making a significant impact on the finances of the Trust and, most importantly, were demonstrating its own ability to improve them. Thanks to a magnificent gesture by Miss Margaret Paterson Barrie, the Trust received the largest-ever sum bequeathed to either NTS or the National Trust, of £1m. An office was established in Glasgow, initially with Murray Scrimgeour and then Trust Deputy Director Findlay McQuarrie, responsible for promoting the Trust in the city and the south-west. The Glasgow Advisory Panel was set up in 1970.

The 40th anniversary of the Trust was celebrated in 1971. Seven years later, the first international conference of National Trusts was held at Craigie College, Ayr, and the CCS Centre at Battleby, near Perth. It was jointly hosted by the NTS and Scottish American Heritage, and attracted 20 delegates from all over the world. A second conference was held in America in 1980 and such events were regularly repeated in future years in other countries.

After the economic difficulties of the mid-1970s, Jamie Stormonth Darling, now NTS Director, was considering options other than absolute ownership, which naturally made the Trust hesitant to accept other offers such as the island of Canna, then under active consideration. He proposed that: 'We should turn more often to a formula, and its many variations, that allows the prospective donor to remain in owner-ship and yet encourage the Trust to build up a supporting fund for the property'.[27] He wanted to encourage the Executive to consider these variations and explore new 'ways and means' of participating in future propositions without it having to be a question of all or nothing. Following the successful operation of the Country Parks at Culzean and later at Brodick, as well as the more unusual example of the Trust owning the plants but not the garden of Achamore on the island of Gigha, Jamie emphasised the desirability of moving into a new world of partnership, consortia and trusteeship.

The Chairman, Lord Bute, began the 48th Annual Report in 1979 with a quotation from William Packer, writing in the *Financial Times*: 'The thought of what this kingdom would be like now had the two Trusts never been is just too hard to bear …' The article commended 'the great work of conservation done on our behalf by the private initiatives of the two National Trusts'. Lord Bute concluded: 'I know of no other organisation – anywhere – whose staff work so hard and do so with such a wonderful spirit. It is fitting therefore that I should end by placing on record Council and Executive's profound gratitude to each and every one – from the Director, who has completed 30 inspiring years as our chief executive, to our newest recruit'.

The Trust had certainly tried, during this period, to fulfil Sir Frank Fraser Darling's appraisal of its position as the leading conservation organisation in the world.

CHAPTER SEVEN
VOLUNTEERING
1931–2001

'the generous partnership'[28]

DONALD HELM, 2000

THE GIFT OF TIME

Membership of the Trust's Council and Executive and all committees is unpaid and thus voluntary, an essential prerequisite. Since 1931, the contribution of these many men and women, in actively promoting the objectives of a leading voluntary conservation organisation, has been crucial to its development and deserves the highest public recognition. Perhaps Lord Wemyss himself best epitomises the volunteer ethic, having worked tirelessly in the service of Scotland and the Trust. A life member of the Trust since January 1938, he was elected to Council in 1945, was Chairman of Council from 1946 to 1968, became President of the Trust from 1967 until 1991, and President Emeritus from 1992, an honour created specially for him. Lord Wemyss still regularly attends Trust meetings and continues to take a keen interest in its affairs. It is appropriate that the splendid new Trust offices in Charlotte Square should carry his name – Wemyss House – in recognition of his service.

In 1997, the Trust invited a member of its Executive, Donald Helm, himself an enthusiastic volunteer, to investigate and report on volunteering in the Trust. A policy on volunteers has since been developed which will guide future management of this key resource. The Trust's Corporate Plan (1999–2004) gives prominence to volunteers, placing them on an equal basis with paid staff in relation to communication, training and recognition. In 2000, some 1,200 volunteers worked on the properties and at Head Office.

This chapter is devoted to all who give or have given time and expertise in whatever capacity to the Trust, which applauds volunteer

Chapter opening picture:
Fair Isle: Stewart
Thomson and volunteer

Above:
Falkland Palace:
a costumed guide

enthusiasm and dedication. It will be possible to mention only a few individuals by name, but that by no means reduces the value of the willing contributions made by so many over 70 years.

VOLUNTEERS AT PROPERTIES

Most Trust property managers offer opportunities for volunteers and many would find it much more difficult and costly to operate without them. The Georgian House in Edinburgh has over 300 volunteer guides including approximately 150 Friends of the Georgian House who organise fund-raising events; 19 flower arrangers; and 30 education guides. The Friends of Greenbank Garden in Glasgow give practical help in the garden, and set up and ran the shop/tea-room, until it became too large an operation. They provide catering for bus parties

Left:
Culzean Country Park:
member of the Young
Naturalists' Club on
the shore with a ranger

Below:
The Georgian House,
Edinburgh: volunteer
with a school party

and lunches for the West Regional Office committee meetings. They are informative guides when Greenbank House opens its rooms to visitors, having done extensive research on its history and contents.

A sewing group has worked for properties in the West Region, for example at Brodick and Culzean Castles, the Tenement House, Hutchesons' Hall, Weaver's Cottage, Holmwood House and Greenbank House itself. According to their constitution, money raised by the Friends must directly benefit the property. Since Greenbank Garden was opened in 1976, they have raised some £160,000 and so enabled most of the hoped-for developments to take place. Kathy Rice is the driving force behind much of what is achieved there.

In addition to raising funds and acting as

Left:
Nellie Jones, widow
of Wallace Jones of
SHUSA, receiving
his George Waterston
Memorial Award from
Lord Wemyss

Right:
Caroline Vevers with
her restored guard book
from Robert Smail's
Printing Works

as well as his great love of people were recognised when he was invited to join the Trust's Executive and Council. He undertook a roving commission for the Trust, visiting all the properties and sympathetically listening to staff about personal matters. He did much to engender a family spirit amongst all those connected with the Trust, receiving the award in 1989, and continuing as a strong supporter of the Stirling Members' Centre until his death in 2001.

Wally Jones was the first person, in 1990, to be given the George Waterston Memorial Award posthumously and so far the only non-British citizen to receive the distinction. An astute businessman and lawyer, Wally was legal adviser from its inception in 1965 to Scottish American Heritage Inc, later Scottish Heritage USA Inc or SHUSA. With his wife Nellie he stirred the American soul to support the NTS in innumer-

able ways, and helped to establish the very fruitful exchange of personnel between the Trust and the US National Park Service, and between Threave and Longwood Gardens, Pennsylvania. He took a personal interest in all who worked for the Trust.

George Russell served the Trust as its law agent for more than 30 years, until his retirement in 1982, when he was rewarded for his wisdom, dedication and enthusiasm by being elected a Councillor Emeritus, a position he still holds today. In 1992, he received a glass bowl specially engraved with illustrations of Drumbuie and Iona, two properties which benefited enormously from George's astuteness and professionalism. He chaired the working group which considered the Trust's response to the proposed construction of the Skye road bridge, taking into account the strong opinions held on that issue.

In 1974, he was the major contributor to a paper on the constitution of the Trust, which became known as the Russell Guidelines. At age 87, he continues to take an active interest in Trust affairs, including reading and commenting on the contents of this book, for which the author is most grateful. For his support of the Trust for 25 years he received the George Waterston Memorial Award in 1992.

Caroline Vevers, first employed by the Trust in 1983, received further training from a master craftsman under the Community Projects Programme and has worked voluntarily in the bookbinding workshop of the Trust on a four-day-a-week basis since 1991. She continues to assist cheerfully in all areas of antique book restoration and repair and has also been involved in picture framing. Caroline takes great pride in the work she does, most notably in the massive task she undertook when she repaired one of the 51 guard books from Robert Smail's Printing Works in Innerleithen. These huge volumes contain an example of each job and the date on which it was printed in the workshop, a practice continued today. The one selected for Caroline was the thickest, requiring each page to be separately repaired and finally bound in two volumes rather than the original one. Caroline spent 769 hours over three years on the job and in 1998 was given the George Waterston Memorial Award for her painstaking skill and commitment.

Tom Hall is a professional librarian, his final post before retirement in 1988 being Acting University Librarian for Aberdeen University. Following a talk on the Trust libraries by Christopher Hartley, then one of the Trust's Curators, Tom undertook the cataloguing of the libraries at Drum Castle, containing some 4,000

Left.
Tom Hall, who spent many years cataloguing Trust library books

Right.
Drumbuie

Malleny Garden
Open Day 2000

volumes, and at Haddo House, where there are some 3,700 volumes in the main library. In addition, he compiled a special catalogue of all the books at Drum and Crathes published before 1700, following British Library practice. As his citation indicated when he was given the George Waterston Memorial Award in 2000, Tom Hall is a quiet and retiring man whose dedicated work fully deserved formal recognition by the Trust.

A full list of recipients of the George Waterston Memorial Award since 1982 appears in Appendix 3.

TRUST MEMBERS' CENTRES

The Trust's first Members' Centres, established in 1974, were in Aberdeen and Edinburgh, the remainder being formed in the 1970s and 1980s. Apart from Suntrap, Malleny and Greenbank,

which came into being in 1977, 1980 and 1981 respectively, all the Friends Groups attached to individual properties were formed in the 1990s.

With a total membership of nearly 8,500, the Centres and Groups represent a significant volunteer bank for the Trust. In 2000, there were 34 Members' Centres, including Friends' Groups, and the London Members' Centre. The Centres are fiercely independent, each with its own constitution and freedom of action within the general purposes of the Trust.

Typical aims and objectives of Members' Centres and Friends' Groups are: to act as a local centre for furthering the work of The National Trust for Scotland; to bring the charitable aims and work of the Trust to the notice of local residents; to obtain new members for the Trust and to raise money for its appeals; and to make

*An Edinburgh Members'
Centre excursion to
St Abb's Head*

membership of the Trust more enjoyable and more effective.

The ways in which such objectives are achieved are as various as the number of Centres, but there are common threads. Annual programmes, carefully put together by Centre committees, offer a combination of summer excursions, including guided walks and winter lectures. Some Centres organise longer periods away to look at cultural or historical places of interest, mostly within Scotland but occasionally throughout the United Kingdom and even abroad. Then there are the events specially designed to support specific properties or occasionally departments at Head Office such as the Little Houses Improvement Scheme, the ranger service and NTS Conservation Volunteers. In 1998-9, the most creditable sum of £111,314

was raised for Trust projects.

There is little doubt, judging by the enthusiastic level of response, that Members' Centres organise enjoyable programmes and make a positive contribution to the work of the Trust. The members enjoy the company of other enthusiasts and derive much satisfaction in getting to know and being identified with the properties in their area.

CONSERVATION VOLUNTEERS

The first Conservation Volunteers were those concerned with the repair and maintenance of the cottages in Village Street on Hirta, the main island of St Kilda (see Chapter Three). George and Irene Waterston, of Fair Isle fame, led the first work party to Hirta in 1958. Since then work parties, who pay for the opportunity of visiting St Kilda, have continued to repair these buildings and the 'cleits' or storage structures every year. More recently, archaeological work parties have also carried out useful surveys, adding to our knowledge of this well-researched archipelago.

The first volunteers to Fair Isle arrived in 1963 under the auspices of the International Voluntary Service (IVS), followed by the Scottish Community Education Centre (Enterprise Youth). These groups were ably co-ordinated over many years by the Trust's representative on the island, Stewart Thomson, a recipient of the George Waterston Memorial Award in 1983. Supervision of many improvements beneficial to the local community was carried out by Alex Warwick, then Master of Works for the Trust. Fair Isle remains a popular work site for volunteers today.

Adventure Camps run by the Trust's Field Officer, Jock Nimlin, were first established in existing buildings at Balmacara, Kintail and Brodick in 1963, with a tented camp at Burg in 1966. Initially, the camps were financed through the charitable funds of the Trust, but in 1967 the buildings were offered on a rental basis to outdoor groups. Three days' voluntary service per week were optional, although the Trust clearly anticipated that parties would include work in their programme as 'it is our conviction that it not only satisfies a natural, healthy and laudable ambition in youth, but also provides the contrast which makes the days of freedom and adventure the more enjoyable'.

It is a continuing practice that volunteers are given at least one day off to relax during what is usually quite strenuous work and to enjoy and learn about the local area. Later Adventure Camps became known as Base Camps. After something of a hiatus, a new programme to establish additional or replacement Base Camps with funding from the Daniel Rutenberg Bequest was initiated at House of Dun and followed with camps at Torridon and, more recently, at Shore Lodge, Brodick.

NTS Youth in Trust was established in 1980 and run from Head Office. Local conservation groups were set up in 1983, covering the Lothians, Glasgow, Highland and Grampian, followed later by Tayside. In 1999, these local volunteer groups carried out 106 weekend projects totalling 11,286 hours' work on 34 Trust countryside properties all over Scotland. Tasks included footpath repair, woodland management, rhododendron control and fencing. Other work included stone dyking, gardening, pond clearance and litter picking.

In 1985, Thistle Camps became an integral part of Youth in Trust, offering week-long projects in some of the finest landscapes in Scotland. Such was their popularity that it became necessary to appoint a co-ordinator for Youth in Trust: Richard Miller was followed by Caroline Crichton Stuart, an enthusiast who inspired volunteers for two years before her tragic death in a road accident in 1984. Then John Mayhew, Jim Ramsay and currently Julia Downes have successively filled this important role in the conservation of the Trust's countryside properties. Supervision by Stewart Thomson of the IVS work camps on Fair Isle ceased in 1984 when John Mayhew based in Edinburgh took over that

Burg:
Thistle Camp volunteers
receiving instructions on
tool safety

Torridon:
dyking on the Farm

*Burg: Thistle Camp
repairing road*

task. The standard of accommodation and facilities on Thistle Camps has vastly improved in recent years, not least in response to health and safety considerations. Minibuses to transport volunteers have specially adapted safety compartments for tools, and volunteer accommodation on projects is comfortable, including good washing facilities, vital after dirty work.

Youth in Trust changed its name to NTS Conservation Volunteers in 1989 in order to meet the strong desire by its members and co-ordinator, then John Mayhew, to reflect more accurately what was done, and the much wider age range of people who were flocking to join the organisation. John's remit had been to expand the work of Youth in Trust, which he certainly achieved by more than trebling the number of Thistle Camps in five years, before he moved on to the Policy Research Department of the Trust. Several other early Youth in Trust and Conservation Volunteers have gone on to hold responsible posts in both the Trust and other

conservation organisations. Arthur Martin, who began with Youth in Trust, became a leader, then seasonal ranger and senior ranger at Crathes, where he is currently Resident Property Manager. Duncan Stevenson, also an active Youth in Trust member, rose to be senior ranger at Brodick Country Park and has now filled one of the newly created Countryside Manager posts, based in the north-east Regional Office at Castle Fraser. Another volunteer, Chris Cairns, went on to become Environment Correspondent for *The Scotsman*.

In 1999, in order to improve volunteer training, safety provision, communication and the standard and support of work carried out at the properties, responsibility for the five local groups was devolved to the Regions. That same year, 36 Thistle Camps were in operation on 21 properties. Key tasks undertaken were the construction of the 11-metre (36-feet) Galloway footbridge at Dollar Glen, corncrake habitat management at Balmacara and Iona, woodland management at Killiecrankie and Glencoe, rhododendron clearance at Brodick and bracken control at Burg and Inverewe. Over half the volunteers at these camps are under the age of 26, with slightly more women applying than men. A good percentage of these return, taking part in two or more projects. Local groups and Thistle Camps accomplished an impressive 27,262 hours of work in 1999, equivalent to a cost saving for the Trust of some £124,200.

Training young people to appreciate the environment of Scotland is a major objective of the Trust in running such projects. Participants who become involved with the Trust in this way

Left:
Mar Lodge: Thistle
Camp constructing
a wall

Right:
Iona: Conservation
Volunteers fencing
on the dune system

are an investment in its future and thus in conservation in Scotland. Work on a weekend task or a Thistle Camp provides valuable experience and a useful reference for future employment, as well as satisfaction and enjoyment.

Other groups that, in different ways, make a thoroughly worthwhile contribution, include the army's HQ in Scotland under its Military Aid to the Civil Community Scheme, and the early government Manpower Services Commission schemes. The former carried out a wide variety of property-based projects, otherwise unaffordable, which required ingenuity and resourcefulness, for example the creation of adventure playgrounds, bridge building, demolition of wartime structures and new path development. The latter provided constantly changing teams of mainly young unemployed people, who cheerfully undertook tasks varying from book-

binding, needle and metalwork to the restoration of 700 18th-century flintlock service pistols and 300 hanger swords in the Culzean Castle armoury. The Trust employed permanently two talented youngsters from these schemes. Stewart Colquhoun, in charge of bookbinding, still works for the Trust and Rodney French, architectural metal worker, spent many years with the Trust before going on, with the encouragement of Curator David Learmont, to run his own business.

CONCLUSION

The conclusion to this chapter is simple. With the knowledge of what is being achieved, one has to ask where, if anywhere, the Trust would be without such outstanding support in so many of its activities?

CHAPTER EIGHT
EXPANSION AND REORGANISATION
1981–1990

'As the Trust grows so must its

organisational structure adapt.'[29]

THE SIXTH MARQUESS OF BUTE, 1980

A WIND OF CHANGE – REORGANISATION

The Trust celebrated its Golden Jubilee in 1981 with a momentous, event-packed year which attracted favourable publicity and provided a much-needed financial springboard for many future projects. The year had, more poignantly, been the 50th anniversary of the evacuation of the last residents of St Kilda. On 27 August, with the co-operation of the army and the navy, some 20 St Kildans visited their former homes, and were able to worship in their church, restored by the Trust. At the service four clergy (including a Canadian St Kildan) took their place in the pulpit, said to be the largest in the Hebrides. Other notable anniversaries included

that of Sir Jamie Stormonth Darling's exceptional tenure as Secretary, then Director for 34 years, in 1983, and 40 years of continuous service by the Trust's President Lord Wemyss in 1987. The Trust was to enjoy the wise counsel of Lord Wemyss for many years to come but Jamie retired in 1983, ending an era in which their combined leadership had been outstanding. Jamie's personal contribution to the success of the Trust was recognised by a knighthood in the New Year's Honours list the same year.

The Trust began to forge more imaginative partnerships. It had already provided public access and the necessary facilities for the enjoyment of its properties, but it recognised that the Scottish Tourist Board's grant-aid for the promotion of tourism in Scotland could further its success. Brief hesitation on the Trust's part at the possibility of being labelled a tourism organisation, was quickly dispelled and the relationship flourished. More than £500,000 came the Trust's way, in the form of grants to improve visitor facilities at its properties.

When Sir Jamie Stormonth Darling retired in 1983, Lester Borley, formerly Head of the Scottish Tourist Board, was appointed as Director of the Trust. The appointment of an expert in cultural tourism signalled a new direction, but also a change in atmosphere within The National Trust for Scotland. Reorganisation both in Head Office and countrywide became the new priority and was inevitably to change the character of what had been a close-knit, almost patriarchal institution. On becoming its Director, Lester comments that his assessment of the Trust was that 'its work was very important and vital. What obviously I could see was, and this is no criticism, that it had grown like Topsy, and was dominated by Jamie, a charismatic figure, who was like a Sun King, with everyone depending on him. My first job was to delegate and create a broader system of management using existing skills and experience of staff who had served the Trust for years'.[30]

Lester opted to reorganise Head Office into Administrative, Property Management, Financial Services and Marketing Divisions, retaining control of the new Central Policy and External Relations team. Regional Directors managed the properties and represented the Trust countrywide through five regions: Central and Tayside; Grampian; Highland; Lothians, Fife and the Borders; and West.

He also drove home his policy on reorganisation with an initiative to build on existing staff expertise through training. John Mayhew, for example, in his new role as Planning and Research Officer, undertook a three-year day-release course on planning, and buildings surveyors studied the latest building conservation techniques. An exchange programme for management staff between the Trust and the United States National Parks Service was instituted in order to expand the Trust's body of professional experience, using funding from Scottish Heritage USA Inc (see Chapter Four). Curators, regional directors, factors, rangers, gardeners and my own team of interpretation staff all benefited from these training courses. Other staff, with encouragement from the centre, developed working relations with kindred organisations in other parts of Europe. Regional Buildings Surveyor Iain Davidson linked with conservation workshops in Estonia, and Margaret Cameron, Education Adviser, worked with the King Baudouin Foundation to arrange the exchange of ten NTS Conservation Volunteers with ten Belgians. Neal Sharp went off to Croatia to advise on the restoration of old Venetian village houses, and Charles Strang gave advice to an incipient conservation trust in northern Cyprus.

GOLDEN JUBILEE YEAR 1981

The Golden Jubilee Appeal for Places in Peril was launched in January 1981 'to continue and expand the work of the Trust – saving for posterity many of the country's finest buildings,

beautiful places and historic shrines'. The Golden Jubilee Appeal Committee was led by Sir Robin MacLellan as Chairman and ably organised by Alex Paulin (Controller, Finance and Investment). Hervey Stuart Black was Chairman for Scotland, the Duke of Atholl in London, and Sir Peter Boon was Chairman of the International Committee. The Trust's Chairman Lord Bute and his wife travelled the world as part of the Appeal effort, visiting local committees in Hong Kong, Australia, New Zealand, Canada and the United States. The Golden Jubilee Appeal raised over £2m for Trust causes.

High-profile events that year included a thanksgiving service in Glasgow Cathedral, receptions hosted by the Secretary of State for Scotland in Edinburgh Castle and the Lord Provost of Glasgow in its City Chambers, and a garden party at Falkland Palace, graced with the presence of our Patron, Her Majesty Queen Elizabeth The Queen Mother. The *Treasures in Trust* exhibition at the Royal Scottish Museum, opened by HM The Queen and HRH the Duke of Edinburgh, attracted a record 50,000 visitors. About 50 Trust staff from all over the country were invited to attend a royal garden party at the Palace of Holyroodhouse, including Chrissie McGillivray from Burg, Lea and Margaret MacNally from Torridon and Stewart and Annie Thomson from Fair Isle, illustrating again the great family spirit and care for people which the Trust exemplified. Lord Gibson, Chairman of the National Trust, spoke as the honoured guest at the NTS AGM and *Treasures of Scotland* by Magnus Magnusson, a book about Trust-owned properties, was published.

The Members' Centres of the Trust organised a plethora of Jubilee events across Scotland 'flavoured with a family feeling, so pleasant and characteristic an ingredient of Trust activities'.[31] There was a popular 'Open Day' at properties when some 10,000 crocus bulbs were planted in Charlotte Square with the help of pupils from five Edinburgh primary schools.

The following three property acquisitions during this period – a west coast island, an intriguing Glasgow tenement and a famous mountain, all eminently worthy of conservation – illustrate well the diverse subjects which the Trust has had to consider. Each has been declared inalienable.

THE ISLAND OF CANNA

As early as 1956, Dr John Lorne Campbell, owner of the island of Canna since 1938, was considering the Trust as the possible recipient of his property, including his valuable house and library. Correspondence appears again in 1973 about the possible conveyance of the island to the Trust during the lifetime of the owner. Dr Campbell was anxious to give up his farming enterprise in order to devote more time to his literary projects.

Jamie Stormonth Darling realised that Dr Campbell's generous gift of Canna, to include the island of Sanday, integral to the farming community, his extensive Celtic and Scottish library and his wife Margaret's unique recordings of Gaelic songs and photographs, could only be transferred to the Trust's care with the financial support of the National Heritage Memorial Fund (NHMF). This had been empowered to purchase parts of the national

heritage under threat. It was also relevant because Jamie, with others, had worked hard in the debates over the Fund to ensure the importance of collections remaining *in situ*.

Acceptance of Dr Campbell's gift was made possible by generous financial assistance from NHMF in the form of an initial contribution of £335,000, the first of several major allocations to the Trust. To this the Trust added its own contribution of £150,000 from the 1981 Golden Jubilee Appeal. Canna House was bought for £50,000. One of the conditions of grant was that the library would remain on Canna for all time.

John Campbell and his wife, Dr Margaret Fay Shaw, had devoted their lives to the island and its community and wished to ensure that their 50 years of careful husbandry would be continued. They had strong literary connections with St Xavier University at Antigonish, Nova Scotia. In order to keep alive this link Alan Boyd, son of the conservationist and naturalist Dr John Morton Boyd and student of Gaelic at Glasgow University, was invited to St Xavier for six weeks in 1981 to research into Gaelic in Cape Breton.

The endowment for Canna had been calculated on the basis that the farm would not be managed by the Trust. When John Campbell became older and less fit in 1983, the farm was taken in hand by the Trust and managed by Ian Mackinnon and his family. Difficult years followed, largely due to the Trust's failure to realise the inherent problems of managing a remote island property from the mainland. Despite these setbacks the Trust, with help from grant-giving agencies, carried out a variety of structural improvements to the estate housing, farm buildings and other vital infrastructure. In the first ten years some £400,000 worth of repair and restoration was accomplished and in the next five years over £1m was committed to Canna, including a contribution to the costs of a new pier. During a reorganisation of the Trust in 1995, under Chairman Hamish Leslie Melville's direction, a regional Trust office for Argyll, Lochaber and the Western Isles was established in Oban. A part-time factor charged with particular responsibility for the care of the island and its farming community was appointed. An experienced contract farm supervisor, a native of Benbecula, currently manages the farm.

John Campbell's extensive libraries and sound archive, together with the photographic records compiled by Margaret Campbell, are outstanding. Canna is remarkable for its natural beauty and the rich variety of interest it offers to both the serious student and the enthusiastic amateur. Archaeologically, it illustrates Mesolithic and Neolithic, Bronze Age and Iron Age periods, as well as more recent settlements. It is sheer joy to walk over the springy wild-flower-rich grasslands of Sanday in spring or summer. The Special Protection Area under the European Birds Directive is designed to conserve the varied seabird colonies. The marine environment, particularly rich in the offshore clear waters, also attracts human as well as ornithological divers.

Positive steps in Trust recognition of Canna's unusually rich combination of interests were taken in 1992 when Lord Bute, President of

Above left:
Canna: the Celtic Cross

Above right:
Canna: spring flowers

Left:
Dr John Lorne Campbell
on the steps of Canna
House

the Trust and Chairman of the Trustees of the National Museums of Scotland (1985-1993), invited Hugh Cheape of the Museum of Antiquities to 'look at the Canna situation'. Hugh accepted and was astonished when on his first visit to Canna, John Campbell quietly presented him with a file which turned out to be the catalogue of his archives of 600 box files of papers, detailed and cross-referenced! Hugh was greatly excited by this and later, on board John Bute's boat the *King Duck,* told the others: 'This is absolutely incredible, what is now in the Trust's hands – we have to do something.'[32]

Hugh wrote two reports for Lord Bute, strongly emphasising the value of the collections accumulated by the Campbells and making recommendations on what he believed the Trust should do. The Trust was developing its management plan for Canna (1994–9) which recommended that a 'core group' should be established to produce a detailed 'citation' for the island. Written by Hugh Cheape in collaboration with Dr Morton Boyd, who knew the Campbells and Canna well, the *Citation of Heritage* defined the island's assets and its resources, met with academic approval and led to the formation of the Canna Advisory Group. The first meeting took place on Canna in September 1995 when the group undertook the conservation of Dr Campbell's recordings made in the early 1930s, and produced an index to the Canna sound archive. The copyright of all Dr Campbell's published and scholarly work was secured by the Trust in 1996.

Lester Borley arranged visits to Canna in the 1980s for the Highlands and Islands

Development Board (HIDB) and the Hebridean Trust. NTS developed co-operation with the latter body, which secured major funding, mainly through the Heritage Lottery Fund, for the conversion to a hostel of the deconsecrated St Edward's Roman Catholic Church on Sanday and the associated Point House. The church has been designed to accommodate visitors as well as students studying the archives in Canna House and the cultural and environmental aspects of the two islands. Future uses of this highly successful conversion, finally completed in 2001, will integrate fully with the farming community on the island. In promoting these developments, the Trust has always been careful to seek and confirm the agreement of the residents of Canna, including the Campbells and the Gaelic community. Dr John Campbell died in 1996 aged 89, and is survived by his wife. Hopefully, the Trust's current plans will benefit the island and the islanders and create a fitting memorial to the life work of Dr John Lorne Campbell and his wife, Dr Margaret Fay Shaw.

THE HILL HOUSE

Charles Rennie Mackintosh's Hill House, situated high on sloping ground overlooking the Clyde estuary, is aptly named. In 1902, Walter Blackie, the Glasgow publisher, commissioned Mackintosh to design an indubitably Scottish and thoroughly modern family home. Blackie took possession of the house two years later and lived there until he died in 1953. There was discussion between the Estate Duty Office and the Trust at this point to assess whether the property might be offered in part payment of

*The Hill House:
the hallway*

death duties, through the National Land Fund, and acquired by the Trust. Nikolaus Pevsner, Slade Professor of Fine Art at Cambridge, worried that the house would be put up for sale and the furniture scattered, exhorted the Trust to save 'this foremost example of Mackintosh's domestic architecture'. [33] Basil Spence and other prominent architects wrote in similar vein. With no prospect of endowment, however, the Trust was reluctant to proceed with negotiations. Blackie's trustees accepted an offer of private sale to T Campbell Lawson, who cared for and generously showed the house to any one interested. He continued to live there until 1972. As a result of subscription notably from architects,

the Pilgrim Trust and the Royal Scottish Museum, the house was then acquired on favourable terms by the Royal Incorporation of Architects in Scotland (RIAS).

By 1980–1 RIAS, the Landmark Trust, the NHMF and NTS were in discussion on the future of the house. The Hill House Trustees, set up after Walter Blackie's death, offered to convey the property to the NTS. This was conditional on NHMF giving a sufficient grant to NTS to meet the cost of outstanding repairs and improvements, with an endowment for the future. Existing commitments, particularly over Canna, then under discussion with NHMF, caused Jamie Stormonth Darling to request the

RIAS to remain in charge during the 1981 season. NHMF provided £400,000 towards endowment and £25,000 towards purchase of The Hill House, together with some major Mackintosh furniture, which the Blackies had allowed to remain in the house. Some items, which had left the house with the Blackies, have since returned. The property was accepted in May 1982 and declared inalienable.

Following serious leaks in the roof, Geoffrey Jarvis, the Trust's Consultant Architect, produced a report on the deteriorating condition of the building and the major repairs required. Extensive restoration was necessary, which included a controversial rebuilding of the north gable. In consultation with HBCS, the original harling was retained and, after research, the exterior of the building repainted in its original grey colour. Painstaking research into the original interior wall decoration was undertaken by Rab Snowden of the Stenhouse Conservation Centre. Where possible, the patterns rediscovered were preserved and elsewhere replicated to complete the scheme.

In 1988, professional and academic criticism was levelled at the Trust's presentation of the interior of the house, which was shown as designed and furnished by Charles Rennie Mackintosh for Walter Blackie, but without, some felt, sufficient emphasis on the famous architect. The Trust agreed that in the four principal rooms precedence would be given to the Mackintosh theme, and throughout the rest of the interior the Blackie family interest would continue to be made evident. Such a contrast was intended to reflect and illuminate the client/

architect relationship as well as maintaining the important character of the family which built it and who were historically interesting in their own right.

Thanks to the Trust's policy of not reletting flats when they became available, over the next decade a number of changes became possible. On the upper floor is an information room and exhibition of modern domestic design masterminded by the gifted and enterprising Property Manager, Anne Ellis. Damage to ceilings and plasterwork caused by the number of visitors obliged the Trust in 1995 to control admissions through timed visits to the house.

Only a small number of pieces of

The Hill House: exhibition of modern design

Overleaf: The Tenement House, Glasgow

Mackintosh furniture have been acquired, although the Trust is still hopeful of purchasing or being given or lent further Mackintosh originals. The Trust was, however, particularly fortunate to receive as a gift from Donald and Eleanor Taffner of New York, a washstand, originally designed and made for the house. This had come up at auction some six years earlier but the Trust had been unsuccessful in securing a purchase. Thanks to the generosity of the Taffners, devoted Mackintosh enthusiasts, The Hill House is now much richer.

The garden has been developed to retain design features known to be attributable to either Mackintosh or Blackie with further planting reflecting a typical suburban garden of a large house at the beginning of the 20th century. An interesting mobile sculpture, designed in 1997 by George Rickey, alludes to the design of the adjacent rectangular-shaped windows. The Hill House has international status for the qualities of its architecture and design. Visitors are unfailingly inspired by Mackintosh's astonishingly modern style with its ever-fascinating interior decor and designs, which delight the eye in a play of light.

THE TENEMENT HOUSE

The Victorian tenement flat at 145 Buccleuch Street, Garnethill, Glasgow was offered to the Trust in 1982 for £20,000, ahead of being placed on the market by the then owner, actress Anna Davidson. She had had the foresight to preserve its original features and many of the contents accumulated by its previous owner and wished to secure their future. Findlay

McQuarrie, then Deputy Director, and the Trust's Glasgow Advisory Panel who, in the past, had already discussed the Trust acquiring a tenement property, immediately supported the idea. Jamie Stormonth Darling, on an early visit, felt 'it looks as if through this property we could bring a fresh dimension to the Trust and especially its image in Glasgow'. [34] The Glasgow membership, when consulted, agreed and offered a voluntary guiding service.

Acquisition was by no means universally supported within the organisation. The unique challenge, beyond critical questions of conservation, was to manage visitors without causing disturbance to the occupants living in the five other flats that shared a common entrance.

There was no time to launch an appeal for the purchase price but using the Golden Jubilee Appeal Fund, which was, after all, 'for places in peril', solved the immediate difficulty. The Carnegie UK Trust and the Scottish Tourist Board both helped and Strathclyde Regional Council offered a grant towards the service for schools.

The Trust was praised for taking on the challenge and, with an eye to acquiring a second flat, its Council took the plunge in 1982 and bought the property. The Tenement House welcomed visitors the following year and soon received the 'Come to Britain' Award. Two further flats were acquired on the ground floor in 1985 and 1990 respectively, providing more interpretation for visitors, staff accommodation, reception, school and exhibition space.

Head of Education, Marista Leishman, had engaged Bill Ritchie, Lecturer in History at

Previous page:
The Tenement House:
kitchen with box-bed

Right:
Ben Lomond:
Blairvockie Farm

Moray House, to write the BP-sponsored *Educational Guide to The National Trust for Scotland* in 1982. The extensive collection of personal papers left to NTS with The Tenement House allowed Bill, as education adviser, to produce the Tenement House Wallet schools pack, also sponsored by BP, about the long and fascinating life of its tenant, Miss Toward. She had lived there from 1911 to 1965 and, squirrel like, kept almost everything as it was until she had to go into hospital. The house has a splendid view over the north of Glasgow – how many travellers on the busy M8 below realise what a treasure awaits them if they care to take a short detour?

BEN LOMOND

It is due to Sir Iain Colquhoun's foresight and pragmatic approach to conservation that the west shore of Loch Lomond has been preserved as a crucial part of this well-loved landscape. The Trust remains in Sir Iain's debt not only for the care of his estate of Luss, including the working hill sheep farm, but for acting as the Trust's Chairman for its first 15 years and as a Vice President for two years. As stated in the Trust's Annual Report for 1946: 'It is openly acknowledged that the notable successes that have been achieved by the Trust in so short a time are primarily due to Sir Iain's vision,

counsel and driving force, and the public spirited manner in which he freely devoted his time to the furtherance of its interests.'

In 1950, Ben Lomond, 974 metres (3,194 feet) and some of the lower ground near Rowardennan was bought for the nation with support from the National Land Fund (NLF) set up following the Second World War to commemorate those who lost their lives while fighting for their country. The land was given by NLF to the Forestry Commission.

It is no surprise that accolades have been showered on the Ben and the loch. It was amongst the outstanding regions described by W H Murray in *Highland Landscape*; as 'epitomising the landscape of Scotland' in the CCS publi-

cation *Scotland's Scenic Heritage*; and designated, at least in part, as a Site of Special Scientific Interest by the Nature Conservancy Council. The area is to become Scotland's first National Park in April 2002.

In the 1980s the Forestry Commission (part of which is now Forest Enterprise) had a policy of selling off non-forestry assets to raise capital. Realising the public outcry there would be were it to sell to a private developer, it offered Ben Lomond, including Blairvockie farm, to the Trust for £142,000. CCS made the purchase possible with a special grant to the Trust and NHMF gave £100,000, matched by the same amount by the Trust from its Golden Jubilee Fund. The Trust then promoted an interna-

Left:
Ben Lomond, from
Duncryne, Gartocharn

Right:
Ben Lomond:
sculpture for the National
Memorial Park

tional appeal towards the endowment, with a target of £350,000. This popular property was bought in 1984 and declared inalienable, forming part of the Loch Lomond Regional Park designated in 1988.

The National Heritage Memorial Park of Ben Lomond was declared in 1995 by Michael Forsyth, then Secretary of State for Scotland, and formally opened in 1997 by his successor Donald Dewar, later First Minister of the Scottish Parliament. The stone memorial close to the car park was designed to symbolise the freedom won for us at such cost by those who gave their lives in the Second World War.

The Trust appointed a ranger-naturalist for Ben Lomond in 1992 and built a house at Ardess in 1997 as ranger accommodation, a countryside centre including an office, volunteer accommodation and a tool store. The Trust signed a Concordat with Forest Enterprise in 1996 for active joint management. Fencing exclosures (see Ben Lawers – Chapter Two) on the lower slopes, coupled with a reduction in sheep numbers, are encouraging natural regeneration of the many habitats on the Ben. In 1998, as a result of co-funding from Europe and from Scottish organisations, habitat restoration, interpretation and footpath improvements were all carried out.

FYVIE CASTLE

It was in 1972 that the Trust first negotiated with Sir Ian Forbes-Leith over the possible acceptance of Fyvie Castle with its valuable collection of pictures and paintings. Although it already owned some of the prize castles in north-east Scotland, the Trust fully appreciated

Fyvie's outstanding architectural and historical interest. Not only had it been a royal castle until 1370, six of the principal Scottish families in the north-east – Lindsay, Preston, Meldrum, Seton, Gordon, and Leith – had links with the Castle spanning more than seven centuries. Here was the opportunity to tell the story of the famous Castles of Mar. The National Land Fund, as it still was in 1972, was likely to be the main source of the necessary finance but in the end Sir Ian and his son, Sir Andrew, decided that family resources could not provide the endowment fund which the Trust specified, and withdrew from negotiations.

With the death of his father in 1979, Sir Andrew Forbes-Leith instructed his lawyer to return to NTS over the future of Fyvie. Transfer of lands adjoining the castle to a family trust had made acquisition more difficult for NTS, and the Trust had already absorbed a good proportion of available public funds for Haddo House and Brodie Castle. Jamie Stormonth Darling was in favour of an approach to the Secretary of State on the basis of the wider context of Fyvie. He proposed a high-level meeting with Sir Andrew to discuss, 'openly and frankly', the future of his property. In August 1982, however, Sir Andrew Forbes-Leith put the property on the market at an upset price, while the family retained the wider estate. Some of the paintings and more valuable items in the Castle were to be sold.

Sir Andrew agreed to postpone the sale of Fyvie and to delay the planned auction of its contents by Sotheby's to allow a search for means to preserve the buildings with their contents as an

*Fyvie Castle,
Aberdeenshire*

entity. The Trust continued to take the initiative: it set up the Fyvie Technical Group and held discussions with the now more relevant National Heritage Memorial Fund. The Chairman of the Fund, Lord Charteris, the President of NTS, and the Chairman of the Historic Buildings Council for Scotland (HBCS) the Earl of Crawford and Balcarres took prominent roles in promoting the preservation of Fyvie.

Lester Borley revived negotiations with the family and secured the Castle and its contents for £1.75m. Meanwhile, support for Trust ownership grew and NHMF offered £3m over three years for the whole property, while HBCS also offered to assist with longer-term maintenance grants. Fyvie finally came into the Trust's care in 1984 and was declared inalienable. Lord Charteris always reckoned that the acquisition of Fyvie was one of the best bargains ever struck.

The Banff and District Tourist Board allocated special funds to make Fyvie Castle – the only stately home in its area – the centrepiece of its publicity campaign. The National Galleries of Scotland negotiated with the Trust Curator, David Learmont, to borrow a selection of the best of the paintings for a *Treasures of Fyvie* exhibition to be held in the National Portrait Gallery during the 1985 Edinburgh Festival.

The exhibition also included a marvellous selection of furniture, sculpture, ceramics and glass, and arms and armour from the rich collections at Fyvie, including some items on loan from Sir Andrew Forbes-Leith. A first-class catalogue was produced. The pictures were also exhibited at Agnew's in London, thus attracting nation-wide interest in this magnificent property.

The Curator prepared plans to present the Castle as it was in its heyday of 1890–1914. Some proposals had to be deferred until more funds became available, for example for the refurbishment of the famous Gallery, hung with 17th-century tapestry, in the Leith Tower and some of the bedrooms. Much redecoration, restoration and refurnishing was undertaken. The property was finally opened by Lord Charteris of Amisfield on 1 May 1986 and attracted 65,000 visitors in that first season. The following year a *Castles of Mar* exhibition was on display at Fyvie.

NHMF agreed to provide further funds for additional restoration work, which lasted five years.

The Trust has since created in the old rose garden an area devoted to the cultivation of North American plants, which reflect the association of the USA with the family of Alexander Forbes-Leith, who made his fortune in the steel industry there. At the time of writing, an attractive project based upon the designs of plaster ceilings in the castle is being developed in the walled garden. A two-acre Garden of Scottish Fruits and Vegetables has been carefully researched and designed by the Gardens Adviser for the North-East Region, Robert Grant. Every Scottish soft fruit known to the Trust to be in cultivation will be represented as well as Scottish apples and other fruit. The final stage of this exciting project, the tree planting, was carried out in the autumn of 2000 ready for the Trust's 70th anniversary in 2001.

Opposite:
Fyvie Castle:
portrait of General
the Hon William
Gordon of Fyvie by
Pompeo Batoni

Above left:
Fyvie Castle:
the Drawing Room

Above right:
Fyvie Castle:
the Gallery

Left:
Robert Smail's Printing
Works, hanging sign

Right:
Robert Smail's
Printing Works:
the office

INDUSTRIAL HERITAGE

Lester Borley was enthusiastic that although the Trust already owned some industrial properties such as Preston Mill, the Angus Folk Museum and the Kippen Smiddy, it should develop a policy to save the increasing number of sites which were in terminal decline, in danger of being destroyed or converted for other purposes. Opportunities arose when two such properties became available in quick succession – a rare example in the Borders town of Innerleithen of a still functioning print works and a recently disused meal mill in Angus. Each property had been owned by several generations of the same families.

ROBERT SMAIL'S PRINTING WORKS

It was thanks to Cowan Smail's habit of not dispensing with any contents that his printing works attracted the attention of Maurice Rickards of the Ephemera Society, who happened on the works during a holiday in Scotland, and realised that here was something eminently worthy of preservation. In 1984, he carried out a three-day examination of the contents, then owned by Cowan, grandson of the enterprising Robert Smail, and with Cowan's somewhat bemused consent took some of the irreplaceable archives to Innerleithen Town Hall for safe-keeping. He contacted Richard Miller, then NTS Regional Director for Lothians, Fife and Borders, to alert him to his discovery. The following year, Cowan decided to retire and put the property on the market. Lester Borley sought expert advice from Ian Wilson of the printing firm Pillans and Wilson on possible acquisition. The NTS Chairman, Willie Cuthbert, also lent his weight to those in support and the property was acquired in 1986, despite an early belief on Cowan's part that he had been graced with a visit from the *National Front* instead!

The Printing Works has records dating back to 1873, mostly stored in brown paper parcels, tied up with string. The printing machinery, case upon case of lead type, and the 50 or so enormous 'guard books' holding examples of every job printed each day between 1876 and 1956, are unique to Smail's. The guard books, which derive their name from the paper 'guard' that separates the pages and allows them to have inserts pasted on each side, may look untouched but they have been de-acidified. They are now kept for reference in an outhouse formerly designed for Cowan's coal!

The story could have had a different ending, had Richard Miller not awoken early on the morning of the sale with a premonition that he should get there quickly. He arrived just in time to retrieve most of Smail's invaluable records from a row of polythene sacks – the product of a final overnight clear-up by the conscientious owner – lined up on the edge of the road waiting for the bin-men!

The Trust was fortunate in having two time-served printers on its Head Office staff, Ian Boyter and Eric Rooney, both compositors to trade. Their advice was invaluable to the sympa-

thetic interpretation of Robert Smail's. It speaks volumes for the significance of Robert Smail's and the staff who continue the tradition of hand-set printing there, that in 2000 the American Quinque Foundation, through the Royal Oak Foundation, provided a most generous sum of $600,000 (£372,000), which endowed the quirky, characterful 101st property of the Trust with a sound financial future. Any visitor (and especially those who still remember the smell of printer's ink) will find the Printing Works intriguing.

BARRY MILL

Barry Mill became the 5th industrial property acquired by the Trust. It was bought for £27,000 in 1988 from Mrs Catherine Lawrence (née Gunn) and partly funded from a legacy of £61,000 from the estate of Miss Isobel Nish, 'for use by the Trust at a property in Angus' and partly with the aid of a bequest from Miss Isabelle Tyrie. Mrs Lawrence, who occupied the mill cottage for the remainder of her life, greatly contributed to the subsequent interpretation of the history and use of the meal mill, on the site of which there was evidence of milling since the early to mid-18th century. Barry Mill contains an example of an overshot waterwheel where the water, which powers the mill, flows over the top of the wheel, in contrast to Preston Mill in East Lothian which has an undershot wheel.

Barry Mill is an early example of project management which proved the prototype for Project Planning and Management Guidelines designed by David Hickling, who was appointed as the Trust's Director of Property Management

Barry Mill, Angus: Manager Peter Ellis explains the milling process

Services in 1990. Project management teams followed the five stages of project planning and management from conception to completion. A new path and visitor car park were efficiently built by a Military Aid to the Civil Community scheme in 1991 and a permanent representative for the property was also appointed that year. The mill machinery was repaired and restored by John Ridley of Blair Atholl Mill. The Trust also extended the orchard by planting 25 additional historic apple trees, to increase visitors' interest in the property.

THE ISLAND OF STAFFA

The romantic and uninhabited island of Staffa lies some seven miles west of Mull and the same distance north-east of Iona. It is about half a mile long, quarter of a mile wide and contains 28 hectares (70 acres) of land. Staffa is famous for its cathedral-like geological structures including Fingal's Cave, immortalised by Mendelssohn in his celebrated *Hebrides* overture. Staffa was also visited by the artist J M W Turner whose painting of the subject is well-known and by Wordsworth, Tennyson and Sir Walter Scott. Queen Victoria was there with Prince Albert in 1847 and wrote in her *Journal of our Life in the Highlands*: 'When we turned the corner to go into the renowned Fingal's Cave the effect was splendid, like a great entrance into a vaulted hall'. The island is designated a Site of Special Scientific Interest on account of its outstanding rock formations. It is also home to a rich variety of seabirds.

In 1971, Staffa was owned by Captain the Rev G F W Newell who planned to develop the island by the construction of a marina, possibly using stone quarried from the island. The proposal was the subject of a Public Inquiry in 1972 at which the Trust, NCC and CCS all lodged objections. The proposal was turned down and the island subsequently sold to Robert Munro Lang who bequeathed the property to his sons. They sought a grant to put the landing jetty into good repair and the Trust, acting as catalyst, brought the army into the discussions and took soundings from CCS, NCC and NHMF for the possible purchase of the island for £150,000-£200,000. The Trust's Executive Committee was divided on acquisition but Council agreed to continue negotiations. In 1986, Lester Borley reopened discussions with the Lang family. Then Jock Elliott, a New York-based supporter of the Trust's work, acquired the island as a 'birthday present' for his wife Elly,

Left:
Staffa from the sea

Below:
Staffa handover day,
August 1980: Lord
Wemyss, Jock and
Eleanor Elliott

and presented it to the Trust. Elly remains Steward of Staffa for her lifetime. Because of the tax relief on both sides of the Atlantic, the Trust acquired Staffa for £75,000, a quarter of the asking price. Jock even composed a poem to mark the event, proving that romance was well and truly alive, on Staffa at least:

There was a besmitten old gaffer
Who believed in whole hog more than half-a
I'll give her an isle
He said with a smile
And so Elly's the Steward of Staffa.

The transfer of Staffa to the Trust was another of these delightfully appropriate occasions for giving and taking sasine, observed on the island on 15 August 1986. Although the Elliotts knew

Geilston House

the area well, it was their very first landing on the island. Staffa was the 100th property to enter the Trust's portfolio.

GEILSTON

Like Greenbank, Geilston is one of the mid-18th-century merchantile villas, which once abounded around Glasow and the Clyde coast. It makes an interesting contrast with Greenbank, the original villa being a simple and wholly unpretentious vernacular rectangle, low in proportion, but with furnished interior work

still largely intact. Circa 1780, a single-storey wing was added at right-angles, the old house becoming a service core. Although no early views have been found, the chimney heads indicate that the enlarged house was a thatched cottage, once similar in character to Clerk of Eldin's famous cottage at Lasswade. The arrangement of this new wing is of considerable interest, the plan-form of the alcove of the bedchamber, the remarkable fitted dressing room and split service buffet and sideboard recess of the dining room, being ingeniously

Geilston:
colour in the garden

interlocked. The drawing room was clearly intended to command the prospect of the Clyde, suggesting that the owner had maritime interests. Although the house was subsequently slated and slightly modified in the earlier 20th century, the 18th–century interiors are still largely intact, similar to the now-lost Glasgow mansions of the same vintage.

West of the house is a stable and farmcourt, which together with the large doocot, is more architecturally treated than the original house. The house is not open to the public.

Towards the Clyde, Geilston's large garden was enclosed by a dwarf wall and railing (lost in the Second World War, but to be replaced) in order not to interrupt the view. The garden, formalised in the earlier 20th century, and making good use of the stream and the lade works associated with the former mill, is rich in rhododendrons and azaleas.

COUNTRYSIDE MATTERS

Through long and well-established consultative procedures with government agencies as well as voluntary organisations, the Trust has always contributed constructively to debate on important issues affecting the Scottish countryside. During this decade concern grew over the increasing attrition of prime mountain areas. CCS was merged with NCC to form Scottish Natural Heritage (SNH) in 1992 when CCS had just published its thought-provoking paper on *Mountain Areas in Scotland – Conservation and Management*. By this time both the Trust and CCS were convinced of the urgent need for National Parks in Scotland. The areas recommended, not surprisingly, coincided with existing Trust properties – Ben Lomond, Glencoe, Torridon and, later, Mar Lodge Estate in the Cairngorms. Ben Lomond and the Trossachs are to be created as Scotland's first National Park in April 2002.

Scottish Natural Heritage developed the consultation to focus on general access to the countryside, producing first a Consultation Paper and then a Programme for Action in 1992 and 1994 respectively, under the title *Enjoying the Countryside*. The action plan proposed the establishment of an Access Forum to allow for comprehensive consultation on the subject. The key proposal from the Forum, chaired by Roger Wheater (later to become Chairman of NTS) was to seek new legislation based on 'a right of access to land and water exercised responsibly, for informal recreation and passage'. This has been accepted by the Scottish Parliament. Its success will depend on responsible behaviour, and to that end a new Scottish Outdoor Access Code is being formulated to coincide with the new legislation.

SUMMARY

The 1980s were years of notable development for the Trust. One of the important purposes of developing the regional structure was to bring it closer to members and the public at large. At the same time, the number of Members' Centres rose to 26. The appointment of Elizabeth Brown ('Broon') at Culzean, who went on to be Head of Central Buying in Edinburgh, and the employment of Katrina Munro as designer for shop goods in 1983, made a huge difference to the popularity and the commercial success of the Trust. All Trust business flourished, with shop and mail order, catering, cruising, holiday cottage lets and visitor numbers at the properties all significantly increased. Additional office and warehouse facilities were acquired at 30 Dean Street in Stockbridge, Edinburgh. The Trust entered the computer age, with Membership being the first department to benefit.

The Trust continued to be active on the American and European fronts in co-operation with like-minded organisations and individuals, in a concerted effort to spread the ethos of conservation of landscape and buildings far beyond these shores. The 4th International Conference of National Trusts was organised in 1987 by the National Trust at Bath in co-operation with NTS and Scottish Heritage USA.

The Director, Lester Borley, took every opportunity to publicise the Trust by ensuring that any anniversary or important event reached the eyes and ears of Scotland. When the Royal Burgh of Culross was twinned with the Dutch town of Veere in 1981, for example, the occasion was celebrated with a presentation to Gaby

Culross: twinning ceremony with the Dutch town of Veere, July 1981. The Marquess of Bute (left) and Gaby Geluk (right centre)

Geluk, President of the Friends of Veere, of a piece of Fife coal and a lump of Scottish salt at Culross Town House. In return Mr Geluk presented the Marquess of Bute with tulip bulbs and specially commissioned pictures of two Scottish buildings in Veere, which remain from Scottish-Dutch trading links of four centuries ago.

The Trust featured in a highly successful TV series entitled *Held in Trust*, broadcast on three channels. During the 1988 Glasgow Garden Festival, a quarter-acre Trust garden planted in co-operation with Dobbie's Garden World and an exhibition on the Scottish plant hunters, called *Lilies, Lamas and Leeches*,

welcomed 438,000 visitors. The garden was ultimately sold. As a result of a signally successful recruitment drive organised by Micky Blacklock, then Director of Marketing, membership more than doubled to over 230,000 between 1984 and 1992.

With a substantial bequest from Mr Scott-Davidson of £750,000 and generous help from HBCS, the Trust was able to make considerable inroads into an important structural review of its major buildings, a process then estimated to cost £3m.

Chairman Charles Tyrrell said in the Annual Report for 1990: 'Staff can make or break an organisation – but ours make it'.

CHAPTER NINE
THE WHEREWITHAL
1991–2000

'Each case according to the context
of its time is judged on its merits.'[35]

SIR JAMIE STORMONTH DARLING, 1999

INTRODUCTION

This most recent decade is remarkable for the variety and number of properties acquired by the Trust and the pace of development it has experienced. The period began with financial optimism. Membership had broken the 200,000 barrier and, despite declining government grants, the General Income Fund, on which so much of the Trust's work depended, was showing a healthy surplus. With financial support from a variety of organisations and individuals, the Trust was able to consider and finally purchase several major properties, as well as provide high-quality reception and facilities to cope with an ever-increasing number of members and visitors. It was, for example, able to invest in major developments at existing properties such as the Killiecrankie Visitor Centre and a new restaurant at Inverewe Garden in Wester Ross. As the decade progressed, however, there was a change in the pattern of the Trust's income, and while there was a welcome increase in legacies and income from the Lottery, there was a decline in membership, persisting for several years.

Corporate Plans covering the years 1992–7 and 1998–2004 were produced, the more recent plan containing targets, whose implementation would significantly alter the way in which the Trust is managed. Staff prepared management plans for more Trust properties and Planning and Management Guidelines played an important role in controlling all major projects. There was a continuing dialogue in the countryside access debate, especially over the mountainous country, access to the countryside and the creation of a system of National Parks in Scotland. The Trust played an active role in the Public Inquiry on the new road bridge connecting Skye with the mainland and in the continuing extensive public discussions on ski-related developments in the Cairngorms.

The Trust's Diamond Jubilee was thoroughly celebrated in 1991. Royal occasions, civic and government receptions, church services, many events organised by the Trust's Members' Centres and the decision to plant 100,000 trees at properties throughout Scotland, all contributed to a memorable year. One of the principal aims was not only to encourage more visits to the properties but also to boost membership. By the end of 1991 it had increased by 38,000 to 234,500 and subscription income had risen by 17% to £2,720,000.

Unprecedented change in the Trust's leadership saw an end to the continuity of earlier times. Four Presidents, four Chairmen and three Directors held office during the decade. Such dramatic changes had a marked influence on the development of the organisation. This chapter will review the work of the Trust during the 1990s and will conclude with an assessment of the Trust at the start of a new millennium.

PLANNING

In 1984 the first NTS management plan was produced for Balmacara Estate. Others were to follow, their structure, whether for buildings or countryside, being strongly influenced by the Countryside Commission for Scotland's *Management Plans for Country Parks – A Guide to their Preparation* (1988). Subsequently, the Trust appointed a dedicated management planning Team, which developed a standardised planning process, resulting in a high quality of document in both content and presentation. This method was adopted until a modified plan structure was developed in 1996 for Iona, which followed the earlier practice of consultation with island communities such as on Fair Isle and Canna. The Mar Lodge Plan, also written that year, but in consultation with Scottish Natural Heritage, developed a statement of significance for the property and a clearer rationale for each declared objective.

By this time the Buildings Committee, formed in 1995, was providing valuable specialist advice to the Trust Council and Executive. It recommended guidelines for the conservation of Trust buildings based on the Australian ICOMOS Charter for Conservation of Places of Cultural Significance, the so-called Burra Charter, named after the historic mining town of Burra in South Australia. Here, conservation philosophy was refined, and the concept of a conservation plan – essentially based on a historic concept of the significance of the place – introduced. Trust surveyors and curatorial staff were already following the Venice Charter principles of conservation of places of cultural significance. One important outcome has been the preparation of conservation plans, which are intrinsic to most new property management plans.

An event with far-reaching effects on NTS management of its properties was the disastrous fire, which engulfed the National Trust house of Uppark on the Sussex Downs on 30 August 1989

Chapter opening picture:
The Five Sisters of Kintail

Opposite:
NTS Diamond Jubilee.
Left: The Duke of Atholl, President, with Charles Tyrrell, Chairman, planting a European larch in the grounds of Dunkeld Cathedral to commemorate the start of Diamond Jubilee Year, 1991. It was one of only six trees planted on Trust property and the only conifer

The National Trust
for Scotland

The conservation charity that protects and promotes Scotland's
natural and cultural heritage for present and future generations to enjoy

CORPORATE PLAN
1999 - 2004
persuasion
influenceresources
conservation
education

The Corporate Plan

Tragic though this was, the experience alerted not only both National Trusts, but also many private owners, to the need to plan methodically emergency fire procedures, as well as to set up fire prevention measures where this had not already been done. The Trust took the opportunity simultaneously to upgrade security systems, necessary as a result of increasing theft.

Project Planning and Management Guidelines published early in 1992 were followed for all major projects during the rest of the decade. In 1994, a working party chaired by Colin Donald, considered the government of the Trust and brought forward some 30 recommendations. Largely implemented in the following two years, these included the creation of the Buildings

Committee. The Donald Report stopped short of recommending the establishment of regional committees, believing them to be neither necessary nor desirable. Only a year later, however, under Hamish Leslie Melville's chairmanship, regional committees were set up to be the Chairman's 'eyes and ears', to advise the Executive and to provide a stronger Trust link with members, staff and the communities in which they were situated.

The increasing size and complexity of the Trust made it urgently necessary to revise the *Corporate Plan*, the most significant of all the management documents to be adopted by the Trust's committees and staff. The Plan recognised the huge contribution made by volunteers in many spheres, and recommended changes in organisational structure to ensure the Trust's effectiveness and efficiency. The Working Practices Review (see later in this chapter) and its implementation over 1999 and 2000 was the result.

POLICY MATTERS

The Trust's Council must approve all Trust policies – a small number of these, such as fish farming and crofting, being of national significance. Many of these policies result from the deliberations of the Trust's special advisory committees or working groups, including those on archaeology, catering, grazing and nature conservation. Such policies first appeared in the Trust's record in 1937 when Unna's Principles were drawn up for the management of mountain properties, funding of which was provided through Unna funds. They cover a wider range

*Ranger-naturalist
Seamus MacNally
guiding visitors over
the Torridon summits*

of activities from deer management to use of metal detectors, from farming and woodland to dogs and the use of peat in Trust gardens. Most policies relate to the Trust's internal organisation, for example those on building conservation and education.

Responding to consultation documents from government, statutory agencies and others, has been an important feature of the Trust's work. This responsibility arises from the legislation establishing the Trust and responses are always based on the Trust's practical conservation experience, careful research, consultation and discussion. The considered views of the Trust are actively sought, reflecting the high esteem in which its opinion is held by both government and the public.

ECOLOGY

The creation of a Nature Reserves Committee in 1946 was the first significant step taken by the Trust to recognise the importance of flora and fauna. It may have been its unwieldy size that led to its being disbanded in 1956 (when it had 33 members) or it may have been because the statutory body, the Nature Conservancy, established in 1949, had begun to take the lead in nature conservation. The Trust had, after all, leased the St Kilda archipelago to the Nature Conservancy in 1957 and perhaps did not believe it was essential to become too involved in this sphere.

It was to be many years later, in 1969, before the Trust appointed trained ranger-naturalists to its properties. Initially, they were a mixture of experienced countrymen and women and recent graduates in the field sciences, all with a keen interest and expertise in natural history – hence the continuing use in the title of 'naturalist' rather than simply ranger, ecologist or warden as used in the Countryside (Scotland) Act 1967. Conserving and managing the countryside properties and conveying their interest to visitors are primary responsibilities.

With an increasing need to provide a Trust view of developments taking place in the Scottish countryside, a Countryside Advisory Panel was set up in 1985. As the Trust acquired important countryside property this was renamed the Nature Conservation Working Party, with Professor Ian Cunningham as first Chairman. In particular, it suggested that the Trust must improve its nature conservation management and that a Countryside and Nature Conservation Committee (CNCC) should be established. In 1992 the working party strongly recommended that the Trust appoint an ecologist and zoologist. Dr James Fenton, whose formative years had been spent at Inverewe, where his parents looked after the busy Information Centre, had five years' experience working for the British Antarctic Survey and at Brathay Hall Field Centre in the Lake District, before being selected as the Trust's first ecologist.

James initiated habitat vegetation surveys, created an ecological survey system, and set about ensuring that ecological principles formed a vital part of property management plans. He has been integral to several important studies conducted to provide more informed nature conservation management. For example, James was involved in a major investigation into grazing practice. To assist in this a partnership was forged between NTS, Scottish Natural Heritage (SNH) (an amalgamation of the old Nature Conservancy Council and the Countryside Commission for Scotland), the Scottish Wildlife Trust (SWT), the Institute of Ecology (ITE) and the Macaulay Land Use Research Institute (MLURI). With support from the European LIFE Project, a two-year programme of study was targeted at designated upland Natura 2000 sites on Ben Lawers, Torridon, Glencoe and an SWT site, Greyhill Grasslands in Ayrshire. The object of the programme, to publish and circulate grazing plans for these properties as well as a practical manual on how to produce such plans for upland sites, was realised in 1998. On Ben Lomond, for example, the Trust commissioned the Scottish Agricultural College to consider the economic viability of running Blairvockie hill farm under different grazing regimes. This has led to practical action on the ground to promote native tree regeneration and a richer flora.

Another important step taken in recent years was the appointment of Abbie Paterson as the Trust's Species Recovery Officer in the Highlands and Islands Region, based in Oban. The post was funded for two years by SNH and the Trust's successful Highland Appeal, and in the light of the importance of the work done, was made permanent in 2000. Abbie has co-operated with farmers and crofters to help conserve populations of corncrake on Canna, Iona and Balmacara, as well as the slender Scotch burnet moth and the white-tailed sea eagle, Manx shearwater and red squirrel. Loch Skeen in the Moffat Hills above the Grey Mare's Tail has been selected as suitable water into which to introduce the rare vendace fish.

In 1998 the NTS and SNH, recognising their shared interest and responsibility for the conservation and enjoyment of the natural heritage of Scotland, entered into a partnership or Concordat, which focused on the 74,870 hectares (185,000 acres) owned by the Trust and designated for their natural heritage value. This agreement allowed money for individual ranger services to be transferred to an SNH-funded programme. SNH supports both individual properties, through management agreements linked to NTS property management plans and some property acquisition. Ranger-naturalists contribute to local biodiversity action plans, which will lead to relevant prescriptions being built into property management plans.

ARCHAEOLOGY

'We do not have a lot to say about archaeological sites on our properties, beyond the fact that we are aware of the location of some of them.'[36] This was the frank response by Director Lester Borley in September 1985 to an invitation that the Trust might provide a speaker at the autumn meeting of the Association of County Archaeological Officers. He followed it with a request to Edwina Proudfoot, representative on the Trust's Council for the Council for Scottish

Left:
Species Recovery
Officer, Abbie Paterson,
assessing vegetation for
its suitability as habitat
for corncrake

Below:
Corncrake

St Kilda:
Archaeological dig in
a precarious spot! – a
possible Bronze Age site

Archaeology (CSA), for advice on how best to handle the research and recording of sites on Trust property. Criticism by professional archaeologists of the Trust's treatment of some sites, coupled with a growing appreciation of their importance and the need for their interpretation to the public, certainly spurred the Trust to action in this field.

Edwina recruited the help of Charles Strang, also a keen archaeologist and at the time Head of Policy Research, in the belief that the Trust should raise its profile on the subject. Authority was sought to appoint a seasonal member of staff for four months to carry out initial mapping and recording of sites. Through the Countryside Advisory Panel, an archaeological working group was established in late 1991 to bring forward a strategy for archaeology within the Trust. The following year, with persistent encouragement from Edwina Proudfoot, the Trust appointed Patrick Begg as seasonal archaeologist; Patrick did useful work on the Sites and Monuments Record from the Royal Commission to establish what archaeology existed on Trust properties. Robin Turner was then recruited on a two-year fixed contract and later as permanent Archaeologist to the Trust. These efforts to recognise the national importance of the subject were duly applauded by the Council for Scottish Archaeology, the Royal Commission on the Ancient and Historical Monuments of Scotland (RCAHMS) and the Society of Antiquaries of Scotland.

Robin found a sympathetic ear among staff

*Ben Lawers:
Archaeological Field
School in action*

who had already been closely involved with the RCAHMS work and publication of the archaeology of Fair Isle and St Kilda. He had relevant experience in desktop publishing and began the regular issue of the informative *Archaeology Bulletin*, which has done much to highlight work based on the properties. Robin has also been instrumental in underlining the importance of both outstanding buildings and landscape archaeology, carrying out investigations into properties such as the bothy on Canna, Alloa Tower, the Trust's new offices in Charlotte Square, and the archaeology of Unst, in Shetland. There have been major excavations using Conservation Volunteers for three years at House of Dun Bronze Age fordhouse barrow and during the archaeological field school on

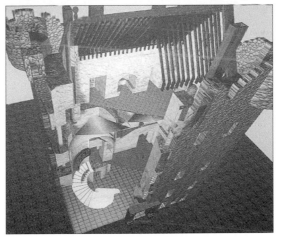

*Alloa Tower: 3 D
computer-generated cut-
away of the Tower*

Ben Lawers, which will ultimately extend over seven seasons. Under the supervision of professional archaeologists, many young people have thus developed their skills, while at the same time revealing much of archaeological interest.

The Archaeological Appeal raised £110,000 and, with matching finance from Historic Scotland, has financed archaeological surveys of most countryside properties which, together with action plans, have provided invaluable information. Following the Working Practices Review of 1999, the Trust has created three new Regional Archaeologist posts in Highlands and Islands, North-East and West Regions. Robin Turner as Senior Archaeologist, based in Edinburgh, services the South Region. These new appointments will allow archaeological initiatives to be continued and extended on the Trust's properties throughout Scotland.

NEW PROPERTIES

ARDUAINE GARDEN

Arduaine Garden, or 'the green point' as it is aptly named in Gaelic, is situated on comparatively fertile green land forming the foreground to rocky and wilder hills surrounding Loch Melfort in Argyll. The garden has strong parallels with its northerly counterpart, Inverewe, in Wester Ross. James Arthur Campbell, who bought Arduaine in 1897, visited Osgood Mackenzie at Inverewe in 1907, no doubt sharing his enthusiasm for rhododendrons and gaining knowledge from him on how best to protect the site at Arduaine. Campbell planted 2,000 Japanese larch seedlings to shield his collection of plants from salt-laden winds, and created a garden developed to his design.

After James Campbell's death in 1929, his son Bruce and his family devotedly cared for the garden until advancing years overtook them. In

Above:
Portrait of James
Arthur Campbell,
founder of Arduaine
Garden

Opposite:
Arduaine Garden: pond

1971, having decided to seek a sympathetic owner, they sold the property to Edmund and Harry Wright, brothers who had previously been nurserymen in Essex. The Wrights' knowledge and hard work ensured that Arduaine, and particularly its rhododendrons, were maintained and further developed. The garden became well known for its plant collections, a mecca for garden lovers and specialists alike, until the Wrights had to find a long-term solution to its maintenance.

The Trust realised that Arduaine was nationally important, and that it could not survive without investment and staff. In the certainty that there would be sufficient financial support forthcoming, the Garden was accepted in 1992 without endowment. A successful appeal covered the initial capital costs of bringing an essentially private garden to the position where it could receive a greatly increased number of

Holmwood House,
Cathcart, Glasgow

visitors, and provided an endowment for its future operation.

A series of ponds, originally laid out by the Wright brothers, accompanies the attractive plantings near to the specially designed reception centre. The remainder of the site is essentially a woodland garden interplanted with a rich variety of rhododendrons and other species, viewed from a network of well-surfaced paths taking the visitor conveniently to the points of principal interest. A circular route through the woodland garden, including a viewpoint to the sea, takes about an hour to complete and gives a fascinating insight into this absorbing property.

HOLMWOOD HOUSE

In advising the National Heritage Memorial Fund (NHMF), Professor David A Walker,

former Principal Inspector of Historic Buildings with Historic Scotland (HS), assessed Holmwood, as the architect Alexander 'Greek' Thomson's finest villa, a building of the very highest class, the preservation of which is a matter of importance not only to Glasgow or even Scotland, but to the western world.

In June 1991, the Marquess of Bute wrote to the Director, expressing his concern for Holmwood's future, and hoping that the Trust might take an interest. The threat, which gave rise to his letter, was a planning application to build 93 flats in its 2 hectares (5 acres) of grounds. Holmwood was about to close as a convent primary school, owned by the Sisters of Our Lady of the Missions, and leased to Strathclyde Regional Council (SRC). Following closure of the school, a developer, Carvill Ltd,

Holmwood House:
the Dining Room

had acquired an option to purchase, subject to planning permission.

Gavin Stamp, chairman of the Alexander Thomson Society, encouraged the Trust and other amenity interests to oppose the application. Glasgow District Council refused to grant planning permission. Meanwhile, discussion with HS and NHMF indicated support for acquisition by the Trust. Carvill resubmitted applications for two revised schemes, both of which were refused. The city included Holmwood in proposed additions to the green belt. In the face of such opposition Carvill withdrew their interest. This left the way open for Regional Director Michael Hunter to negotiate purchase, which was achieved in March 1994. Acquisition was made possible by an exceptional grant from NHMF, which also provided an endowment fund, and support from Glasgow City Council, Strathclyde Regional Council and a number of conservation bodies. The Historic Buildings Council for Scotland funded conservation repair. Glasgow City Council and the European Regional Development Fund underwrote other repairs and development for visitors. A successful appeal raised the balance of funding for the project, maximising the share of NHMF grant for endowment.

Interest in Thomson's architecture was on the increase and helped Glasgow win the title of UK City of Architecture and Design 1999. A project team, comprising Trust staff and conservation consultants led by Page and Park Architects, began work on research and planning the necessary major conservation and improvement work in time for opening to visitors in

Holmwood House,
the Parlour

1999. An early recommendation from the Trust's Buildings Committee to conduct a trial of the methodology of the Burra Charter (see earlier in this chapter), led the team to undertake the project as an exemplar of best practice. The guiding principle was that the original design and construction of the villa by Thomson for paper mill owner James Couper were so much more significant than later changes by other owners, that these changes should be recorded and removed. Elements which had been taken away should be faithfully reproduced. Archaeological work on the buildings, a few early photographs and Thomson's own published drawings formed the evidence for this work.

Under the protection of a large temporary roof, the minimum necessary new rafters, sarking slates and lead replaced the existing defective roof, and repairs were made to the stonework. A wall linking the villa with the coachman's house had been removed in the 1920s and this was replaced, recreating the exceptional asymmetrical composition of the garden front of the house. Whilst this work was proceeding, research into the history of decoration began. This work continued slowly and carefully into the new decade and developed into a programme of conservation, restoration and reproduction of Thomson's final scheme of painted decoration in Holmwood's principal rooms, almost all of which, remarkably, had survived. Visitors may be able to see conserva-

*Wester Kittochside
farmhouse*

tors at work until the restoration is complete.

Gavin Stamp, architectural historian and writer, regards Thomson's interiors as important, if not pivotal, in the development of decoration, particularly of the Aesthetic Movement. In Holmwood the Trust is able to preserve his finest domestic work.

WESTER KITTOCHSIDE

Following her late husband's suggestion, Mrs Margaret Reid, whose family had owned Wester Kittochside for the previous 400 years, first approached the Trust in 1983, to enquire if it might be interested in accepting the property as a gift with 'a substantial cash endowment'. Knowing the crucial position and quality of this

classic pedimented 1783 farmhouse and its 57-hectare (140-acre) farm in the green belt, sandwiched between the conurbations of Glasgow and East Kilbride, the Trust was immediately interested.

The problems, common to most acquisitions, were the source of finance and the practical use to be made of the property. During negotiations Donald Erskine, by then a Deputy Director of the Trust, wrote to Dr Sandy Fenton of the Scottish Country Life Museums Trust (SCLMT) which NTS had helped to set up, attempting to interest him in a possible agricultural museum at Wester Kittochside. SCLMT was already considering an alternative site to their industrial shed at Ingliston and Dr

Fenton advised that any lease arrangement would require to be made through the National Museums of Scotland (NMS) and not SCLMT.

Discussion with the Reid family continued at a low key, and Mrs Reid again approached the Trust through her lawyer in 1991, saying that she would like to donate Wester Kittochside, provided the Trust could guarantee future use as an educational farm. Regional Director Findlay McQuarrie, then about to retire, established a firm case for Trust acceptance. He did so with typical enthusiasm, stimulating interest from the local authority and the Countryside Commission for Scotland.

Mrs Reid proposed to leave a generous bequest of £50,000, as well as the house, its furnishings and the equally important threshing plant and agricultural equipment of the adjacent steading and other buildings, listed along with the house. Mark Jones, Director of NMS, having visited the site with key staff, had seen the potential for development and was very enthusiastic. With Mrs Reid's continuing co-operation the Trust carried out a thorough feasibility study to take over the property and, with the real possibility of the involvement of NMS, Council agreed to accept Wester Kittochside in 1992. The long-term aim was to present the Farm as it was in the 1930s–1950s period, one of major agricultural change from horses to tractors.

The Trust, in close liaison with the staff of NMS, and the Scottish Agricultural Musem responsible for the National Country Life Collections, particularly Gavin Sprott, then set about publicising and promoting the project.

Applications were made for financial support from local East Kilbride authorities and the Lanarkshire Development Agency, from the Heritage Lottery Fund (HLF) and the European Regional Development Fund (ERDF). A joint working group of NMS trustees and NTS Executive Committee members was appointed to oversee this very ambitious project and another to implement the scheme. The plans include a sensitively sited new building to house the Museum of Scottish Country Life, with space for exhibits, storage and a research base as well as live interpretation of a working 1950s, farm including demonstrations and events, and guided access to the house and steading buildings. A Countryside Premium Scheme was entered into with South Lanarkshire Council over 24 hectares (60 acres), to enable capital works such as hedging and fencing to take place.

After the success of their funding applications, which provided £3.78m from HLF and ERDF, NTS and NMS drew up a lease and operating agreements in 1998. The partnership applied the principles of the Burra Charter, undertook a historic buildings and landscape survey, and drew up a statement of significance and a management conservation plan. Each alteration proposed was subjected to a heritage impact assessment in which any change had to be justified and any loss of significant fabric argued.

Contractors began work in January 2000 on the museum building whilst the Trust restored the farm steading. The Reid's confidence was fulfilled and this exciting project was completed in 2001.

The Museum of
Scottish Country Life

Kittochside Fair, 2000

Kintail and Loch
Duich: map reading

WEST AFFRIC AND KINTAIL

When West Affric came on the market in 1992, the Trust already owned the adjacent property of Kintail. This included the spectacular Falls of Glomach with the dramatic mountain landscape of the Five Sisters and Ben Attow (or Ben Fhada) Kintail, Glen Lichd, the Morvich Countryside Centre, and parts of Glen Shiel.

Surprisingly, the Trust's initial response was unenthusiastic. The area in question, although it had high landscape value, was rated low in nature conservation interest and it seemed there would be little threat to either West Affric or the contiguous property of Kintail. Even the Countryside and Nature Conservation Committee (CNCC) and the Highland Regional Office were less than convinced about possible purchase. It had been

almost ten years since the Trust had acquired a significant mountain or open countryside property. Was it 'Trustworthy?'

Frank Bracewell, a member of the Trust's Executive, feared that the estate might be sold to a forestry developer. He anticipated wide support for the Trust if it attempted to acquire West Affric. Chris Brasher, a great lover of wild country who had recently formed the Chris Brasher Trust (CBT), was also involved in the discussions from the outset. The charity Trees for Life (TFL) were planting trees in co-operation with the Forestry Commission. Together they planned a reforestation programme with native woodland species, by culling the excessive deer population and exclosures for the young trees to promote regeneration.

*West Affric
from Glen Affric*

The John Muir Trust (JMT), whose *raison d'être* is the acquisition and management of wild and remote mountain areas, had earlier been in touch with TFL but had declined to take an interest while pursuing another property. TFL then proposed joint management with NTS of West Affric. Unexpectedly the Trust, initially reluctant to purchase the property and doubtful about finding the purchase price, received an offer of £150,000 from the CBT. The executors of a Trust benefactor, Myles Morrison, gave authority that the Morrison bequest, although destined for Wester Ross, should be used instead for West Affric. Trust ownership, coupled with existing management of Kintail and Glomach, suddenly became a logical and desirable goal.

A sale was agreed in 1993 with the owner,

Brian Butler, receiving £405,000 and a lease-back of stalking rights until 1999. A West Affric Management Committee consisting of three members from NTS, one from CBT and one from TFL was set up. A management agreement was established with Scottish Natural Heritage (SNH) in 1994 over land designated as a Site of Special Scientific Interest (SSSI). As a result, the Trust received £50,000 from SNH towards the endowment for West Affric, with further support either financial or in terms of specialist advice. A 25-year lease from 1995 to 2020 was drawn up with the Scottish Youth Hostels Association for the youth hostel at Alltbeithe, a popular facility with walkers through Glen Affric. This agreement enabled the hostel to be renovated.

The property of Kintail was purchased in

1944 with funds left to the Trust by Percy Unna and given to the Trust as his personal gift. As with other properties bought with Unna monies, it is covered by his Principles to protect the wild character of the landscape. The Brasher gift of £150,000 was on a similar understanding, the only exception being recognition that, initially, commercial stalking would be necessary to reduce deer numbers. When the original stalking arrangement with Mr Butler ran out in 1999, the CBT accepted the Trust proposal to re-let the stalking with certain conditions as to the numbers culled and methods of extraction.

In 1992 the Trust set up its Grazing Working Party to investigate the effects of grazing on many of its countryside properties. The working party's report recognised that impoverishment of large areas of vegetation was taking place, and led the Trust to commission a study of grazing effects at Kintail, as part of the wider consideration of grazing referred to in the section on Ecology in this chapter. Using the Macaulay Land Use Research Institute model, the conclusions reached were that valuable heather cover had been seriously depleted by burning and further damaged as a result of over-grazing by sheep, deer and goats.

More recently in Kintail, the Trust has attempted to restore some of the heather and other more interesting and valuable plant communities, especially on the lower ground. In this the Trust has co-operated with the local crofters, using a combination of the Countryside Premium Scheme (CPS), fencing and a reduction of both sheep and deer. In West Affric, which is geologically, scenically, and climatically different from Kintail, the policy is to encourage regeneration by limiting the deer cull, mainly by fencing. Heritage Lottery Millennium Forest for Scotland funds have supported this latter initiative, although recent palaeo-ecological work by Stirling University has suggested that West Affric woodland is disappearing for climatic reasons, rather than because of human activity. Care will therefore be taken in the selection of species to be planted favouring birch, hazel and rowan rather than Scots pine.

In the words of the management plan for Kintail, the Falls of Glomach and West Affric: 'The Trust should ensure the permanent conservation, for the benefit of the nation, of Kintail, the Falls of Glomach and West Affric as examples of nationally important landscapes and remote and relatively unspoilt areas of recreational and nature conservation value.'

MAR LODGE ESTATE

The President, Lord Wemyss, was unswerving in his belief that the NTS, with its power of conferring inalienability, coupled with relevant experience of managing mountains, was the best single organisation to take care of areas such as the Mar Lodge Estate (MLE) in the Cairngorms, provided finance was available. The largest area of land in Britain over 914 metres (3,000 feet), it includes Ben Macdui at 1,309 metres (4,294 feet) and a total of 15 Munros, mountains over 914 metres (3,000 feet), many of which, such as Cairn Toul, Braeriach and Devil's Point, are well-known.

Mar Lodge undoubtedly fulfilled all the criteria of being 'Trustworthy'. It already had

Mar Lodge from Claybokie looking west

numerous international designations for its nature conservation and cultural interests, and was highly popular with walkers and climbers. A not inconsiderable challenge was the fact that its American owner, who had managed the property as a sporting estate, wished it to remain as such and to sell it for in excess of £10m. Its importance was well-known and a conservation consortium made up of the John Muir Trust, the World Wide Fund for Nature and the Royal Society for the Protection of Birds (RSPB) put forward a vision for its management (*Mar Lodge: a new future?*), with a view to purchase assisted by NHMF.

Early consideration by the Trust was given to the potentially sensitive issue of hunting. Roger Wheater, then a member of Trust Council, cautioned: 'There is a big difference between such an estate being owned by a single owner or even a group with sporting interests, and ownership by a body such as the NTS, made up of members with strong convictions about conservation of all aspects of the heritage of Scotland.'[37]

Much deliberation followed on the best way to secure the long-term conservation of the estate. The vendor declined an offer by the Crown Estates to purchase the Lodge, and the Scottish Office refused to use government money to help the consortium to buy the property. After high-level discussions, the NTS helped the consortium to prepare a case for NHMF.

It was then that an anonymous body revealed its interest in funding the NTS, and only the NTS, to the tune of £4m to help to

purchase the estate, if the Trust could attract enough grant for an endowment. The Trust successfully negotiated initially with the trustees of NHMF. Trust staff prepared draft management proposals for discussion with all interested parties In December 1994, Council determined to proceed with the acquisition of Mar Lodge Estate, subject to agreement on terms of purchase and adequate funding. The anonymous body, later revealed as the Easter Charitable Trust, confirmed that it would contribute £4m towards purchase. The Trust's Chairman Hamish Leslie Melville, with Trust Director, now Douglas Dow, and Nigel Fairhead (Director of the Finance Division), successfully negotiated with the Heritage Lottery Fund (HLF) which generously provided £1.5m and an additional £8m for the endowment and £1.2m for capital repairs and development. In recognition of a property outstanding for its nature conservation as well as its landscape, a Management Agreement with SNH for 25 years provided an exceptional grant to the Trust of £125,000 per year, for its first five years.

NTS formally took over Mar Lodge Estate on 30 June 1995, employing all current staff, including factor Toby Metcalfe. The Mar Lodge Estate Management Committee (MLEMC) was established under the chairmanship of experienced landowner Toby Tennant to oversee its management. An early objective was to ensure that Trust members fully understood the purpose of acquisition. Accordingly, two special inserts were published in the Trust magazine *Heritage Scotland* (1995/1996) which explained that 'NTS intended to demonstrate that conser–

Opposite:
Mar Lodge:
the Ballroom

Left:
Mar Lodge:
a mature Scots pine

vation, public access and field sports can be managed in harmony on the estate, although conservation was to be the primary and overriding aim'. The Trust had also been careful to keep the Grampian authorities fully informed of its objectives, and held an Open Day to involve the local community in plans for the Estate.

As part of the discussion the Trust agreed to follow a set of principles, including that no motorised vehicles, other than those associated with conservation, deer management and field sports activity, nor mountain bikes, are to be used beyond the immediate environs of the Lodge. The Trust has accepted the principle of the 'long walk-in' and is discouraging the use of mountain bikes through information and by persuasion, with plans in the longer term for reducing many Estate roads to footpaths.

Since acquiring the Estate the Trust has reduced the number of red deer to a level more compatible with regeneration of the native Caledonian woodland, which is a principal feature of the landscape. Already there are signs that the policy is bearing fruit, with the appearance of young seedlings in some areas. In order to protect the small populations of black grouse and capercaillie, more than half the deer fencing has been removed and, as the quality of the vegetation improves, so it is hoped will the numbers of these exciting and noisy birds. The estate ranger staff and volunteers also tackle problems created by pressure of visitors' feet on

Mar Lodge: Beinn a'
Bhuird, bulldozed track

Mar Lodge

footpaths. In higher and more remote areas, these workers need temporary accommodation flown in by helicopter. Formerly broad tracks are being reduced to a more acceptable width.

Thanks to European funding the Trust has undertaken the massive job of restoration of the high-level Beinn a' Bhuird track, as well as reversing agricultural drainage in the Quoich wetland area to encourage breeding waders and ducks. Automatic people counters have been installed to aid management. The second phase of funding has provided an archaeological survey and monitoring programme for its future management, continuation of the work on the Beinn a' Bhuird track, restoration of footpaths, the removal or downgrading of vehicle tracks and the removal of non-native trees, have all been undertaken. An environmental audit, a monitoring programme for future management of the estate and an interpretative strategy have been funded by the generous total European grant of £321,000.

The management of the Mar Lodge Estate is certainly the largest countryside enterprise which the Trust has undertaken. It will be fascinating to follow how successful the combination of conservation, public access and field sports will be and, in particular, the conversion of an over-grazed landscape to one more in balance with a higher quality of vegetation attractive to birds. A holiday in the splendidly appointed Mar Lodge, built for the Duke and Duchess of Fife in 1895, and now converted to very high-quality self-catering apartments, is an enjoyable way to gain personal experience of this marvellous property.

CONTENTIOUS ISSUES

THE SKYE ROAD BRIDGE

In the late 1980s, the Scottish Development Department came forward with a proposal to construct a road bridge between Kyle of Lochalsh and Kyleakin on Skye. The Trust was involved because of its inalienable ownership of the Balmacara Estate, including the small island of Eilean Dubh, its feudal superiority over Eilean Ban, and its Conservation Agreement over Kyle House on Skye, all of which lay on the line of the road. In March 1990, the NTS set up a working group under the chairmanship of George Russell to consider all aspects of the proposal. It was accepted from the outset that there was an unequivocal need for the bridge. The Trust was convinced, because of the sensitive nature of the proposed location in one of Scotland's finest landscape settings, that the project demanded skills of world standard. It also made clear that any additional costs required to achieve the highest environmental and aesthetic standards should be financed by government. In May 1990, the Trust wrote to the Scottish Office setting out conditions to be met before it would give formal approval to the project.

During subsequent negotiations, notable improvements to the design were achieved, including lowering the height of the main bridge by 5 metres (16 feet). In February 1991, the Trust provided detailed comments on the contractors' tender submissions, stating that none of them was totally acceptable. In particular, no exciting or innovative design of world quality had emerged.

The Skye road bridge

Opposite:
The Glen More
gondola proposal

The Trust was convinced that the proposed toll-finance system combined with the 'design, build and operate' process was driving down the quality of the bridge, although it did consider that the concrete box-girder bridge proposed by Miller Construction was the more acceptable of the two designs put forward. At that stage, the Trust felt that, with suitable detailed design improvement, the Miller proposal could meet most of the Trust's requirements.

Following selection by the Scottish Office of the Miller design, the Trust, the Countryside Commission for Scotland (CCS) and the Royal Fine Art Commission for Scotland commissioned a report from Professor Fritz Leonhardt of Stuttgart, one of the world's foremost bridge designers. Professor Leonhardt, while suggesting that significant improvements could be made to the design proposals submitted by Miller Construction, felt that the best solution would be a cable-stayed bridge. The Trust working party agreed with Professor Leonhardt but at Council in October 1991, the Scottish Office presented costs which directly challenged

Professor Leonhardt's report and claimed that the cable-stay design would be more expensive and could possibly delay or even cancel the project.

The Trust decided to press the Scottish Office for further improvements to the box-girder design rather than to pursue the cable-stay design recommended by Professor Leonhardt. The Trust was influenced by a report commissioned by the Scottish Office which stated that a cable-stay design would 'strike a particularly discordant note' in the land-scape. As there was strong opposition to the design and effects of the bridge from several conservation organisations and individuals, a Public Inquiry was held in January 1992. The Trust had lodged a holding objection while it negotiated for the best possible modifications to the box-girder design. Knowing that this proposal was the one which found favour with most local people and having satisfied itself that the alterations to the design would be carried out, and that the cable-stay design would not be cheaper, the Trust withdrew its objection, although opinion within the organisation was divided.

Overall, the design changes proposed by NTS and CCS for materially improving the appearance of the main bridge were adopted by the reporter who conducted the Public Inquiry and, in practice, by the contractor when building the bridge. The extra expense of these improvements was contained within the total project costs and tolls were not increased as a result.

It would be revealing to ask the local population now what their feelings are about the bridge. Looking objectively at the box-girder design, it does sit unobtrusively in the landscape but some impact cannot be avoided. The cable-stay design would have been lighter but would have made a greater statement in the landscape. Perhaps the outline and grandeur of the Cuillins are better not punctuated by any intrusion into their skyline.

THE CAIRNGORM FUNICULAR

The acquisition in 1995 of Mar Lodge Estate, which is contiguous with the northern corries of Cairngorm and the site of the Cairngorm Chairlift Company's (CCC) proposed funicular railway over tourist development in Coire Cas, sharpened the Trust's appraisal of what always promised to be an intrusive and inappropriate enterprise. The controversy did not lead to a Public Inquiry, despite much intensive argument over the potential effects of what is widely acknowledged to be an internationally important landscape with several designations supporting this description. The alternative proposal put forward in 1996 by Scottish Wildlife and Countryside Link, Save the Cairngorms Campaign, NTS and RSPB, for a 'gondola' from Glenmore to an upgraded Day Lodge at Coire Cas with associated environmental improvements, was not accepted.

Planning permission granted in 1997 for a Cairngorm funicular from the Day Lodge via the White Lady Shieling to a new interpretation centre and Ptarmigan Restaurant at 1097 metres (3,600 feet), carried with it a requirement that CCC produce a plan to manage non-skiing visitors. The visitor management plan eventually

The GlenMore Gondola
a better alternative

produced in July 2000 was less than satisfactory. The Trust maintained its consistent opposition to the funicular and the interpretation centre on account of their probable effects on the Cairngorm plateau, their visual impacts and their potential influence on its Mar Lodge Estate. In constructively criticising the plan the Trust sought to ensure than the proposed closed system by which visitors would not be able to reach the sensitive summit plateau, would remain in place for the lifetime of the funicular.

COMMERCIAL ACTIVITIES

The National Trust for Scotland Trading Company Ltd, renamed the Enterprises Division, was originally established in 1985 to extend commercial opportunities. Trading profits were distinguished from other revenue for tax purposes. By 1997, it was realised that a new Trading Company Board would be necessary to increase the emphasis on commercial activities, in order to seek additional opportunities to generate new funds for the Trust's core conservation purposes. Stephen Spencer was appointed in May 1998 as Commercial Director, and the Board was given an overdraft facility of £1.5m and £0.5m loan from the Trust. Plant sales, licensing, and the promotion of functions in Trust properties have been added to the more traditional shops, catering outlets, holiday cottages and Trust cruises. Every opportunity is being taken to expand and upgrade each of these as well as other enterprises such as mail order and the raffle.

Commercial activities are now integral to the charity. The present financial position of the

Trust demands that it maximises its commercial opportunities to raise money, essential to maintain its expenditure on conservation projects. The Board, although able to make decisions within its area of responsibility, is ultimately responsible to the Trust's Executive. There will always be a delicate balance to be struck between the Trust's primary purpose of conservation, and its understandable desire to realise as great an income as possible to promote this purpose. Currently, the Enterprises Division earns more than £1m a year for the Trust, and it has set itself the target of raising £2m per annum by the year 2005.

26–31 CHARLOTTE SQUARE, EDINBURGH

This fine terraced block on the south side of Charlotte Square in the heart of Edinburgh's New Town, with a façade designed by Robert Adam in 1791, was not built until the early 19th century. It had been the Trust's long-held desire

to house all its head office requirements within one building. The houses were badly altered internally, had lain empty for some years and were the subject of a proposed major office development. The Trust held discussions with and carefully prepared applications to the Heritage Lottery Fund, Historic Scotland and Lothian and Edinburgh Enterprise Ltd, as well as other bodies. With funds in place, the Trust was able to carry out an ambitious proposal to convert the six buildings to modern use.

A condition of the Lottery and other grants was that a significant proportion of the buildings must be open to public access and participation. This has been achieved in an imaginative and attractive manner by the creation of a reception area, restaurant and shop on the ground floor, and an exhibition suite above on the first floor of No 28. The boardroom, appropriately named after Sir Jamie Stormonth Darling who died in 2000, is situated above the coffee shop and restaurant. From his collection of 20th-century

Opposite:
Cairngorm:
ground erosion

Above left:
NTS raffle: Chairman
Hamish Leslie Melville,
with Councillor Robert
Cairns in the 1998
first prize

Above right:
Plant sale at Culzean

canvases Douglas Hutchison, a long-time supporter and active member of Trust committees, thoughtfully presented the Trust with over 30 paintings, which now grace the gallery.

The Trust has achieved its purpose of creating a modern office for its entire head office staff, and in the process it has assisted significantly in the conservation of this world-famous Square. The former Trust offices at No 5 have been occupied by the World Heritage Trust, an amalgamation of the Old Town Renewal Trust and the New Town Conservation Committee, and the Scottish Parliament's First Minister retains official use of No 6, Bute House. The nearby Roxburghe Hotel, under new management, has had its roof restored to its original form and similar restoration is planned at Nos 15, 16 and 17. Confidence has returned to the Square and proposals to pedestrianise the whole of Princes Street and Charlotte Square may enable residents of Edinburgh and visitors alike to appreciate fully the revitalised heart of the city's New Town and this World Heritage Site.

To mark the completion of the work on 26–31 Charlotte Square, now known as Wemyss House, the official opening was carried out by Her Majesty The Queen on 6 July 2000. This was also the year in which the Trust's Patron, Her Majesty Queen Elizabeth The Queen Mother, attained her 100th birthday.

BROUGHTON HOUSE

It is easy to understand why the artist Edward Atkinson Hornel was attracted to buy the 18th-century Broughton House. It sits well back from the line of the High Street in the attractive small

town of Kirkcudbright on the River Dee in Galloway. Hornel was a renowned member of that distinguished group of artists known as the 'Glasgow Boys' who made their mark at the turn of the 20th century. He bought the House in 1901 and lived there until his death in 1933, enjoying the clear atmosphere and mild climate of the south-west.

During that time, as well as making notable contributions to the art world, he also became an avid collector of books written by authors born in the local area or resident there, especially those published in Dumfries and Galloway. The library is outstanding, including a collection of 2,500 works by Robert Burns, said to be one of the finest in existence with a rare 'Kilmarnock' edition of the poet's work, published in 1786. There are several Hornel paintings illustrating his earlier and later work, as well as furnishings and the original studio, which the artist had built and where the

tools of his art still remain. The structure and planting of the long thin garden stretching from the house down to the river reflect Hornel's visits to Japan. The garden, or rather a series of individual gardens, contains a rich variety of species for the visitor to discover.

The Hornel trustees, together with the Friends of the Hornel Art Gallery and Library, made sure that this historic house and its wonderful garden were preserved for the residents of Kirkcudbright and far beyond. Sadly, after a destructive fire at the house in 1992, their finances were not sufficient for them to continue and they approached NTS with a request that it take over the responsibility for management, with a view to ultimate ownership of the property. There was an enthusiastic local response, including that of the Friends, and the Trust's own Galloway Members' Group, which offered support. A visit by members of the Trust's committees and a promise

Opposite:
No 28 Charlotte
Square: the coffee shop

Above left:
Broughton House

Above right:
Broughton House:
the garden

Above:
Broughton House:
the Gallery

Opposite:
Alloa Tower,
Clackmannanshire

of the remaining funds convinced the Trust that the proposal was both feasible and 'Trustworthy'. The trustees provided their remaining funds of £250,000; the Mackay Fund for Galloway pledged £450,000, and NHMF subsequently offered assistance. NTS took over running of the property in the 1995 season and a public appeal for funds was successful.

Although it was anticipated that there would be little difficulty for the Trustees in their application to the Court of Session to transfer Broughton House from their care to that of NTS, almost four years were to pass before it was legally possible. For a good part of that time, there was uncertainty about the outcome, the transfer eventually being completed in 1997.

The Trust has carried out essential repairs, and in the interests of retaining as much as possible of the fabric of the house, has always followed a philosophy of preventative conservation rather than restoration. A conservation and management plan will guide the future for Broughton House. While work is being carried out, it is anticipated that the studio and garden will remain open to visitors.

A NEW STYLE OF PARTNERSHIP

It was Jamie Stormonth Darling who first promoted the idea of partnership with other bodies, but in the 1990s, perhaps because of the number of properties at risk as well as the expense involved, there was even more pressure to extend this notion. In response to approaches by their owners, the Trust agreed that Alloa Tower in Clackmannanshire, Pollok House in Glasgow, and the David Livingstone Centre in Blantyre, were entirely 'Trustworthy', but cannot currently accept ownership because of insufficient funding. If any of these properties were ever to be accepted, they would be declared inalienable and therefore would become permanently the Trust's responsibility. The solution has been, rather as at Broughton House, for the Trust to provide the management expertise, while at the same time negotiating with every source possible to raise the necessary endowment, to enable it to take over the properties for all time. This remains the case.

ALLOA TOWER

Alloa Tower is the surviving medieval nucleus of the late Stuart country house burned in 1800 and not rebuilt. The Earl of Mar and Kellie had formed the Alloa Tower Building Preservation

*The David Livingstone
Centre, Blantyre*

Trust with Clackmannan District Council in 1988, to carry out an eight-year programme on Alloa Tower, to fully restore and furnish it, with 18th-century furnishings and a distinguished collection of family portraits, formerly held in the National Portrait Gallery. The project was co-financed from the European Regional Development Fund (ERDF).

Detailed archaeological recording of the Tower was carried out under the supervision of the Trust's Archaeologist, Robin Turner, while conservation works were being completed. The property was opened under Trust management in 1996 and was officially re-opened by HM The Queen on 9 July 1997 to mark its 500th anniversary.

THE DAVID LIVINGSTONE CENTRE

The David Livingstone Centre in Blantyre is of national importance as the birthplace of the famous missionary explorer. The birthplace is an A-listed building being, late Georgian industrial housing associated with a former cotton mill. It was rescued from demolition by public subscription in 1929. The Trust was represented on the board of Governors of the David Livingstone Centre as early as the 1970s. The property was in constant need of financial support, which at that time the Trust was unable to provide. As with many properties ultimately coming into the Trust's care, a long period of gestation ensued. By 1986, the African Pavilion was fulfilling an important educational function. In March 1998, the

David Livingstone
Centre: the exhibition

Governors of the David Livingstone Memorial Trust formally approached NTS to ask if it would be prepared to offer advice or assistance with respect to the future of the property.

The management of the Centre was transferred to NTS in April 1999 and a partnership formed with the Governors, South Lanarkshire Council and Lanarkshire Enterprise, for the purpose of raising funds for the operation and development of the Centre. Historic Scotland also provided support. The ERDF co-financed four phases in its evolutionary development. While some elements of the original exhibition were retained, new interpretation was introduced. The white 18th-century tenement commemorates Livingstone's life and work: visi-tors move through his childhood home before entering rooms with displays that describe and illustrate Livingstone's African explorations, showing many of his personal belongings and travel equipment. It is anticipated that, subject to funding being raised and agreement by the Court of Session, transfer of the Governors' responsibilities and full ownership will be assumed by the Trust in 2002.

POLLOK HOUSE AND ESTATE

The Trust's interest in Pollok Estate stretches back to its origins in the 1930s when it entered into the first Conservation Agreement in 1939 with Sir John Stirling Maxwell over 452 hectares (1118 acres) of policy land. A Minute of

*Pollok House:
the Drawing Room*

*Opposite:
Camellia House,
Culzean: after
restoration*

Agreement in the 1960s between the Trust, Nether Pollok Ltd and Glasgow Corporation determined the site for the Burrell Collection and established the Pollok Advisory Committee. From 1 May 1998, the Trust was asked to manage the house in partnership with Glasgow City Council, the owners. The ERDF and the Council co-financed improved access and interpretation of Pollok House. It has been possible to bring out of store the majority of the original furnishings, including the internationally important collection of paintings, and with the co-operation of the family to present the House in the style of the period during which Sir John lived there.

Except for the Burrell Collection, which should be managed by people who already manage museums or art galleries, there is little doubt that Pollok Estate would be best preserved as an entity and managed by a single organisation such as The National Trust for Scotland. Negotiations are proceeding with a view to the long-term management of both House and Estate, the property being vitally important as a source of recreation for the citizens of Glasgow and for many other visitors.

CULZEAN CASTLE
AND COUNTRY PARK

A Culzean Stonework Appeal was launched in 1982 to finance a 10-year programme of building restoration in Culzean Country Park, Ayrshire, a priority being the repair of a viaduct on the main approach. Another project in 1990, this time for the restoration of landscape as well as buildings, was given new impetus through a second appeal for £2.5m. Known as the Culzean 2000 Initiative, this restoration project attracted almost double the sum from heritage agencies and was possibly the most comprehensive restoration scheme for any property owned by the Trust. Compatible visitor facilities were developed in several of the restored buildings.

Over 30 individual buildings and structures have been restored at Culzean. Stonework research and extensive repairs on the Castle have been carried out, in addition to the setting up of Culzean's own practical workshops, a landscape survey to aid management of the 227-hectare (560-acre) Country Park, and new interpretation in the Park Centre. The old Castle kitchen has been recreated as closely as possible to the original. It had been known for many years that the wall dividing the two areas of the walled garden was formerly heated by warmed air channelled through an arrangement of flues, and an archaeological investigation in 1999 revealed the mid-19th-century hypocaust underground heating system of ceramic pipes. The Victorian range of greenhouses, demolished in about 1948, has been reconstructed, so completing a major visitor attraction in the walled garden. Amongst other estate buildings the Orangery, Camellia

Pagoda, Culzean,
after restoration

Culzean:
the coast, looking north

House and Pagoda have all been restored. Realignment of the traffic route, coupled with adjustments in the deer-park car park has also been carried out. Croy Shore, a popular beach to the north of Culzean, is managed in partnership with South Ayrshire Council as part of the Country Park. In order to prevent cars from parking on the beach, a new car park with toilet facilities has been introduced.

None of the above could have been executed without the very generous financial support of many agencies and individuals, too numerous to mention. It would be remiss, however, not to acknowledge the support of several local authorities and the hard work and devotion of staff at Culzean, at the regional office and at head office over many years, in bringing to fruition this vast conservation programme. As a result, Culzean Castle, garden and estate retains its distinction as the flagship of the NTS and has kept its position as a pre-eminent historic and natural site in Scotland.

NEWHAILES

The Trustees of the late Sir Charles Dalrymple for Newhailes, near Musselburgh, feeling they could no longer continue with their stewardship of the A-listed house and estate, first approached NTS about its future in 1990. From the beginning there was strong support for Trust involvement, but with the accompanying realisation that the cost of permanently looking after this extraordinarily rich house just east of Edinburgh, with its decayed but recoverable historic landscape, would be enormous and far beyond the Trust's own resources.

Newhailes: the house

The view of Sir James Dunbar-Nasmith, who, both as architect to the Dalrymple trustees, and as an authority on the building's historic architecture, was critically important. In a letter to the Historic Buildings Council for Scotland (HBCS) in August 1993, he described Newhailes as 'a house, especially the interior of which has unique importance. It is designed by James Smith for himself, and possibly extended by William and John Adam with plasterwork by Calderwood and Clayton, paintings by Norie and carvings by Strachan. We must put it in the

Above:
Newhailes: the
Chinese Drawing Room

Opposite:
Newhailes: portraits
in the Dining Room

Overleaf:
Newhailes: the fragile
entrance stairway

first rank architecturally, and its ownership by Lord Hailes, who wrote his *Annals of Scottish History* in the library, with Johnson's annotations, has the same rank historically. Add to this the furniture, pictures and china and the possibility of the books being returned to the library and you have, so far as I am aware, a treasure chest of architecture, history and contents that exists nowhere else in Scotland.' The house and contents have remained virtually untouched for 250 years.

Until the promise of unparalleled financial support from the Heritage Lottery Fund (HLF) and help from Historic Scotland (HS) became more than a possibility, the Trust was naturally cautious. Negotiations between the trustees and HLF over the contents were not concluded until 1995. There was concern that the stable block, situated at some distance from the main building, had 16 individual short-term leases, some of which were without planning permission or listed building consent. A former landfill site for domestic refuse threatened pollution on the site. Not least, there were pressing requirements for interim repairs to the house and urgent security measures to be taken as soon as was practicable. Lady Antonia Dalrymple no longer wished to remain in the house, and later took up residence in the gardener's cottage, which had been improved and extended by the Newhailes trustees.

The Chairman of NTS, Hamish Leslie Melville, had high-level discussions with the Secretary of State for Scotland, Ian Lang, over prospects for funding if the Trust did acquire Newhailes. Matters came to a head when the trustees gave the Trust a final deadline of 1 December 1996, for a firm decision. The National Art Collections Fund (NACF) provided £245,000 to fund the purchase of four important paintings on condition that, as anticipated, the purchase of Newhailes would be supported by HLF. Formal application was made in early 1996. The National Library of Scotland (NLS) agreed in principle that the famous library could be returned to the house, providing environmental conditions, security and access were ultimately in place. Manuscripts were to stay in NLS. NTS will monitor the envi-

ronmental conditions in the library firstly without books and then with some non-Newhailes volumes in place, to help gauge whether it may be appropriate to transfer some of the original books to their former shelves.

The purchase of the contents of the house was agreed between HLF and the Dalrymple trustees at £3.2m. The total funding required for purchase of contents, restoration and endowment was £12.7m of which HLF generously offered £8m, to cover both the endowment for the property and a substantial part of the cost of the contents. It was agreed exceptionally by the then Secretary of State for Scotland, that 60 per cent of the repair costs would be found by Historic Scotland. NTS provided £1.6m towards the contents and restoration. But there was still an immediate shortfall of £1.5m. The Trust decided to appeal to its members and supporters for the considerable sum of £3m for this exceptional property. Five thousand members responded within the first three months, making possible a purchase, which had seemed unattainable. The property was transferred into Trust ownership on 30 January 1997. The European Regional Development Fund (ERDF) gave £500,000 provided that planning permission for the project was in place by 1 April 1998.

From the outset the Trust had been conscious that the revival of the house, its stable block and designed landscape must be treated with as much delicacy as a very fragile oil painting. After much discussion the agreed philosophy for the programme of work was to do as little as possible and only as much as is necessary. The aim is to retain the existing mellowness of both the interior and exterior of the buildings. To guide future decisions and to provide vital information on the origins, development and significance of Newhailes, a management plan, conservation plan (also grant-aided by HLF) – including a topographic survey and historic buildings and landscape survey – have all been meticulously prepared. Three Newhailes Study Days held in Edinburgh, organised by Dr Joe Rock of Edinburgh University, have been well attended and while research has proceeded, have helped to promote interest and discussion. Dr Bill McQueen was contracted to undertake documentary research on the Newhailes papers held in The National Library of Scotland.

Following a detailed tree survey to establish the existence of any early planting, only specimens near footpaths, presenting a danger to the public, were felled. Essential repairs to extensive boundary walls were undertaken, new security services were installed and a fire main was led from the main road to protect the property. On the estate, redundant temporary buildings have been removed and much rubbish has been cleared away. With attention to the drives and clearing of the ha-ha and the former flower garden, the property has taken on a more managed character.

Within the house, experts in the appropriate fields undertook individual surveys on paintwork and of virtually all significant contents. Preceded by a photographic record of every aspect of Newhailes, all moveable contents were temporarily removed to an environmentally-controlled secure store and the house prepared for the management contractors, Linford

Bridgeman, who had done similar work for the National Trust at Chastleton in Gloucestershire. The property is one of the most carefully recorded in NTS ownership. The stable block is being repaired and adapted to provide reception for the visitor, shop, interpretation room, coffee shop and toilets on the ground floor with staff and volunteer accommodation on the first floor. There will be a manager's house, and some areas are likely to be let as houses.

The conservation philosophy of doing as little as possible and only as much as is necessary does raise some dilemmas. Research has been carried out to determine the most appropriate method of repairing the existing lime plaster on the house, and at present there will be no general lime washing of the building. The exterior timber of the windows must be fully painted, whereas all internal finishes will be preserved. The intention is to present the house more or less as it was when the Trust accepted it in 1997, with additional safeguards, but not doing anything which cannot be reversed in the future.

To extend protection of the sensitive interiors of the house, a system of timed access will be adopted, volunteer guides taking previously booked parties through the house. Regular walks will be organised to explore the surrounding historic landscape. Newhailes will offer the rare opportunity of seeing a form of house much as it would have appeared during the Scottish Enlightenment in the 18th and early 19th centuries – a period of outstanding achievements in intellectual, literary, legal, scientific and artistic fields. The projected date for opening the property to visitors is 2002.

Previous page:
Newhailes: an equally
fragile estate building –
the shell grotto

Above:
Professor Ian
Cunningham, Chairman,
left, Miss Joy Sandison,
and the Earl of Airlie,
President, at the official
handover of her Unst
and Yell estates

UNST AND YELL ESTATE, SHETLAND

In 1998, Miss Joy Sandison most generously gifted her 1,780-hectare (4,400-acre) estate on the Shetland islands of Unst and Yell to the Trust. She did so on a leaseback arrangement, whereby she continues to live there and to manage the estate, which consists of ten parcels of land, eight of which lie on Unst. The largest single area extends to 420 hectares (1,038 acres) and is on the island of Yell, while the smallest is a 12-hectare (30-acre) island off the island of Fetlar to the south-east of Unst. The property, although not outstanding in nature conservation terms, contains some of the best examples of typical Shetland scenery and wildlife. Archaeological remains reflect prehistoric, medieval and recent activity in abundance. The Trust's Senior Archaeologist, Robin Turner, rated the estate as 'a very special place, eminently Trustworthy'.

There is a long tradition of knowledge and enthusiasm amongst members of Joy Sandison's family, particularly those in the 19th century, who took a special interest in the natural and

human history of Shetland, describing several subjects in their literature. The otherwise treeless landscape of Unst is broken by a grove of sycamore trees planted by Dr Laurence Edmonston, Joy Sandison's great-great-grandfather. These thrive even today, near to Halligarth, alongside a colourful spring display of bluebells and other woodland plants. At the tender age of 19, Thomas Edmonston, Joy's great-grandfather, became Professor of Natural History at Anderson's University of Glasgow, and at 21 had published the first *Flora of Shetland* (1845). The estate also has a valuable stud of the most appealing Shetland ponies, for whose future the Trust will take responsibility. The most recent co-operation between the Trust and The National Museums of Scotland over Wester Kittochside Farm bodes well for the return of the Saxby/Sandison collection of Shetland artefacts presently on loan to The National Museums of Scotland, with a view to establishing a museum on Unst.

Anyone who has seen the Fair Isle landscape will naturally compare it with that of Unst. The two are quite different in that it would be unusual to spot a ruined cottage on Fair Isle and there are areas on Unst in which it would be difficult to count the number of ruined structures. But the two islands share flora and fauna, rocky coastline, cliff scenery and a windswept landscape as well as a language influenced by Norse. Unst, the most northerly inhabited island in Britain, takes some effort to reach but is eminently worthy of exploration.

THE WORKING PRACTICES REVIEW

There have been several reorganisations of the Trust, notably in 1984 under Lester Borley and in 1994 when the working party under Colin

Top left:
Unst ponies

Top right:
Unst landscape

Left:
A 'luxury' bus-halt on Unst: Roger Smith, Convener: Countryside and Nature Conservation Committee, map-reading

The Ben Lomond National Memorial Park sculpture: the official opening in November 1997. Left to right: Hamish Leslie Melville, Chairman; the late Donald Dewar, Secretary of State for Scotland, later Scotland's First Minister; Sir Peter Hutchison, Chairman of the Forestry Commission; and Trevor Croft, Trust Director

Donald reviewed the structure of the organisation. The Working Practices Review of 1999 is the single most significant review of the internal management of the Trust ever undertaken. It took as its inspiration the Trust's Corporate Plan for 1999-2004, with the purpose of examining the procedures of the Trust and recommending ways to enable it to become more efficient and cost-effective in its core purposes of conservation, access and enjoyment. The target for completion of the review was 1999 with implementation by the end of 2000. The Regions were reduced to four and renamed as North-East, Highlands and Islands (with a sub-office in Oban with responsibility for the Western Isles, Glencoe and Argyll), South, and West. The regional offices have been strengthened by the appointment of specialist staff, for example, in conservation, buildings, archaeology, countryside, gardens, education and finance. This wider range of skills at regional level makes communication with staff at the properties more effective.

NTS is now better equipped to achieve its strategic objectives, of conservation, enjoyment, education, influence and persuasion, and has increased capacity to manage its resources in doing so.

SUMMARY

The 1990s stand out in the history of the Trust, with extraordinary changes in the leadership of the organisation. These might have been expected more radically to change the direction of the Trust; however, a moratorium on future acquisitions was declared after the endowment of Newhailes was not fully realised. All property acquired since then has been funded by gift, or bequest and generous endowment.

Among 29 new properties in the 1990s (only the first period from 1931 to 1944 exceeds this number), 12 may be counted as major acquisitions. The decade was also notable for the level of grants received, reflecting the Trust's national standing and the confidence placed in it by government, its agencies and others. The Heritage Lottery Fund contributed over £29m towards 12 projects, the Millennium Commission through the Millennium Forest for Scotland over £743,665 for restoration of native woodlands at 13 properties, and the Arts Lottery Fund £45,000 to support one project – the granite sculpture for the Ben Lomond National Memorial Park. Historic Scotland gave grants of over £12m towards Quinquennial Survey work and conservation repairs of the Trust's historic buildings and Scottish Natural Heritage over £4m for the conservation of landscape and flora and fauna, including fully supporting the Trust's expanding ranger service through the Concordat

Agreement. Local authorities and enterprise companies gave grants totalling over £4m. From 1991 to 2000 the European Regional Development Fund, the European Agriculture Guidance and Guarantee Fund and the European Social Fund, together provided over £10m towards 41 Trust projects.

Without these major grants the Trust would not have been able to take on the new properties or carry out extensive conservation projects. It is to the credit of the Finance Division, especially its Director, Nigel Fairhead and Grants Officer Danny Nugent, working closely with regional staff, that applications have in a majority of cases been successful.

Revolutionary change and a new emphasis on commercial activities have boosted both membership and income for the Trust's conservation work. The Trust acquired a more positive image for the millennium with its new offices and public face at Wemyss House in Charlotte Square, Edinburgh. Membership of the Trust for most of the 1990s rose and fell, then remained steady, but finally in the last year reached an all-time high of 239,000. Official recognition has been given to the Trust's army of volunteers in almost every sphere of activity and an agreed policy on volunteering in the Trust will result in the appointment, albeit part-time, of a volunteer co-ordinator. The Education Department has also been given new impetus by the appointment of Regional Education Officers in each of the four regions.

The Working Practices Review has upgraded Trust procedures and given it revised objectives. The injection of specialist staff,

Charlotte Square, Edinburgh south side

particularly into regional offices, will provide new inspiration and hopefully bring the operational side of the Trust closer to the membership. The closure of the Central and Tayside regional office with some staff redundancies was a regretted consequence of reorganisation.

This seems an appropriate place to fully acknowledge the hard work carried out by a loyal staff at all levels and in all situations during the Trust's 70 years.

Production of the first Corporate Plan and then, more significantly, the implementation of the second, is helping to concentrate the minds of staff and volunteers on the Trust's objectives and the task ahead. The conservation and presentation of the heritage of Scotland is exemplified through an ever-increasing variety of properties, most of which are owned by the Trust inalienably and managed by it – always *for the benefit of the nation.*

CHAPTER TEN
MISSION FOR THE SECOND MILLENNIUM

'We do not discover the future, we invent it.
And we invent it wisely when we study the
failures and successes of our past.'

ROGER SCRUTON,
FINANCIAL TIMES, 30 DECEMBER 2000

LOOKING AHEAD

Roger Scruton said that 'those who predict the future usually want to control it'. At the end of my career I can confess to no such ambition, but after holding a variety of positions within The National Trust for Scotland over the past 31 years, including the two-year research period for this work, I feel better equipped than many to try to give an insight into the Trust's future challenges.

It was the vision of just a few people which began the Trust movement, a cause served by a responsive and a responsible organisation which has achieved extraordinary support. Will it continue to draw on its traditional strengths, with skills and experiences freely given? Or will it develop like a quango or an arm of government? It is appropriate to ask how relevant the Trust will be to the nation's expectations in the future.

A good starting point for any analysis is to take an objective look back over the high and low points of the Trust's history. Over the last 70 years the Trust's capacity to adapt to internal and external change has ensured its success. During the next 70 years and beyond, the same evolutionary process will continue, requiring the Trust to find fresh skills and resources and the will to adapt to new circumstances. Some of these will be generated internally and therefore, theoretically at least, be within the Trust's control. Others will be as a result of external influences to which the Trust will have to consider its response. Essential will be a strong, yet flexible, centrally conceived strategy around which Trust staff, volunteers and members may

continue to rally. The new Corporate Plan (1999–2004) contains the ingredients for such an inclusive strategy and, if adhered to, monitored and updated as situations dictate, should help to ensure success in the future.

The first ever vote by members of Council was called for during the April 1981 Council meeting held in the newly acquired offices in Dean Street, Stockbridge. The occasion was a debate about whether the Trust should become involved in the future of the island of Rum. Until that moment the Chairman had always managed to achieve agreement by consensus and this is still the case with the majority of decisions taken.

The general policy of NTS, apart from conservation, has been to expend much effort and money on increasing membership, numbers of visitors, income, and revenue-earning use of buildings at properties. This has enabled the Trust to continue to acquire and maintain a variety of properties at a constant rate over the decades.

The balance of membership has always been towards the older, more affluent sector of the population. These people generally have more leisure time, they are mobile, able to travel and have a greater appreciation for and interest in the wide variety of property and activities offered by the Trust. In order to maintain such support in the future, it is desirable to attract a higher percentage of younger people, who already enjoy the benefits of Trust properties, particularly in the countryside. If they can be convinced now, they are more likely to become advocates and enthusiasts in later life. Unlike the experience of

Chapter opening picture:
Newhailes: the Library

Ben Lawers Visitor Centre exhibition

the National Trust, NTS members have tended not to question the decisions made by their leaders. It is likely and desirable that in future more questions will be asked by an increasingly well informed and critical membership, leading to more democratic management. The noticeable dip in membership between 1994 and 1998 has been arrested, as joining has been made more attractive through deliberate recruitment initiatives. Such re-invention is constantly required if the more characteristic upward trend is to be permanently re-established, the crucial source of income maintained, and the attention and support of government retained.

Education and interpretation have always been part of the Trust's mission. The establish-ment of Regional Education Officers is a recent innovation and a strong Trust presence on the Internet and the worldwide web has already changed the way we communicate. Both developments should bring the Trust closer to young people, although the real thing will always be more satisfying than 'virtual reality'! Some visitors remain content with exhibitions as they were when they were created and others appreciate and enjoy regularly updated interpretative techniques and have come to experience these in visitor centres. Within financial constraints the Trust should conduct a regular review of all displays at properties – say a septennial review – and perhaps be prepared to invest funds in new techniques of interpretation. The enormously

*The Hill House:
queue of visitors
waiting to see the house*

rich resources of the properties are also available for adult learning, which could be increased, with the advantage of spreading knowledge of them even further.

The Trust's policy of making its properties accessible to all is in accord with national policies and the public's expectations. The great attraction of buildings and countryside has produced some unacceptable pressures. These effects may be seen in our castles and houses, where the sheer pressure of visitors has led to restriction on numbers at Craigievar Castle, Crathes Castle, The Hill House and Broughton House. Timed or pre-booked entry, apart from helping to conserve the fabric of a property, allows the visitor to appreciate it more comfortably, with

fewer people present. It is likely that if visitor numbers rise in the future, similar restrictions will become necessary at more properties. Such rationale should be explained carefully in advance of implementation, if it is to meet with co-operation and approval.

The number of paying visitors, able to be recorded at properties, peaked at over two million in 1990 and 1991, but seems to have settled more recently around the 1,750,000 mark. The exchange rate, as well as the fickle Scottish weather, midges, and the price of petrol, none of which the Trust can control, influence visits from abroad. It can and does put an enormous effort into ensuring the warmth of welcome to its visitors and maintaining the high

Brodick Country Park:
ranger guided walk

quality of care and presentation of its properties. In remote areas at Inverewe and Culzean, for example, the Trust is a major provider of local employment.

In the countryside the increased numbers of walkers and climbers, triggered by a combination of external as well as internal publicity, has undoubtedly led to degradation of the Trust's mountains. The Trust has long recognised the need to minimise the effects of wear and tear and has in many instances diverted original routes. On Ben Lomond it was necessary to ban large groups involved in sponsored races from using the footpath.

Ranger staff have had to become more specialised. The practice of reinstating tradi-

tional stone-pitched paths, although expensive in time and materials, has the benefit of long life, and is being adopted on many Trust mountains. In very recent times, as Trust expertise has developed, it has taken over national responsibility for footpath maintenance training. A better-informed public has responded enthusiastically to its millennium 'Sole Trading' Appeal, raising funds to help with the repair and maintenance of mountain footpaths.

Greater numbers of visitors to its splendid gardens have caused the Trust to upgrade original path surfaces and provide ever-increasing facilities such as car parks, toilets and plant sales areas, which unless sympathetically introduced can spoil the very focus of attention. The

replacement of stolen garden ornaments, plants, and even of the labels used to make identification easier, is expensive in labour and materials – a difficult problem to solve without a constant staff presence, which is not always practical. There has been an enormous increase in publicity for gardens through the media, especially television. In the not too distant future, and with public interest in gardening at an all-time peak, it may become necessary to introduce some form of visitor control, for example through a reduction in signing or possibly timed tickets as in our castles and great houses.

The element of discovery at properties has diminished at properties such as Culzean, where many feel that the speed of development has overtaken Elisabeth Beazley's often quoted 'essential character and atmosphere'. Her choice of colour and sign design for the Country Park has been compromised by use of different styles close to the three shops, restaurant, coffee shop and snack bars, which are now available. It will be wise to consider carefully the impact of continuing access and development policies prior to their translation into reality. Nonetheless these developments have been combined with skilful restoration of practically every estate building, and have culminated in one of the best-conserved estates in Scotland.

The creation of the first shop in the Trust was a response to the need to raise money for conservation and to improve facilities for visitors. The establishment of an independent Trading Company, and now the Enterprises Division, is a reaction to the same requirement but with the purpose of continuing to support

Opposite:
Kintail: a pitched path

Left:
Fyvie: statue of Pan being removed from the garden for safe-keeping and more secure fixing

the Trust to raise more funds for conservation. Whilst fully recognising the part played by the division, the Trust's *raison d'être* remains conservation and care should be taken not to divert inappropriately or disproportionately from this all-important purpose.

The Trust boosted employment by taking advantage of government schemes which also matched its objectives. This provided valuable assistance for the Trust in gardens, curatorial and education departments. At the same time, involvement in the schemes has benefited many young people by providing them with new skills. As the needs have arisen, Trust departments have encouraged existing staff to develop in new fields. In the Curatorial Department, for example, staff have enhanced their ability to research the historical background to properties and in the conservation of paintings, ceramics and furniture. They have also greatly improved the furnishing of the Trust's many holiday cottages and other accommodation.

At Culzean, the establishment of a workshop primarily to train stonemasons helps to keep alive a diminishing trade as well as providing skilled manpower for the property's own building needs. Similarly at Threave, the courses in the practice as well as the theory of horticulture fill a gap in national provision. Annually, the six trainees help the permanent staff to maintain the quality of Threave Garden. Robert Smail's Printing Works employs young people on a small but crucial scale to learn the all-but-lost art of printing with lead type.

Pollok House: Assistant Curator Christopher Hartley carefully hanging paintings by Sir John Stirling Maxwell, near the family room

If such varied initiatives continue and develop as the opportunities arise, the Trust will strengthen its position as an important force in the evolution and preservation of useful and historically valuable trades and professions. It would be a worthwhile and relevant project, for example, for the Trust to enlarge and build on the achievements of the John Bute Memorial Appeal, which encourages young people to learn some of the historic skills in building and fine art.

The Trust's curatorial Collections Care Policy (July 1999) states that 'it is a prevention rather than cure policy and concentrates on preventing damage and slowing down deterioration, in favour of (but not ignoring) repair after damage has occurred. Conservation work within the Trust had traditionally focused on repair of damaged or deteriorated items. The new policy concentrates on activities that prevent damage from occurring in the first place.' Objects age naturally and it seems inappropriate to restore them to a pristine state. Preventative conservation should also reduce costs, thus permitting a greater volume of work to be done. It also provides the long-term option of adopting more sophisticated or alternative techniques when knowledge may be more advanced.

Such a policy may appeal to the connoisseur but could result in shabbiness, or even appear to the first-time visitor as a lack of care. The Trust may have to explain more of what it is doing to the less knowledgeable public. This could be achieved at properties by holding more 'putting-

Culzean: lime-burning in the masons' workshop

to-bed' days, special behind-the-scenes visits to demonstrate how contents are cared for in the winter months and showing properties in the 'before, during and after' state of conservation. The acquisition of Newhailes with its philosophy of preventative care provides the Trust with an important opportunity to interpret this relatively new policy.

In both buildings and landscape the Trust's capacity to influence the relevant departments of government at the right time has been instrumental in obtaining the best legislation for these interlinked elements of Scotland's heritage. Positive relationships with the personalities in power have been crucial. With the new Scottish Executive in office, the Trust has established ways of ensuring that MSPs are adequately and regularly informed about its activities. At the same time, through consultation the Trust takes the opportunity to comment on legislation such as land reform proposals, which include the abolition of feudal tenure. This has particular relevance to the Trust's feudal agreements over which it is intended to retain a measure of development control by converting at least some to 'conservation burdens'.

Financial support for the Trust from government has been diminishing over recent years and large Heritage Lottery and European grants, from which the Trust greatly benefited, particularly in the 1990s, are no longer forthcoming. Historic Scotland and its predecessors have been the most consistent providers of grant towards the built heritage owned by the Trust.

Newhailes: mangle requiring TLC (tender loving care)

Scottish Natural Heritage and its forerunners have been generous in their support of countryside. Whereas the Trust will always be grateful for the large capital sums made available for purchase of property, adequate finance and endowment for their long-term maintenance will be a continuing call on the Trust's limited resources in the foreseeable future.

The level of personal legacies also varies but has never been of such crucial importance as in recent times. The Trust is grateful for the generosity and thoughtfulness of those people who contribute in this way as it depends on this form of giving in order to carry forward its responsibility to care for the properties. Gifts and donations are also vital in support of the Trust and, like legacies, will only continue if the donors feel the organisation is truly worthy of support.

Ben Lomond and the Trossachs is the first National Park to be to be declared in Scotland. The creation of the National Heritage Memorial Park, coupled with Trust ownership, is unprecedented. The eyes of the nation will be watching to see how Ben Lomond is managed in the future. With arrangements for organisation of the Park now under public discussion, the Trust is in a unique position to advise and participate in its operation. The experience gained will be particularly useful in the consideration and development of future National Parks such as the Cairngorms and Glencoe, where the Trust also has significant tracts of land within probable park boundaries.

The Trust has frequently been the catalyst behind successful partnerships with both voluntary and statutory organisations and indeed

Far left:
Professor Roger Wheater
OBE, Chairman of
The National Trust
for Scotland

Left:
This European larch (see
caption page 225), now
10 years old, mirrors the
Trust's healthy growth
and is a symbol for its
continuing strength in the
future

Below:
NTS Legacy
Appeal leaflet

believes that in order to achieve its objectives such alliances are essential. Notable joint partnerships have been forged with local authorities over Culzean and Brodick Country Parks. In these cases, although the Trust remains the owner and the lands retain their status of inalienability, operating costs are shared with the local authorities with mutual benefits to the participants. The Trust has already entered into joint management of Pollok House, the David Livingstone Centre and Alloa Tower. It could be worthwhile considering some inalienable houses presently running at a deficit and exploring further partnerships with local authorities, without losing the Trust's ultimate control of policy.

The Trust must continue to realise its objectives in the future by emphasising to its members and supporters, as well as the wider public, the balance between income and conservation needed to look after the heritage of Scotland. It must therefore take every opportunity to publicise its mission in the second millennium, not least through the continuing success of the National Trusts' international conferences, which will return to Scotland for the 10th conference in 2003.

In conclusion, the challenge for the Trust is to be as relevant, if not more so in the next 70 years, as it has been for the last. The Trust is fortunate to have had altruistic leaders with high principles, who have often provided inspired leadership. As the National Trust FOR Scotland it will be relevant to the nation's expectations if every generation continues to serve and employ those who believe in its unique mission.

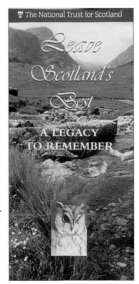

APPENDICES
AND INDEX

THE FORMATIVE YEARS
1929-1935

GEORGE S RUSSELL OBE CA WS,
Councillor Emeritus and former Law Agent to The National Trust for Scotland

As it was wholly the idea of the Association for the Preservation of Rural Scotland – now the Association for the Protection of Rural Scotland (APRS) – that Scotland should have its own 'National Trust' it is right to deal first with the start of the APRS and the people involved in forming and running it.

The APRS was born in 1926 and first functioned in April 1927. At much the same time a body called the Council for the Preservation of Rural England (CPRE) had been formed and the APRS was the Scottish counterpart. It was the brainchild of the Royal Incorporation of Architects in Scotland and conceived by the Edinburgh Architectural Association. The driving force behind the idea was one of Britain's greatest planners of the time, Frank Mears, who was the first Honorary Secretary of the Association and later knighted.

The APRS when it was formed had some very prestigious Presidents and Vice Presidents. The Honorary President was the Earl of Crawford and Balcarres whose son David, the 28th Earl, was to become involved with practically every important body in Scotland to do with the arts and also with the National Trust, the Royal Fine Art Commission, the Pilgrim Trust, the National Gallery and the National Library of Scotland, amongst other important bodies. The President was the young 12th Earl of Haddington, then just 31, who also was to take a prominent part in the arts in Scotland later on in his life. Sir

John Stirling Maxwell Bt of Pollok, was a Vice President.

The APRS also had as their first treasurer Alexander Harrison CA, who was later to play such an important part in the life of the NTS and who until his death on 1 December 1988 in his 99th year was the oldest person alive who had been associated with the Trust in its early days. Also, amongst the original founders of the APRS was my father, Arthur W Russell, who was a Writer to the Signet in Edinburgh, a great walker and climber and who was Secretary of the Scottish Rights of Way Society from 1923 to 1932. He represented that body on the original Council of the APRS.

Although not in at the very start but joining the Council of the APRS in 1928 or 1929 and to be its Chairman for a time, was the youngish Sir Iain Colquhoun Bt of Luss (the 7th Baronet), who also played an important role in the subsequent formation of the NTS. He was not only the first Chairman of the NTS Council in 1931, but continued to hold that position till 1946, when he was elected a Vice President – a position he held till his death in 1948. He was succeeded as Chairman by the 12th Earl of Wemyss and March.

Also involved in the early days of the APRS was the 8th Duke of Atholl and it was these men who were so closely involved with the APRS who were mostly to become the founding fathers of the NTS, ie Atholl, Colquhoun, Crawford, and Stirling Maxwell (who was to

Picture on page 282:
A detail from a tapestry
at Falkland Palace

give the NTS its first property – Crookston Castle), together with Sandy Harrison and Arthur Russell.

The APRS had as its objects the preservation of the countryside in its widest sense taking into account all the competing interests – objects which were embodied later in the constitution of NTS. In 1929 the APRS was offered the Loch Dee Estate near Newton Stewart in the Galloway Hills; the APRS did not have power to hold land and the matter of the proposed gift was discussed with Samuel H Hamer – the Secretary of the National Trust – which had been formed in England in 1895.

While the National Trust was entitled to hold land in Scotland, there was a strong feeling in the Council of the APRS that Scotland should not be 'invaded' by the National Trust from south of the border. Sir John Stirling Maxwell, in particular, was very vehement over the matter and is thought to have been the principal spokesman for the cry that went up – 'let us have our own National Trust for Scotland'.

So it was at that time – in June and July 1929 – that important voices in Scotland were realising that England and Wales had had their National Trust since 1895 and it was high time that Scotland formed a similar preservation body which would be enabled to hold land and buildings in Scotland for the benefit of the nation. The APRS was in the forefront of these thoughts and discussions and the minute books of their Executive and Council meetings show that the matter was discussed frequently in 1929 and 1930, and even into 1931, by which time the NTS had been formed and was getting underway.

To go back however to 1929, discussions took place with Mr Hamer of the National Trust and with Mr Adamson, the then Secretary of State for Scotland; Sandy Harrison was at the forefront of these discussions. It appeared that the government was not too keen on seeing a Trust being established in Scotland on the same lines as the National Trust and there were clearly ideas in the mind of the government at that time that it would be much better to establish a National Parks system – under some form of government quango – and the matter hung fire for some time.

It is clear from the records that enthusiasm for the idea spread in Scotland and, with the possibility of other offers of land being made, the council of the APRS took the bit between their teeth and on 21 May 1930 decided to press on and consider how a National Trust for Scotland could be constituted – either by a Royal Charter, an Act of Parliament, or incorporation under the Companies Acts. The question of who in Scotland should be invited to be the leaders of this new body came under active consideration.

With regard to the constitution, the APRS came to the very sensible decision that to get the new Trust off the ground, by far the quickest and simplest way would be to incorporate a company under the Companies Act and questions of a Royal Charter or an Act of Parliament could come along later. This was undoubtedly the quickest method to get the Trust started.

There were thoughts that the APRS should widen its constitution to enable it to hold land – but the final view was taken that it would be much better if the APRS used its initiative to set up and launch a new body – rather than try to expand the APRS. Accordingly, it was on 22 July 1930 that the Council of the APRS, meeting at their headquarters at 3 Forres Street in Edinburgh with Sir Iain Colquhoun in the Chair, Frank Mears as the Honorary Secretary, and Kenneth Ferguson as Organising Secretary, resolved that they should proceed with the formation of a National Trust for Scotland. It was to be constituted as a company limited by guarantee.

The first task was to find an influential group of persons in Scotland who were prepared to back the new venture and a letter was sent out on 6 August 1930 to a number of people throughout Scotland. This letter – of which only one of the original exists – is now a very important document in the archives of the NTS. The Council of the APRS agreed that the offices at 3 Forres Street and the staff of the APRS and in particular the services of the Honorary Secretary, Frank Mears, should be placed at the disposal of the new Trust in its early stages.

The Duke of Atholl, Sir John Stirling Maxwell, Sir Iain Colquhoun, and the Earls of Crawford, Haddington and Elgin (all Knights of the Order of the Thistle, then or later) were involved in the early stages of the formation of the Trust – along with many other prominent persons in Scotland. Arthur Russell, being an enthusiastic supporter of the idea, and in practice in the firm of Pringle and Clay WS at 14 Melville Street, was instructed to take the necessary steps to get the company established. This was the beginning of Arthur Russell's lifelong interest in the NTS which really continued until his death in 1967 at the age of 94.

The APRS officials must have moved quickly because it was on Monday 10 November 1930 that a distinguished body of people met at 3 Forres Street and constituted themselves as the first meeting of the Provisional Council of the NTS. The Trust archive holds copies of the draft minutes of this meeting, prepared by Kenneth Ferguson and revised by Sir Iain Colquhoun. There is also an explanatory memorandum on the proposed Draft Memorandum and Articles of Association and papers prepared for the meeting by Frank Mears and Mr Samuel Hamer.

The Duke of Atholl took the Chair at the meeting on 10 November 1930 and Sir D Y Cameron moved the motion that The National Trust for Scotland should be registered as a company limited by guarantee. The Duke of Atholl was appointed President with the Earl of Crawford and Balcarres as the first Vice President and Sir Iain Colquhoun as Chairman of Council. Arthur Russell was appointed Law Agent for the purpose of completing the Draft Memorandum and Articles of Association and thereafter to carry through the registration of the Trust under the Companies Acts. Messrs Bryson and Craig CA

Invitation to act as a Trustee of NTS

were appointed as the first auditors of the new Trust. Mr Ferguson, the Organising Secretary of the APRS, was appointed Acting Secretary.

So the first steps were taken towards the formation of The National Trust for Scotland on 10 November 1930. Arthur Russell, no doubt appreciating the significance of the occasion, carefully preserved many of the original drafts and papers which are also held in the Trust's archive.

It is important to realise that this well-represented meeting of 10 November 1930 took place six months before the company was actually incorporated on 1 May 1931. It was very wise of the few original founding fathers to make sure that there was a powerful body of opinion in Scotland actually wanting an NTS to be formed – before the actual legal steps towards formation were taken.

The new body was now fledged and about to be launched on its own. At this point tribute must be paid to the outstanding work which the APRS did in getting the new Trust launched, from the time the idea was thought about in June and July 1929 until November 1930, when it all happened. The whole thing was obviously carried through by the APRS with energy and efficiency and the Association still holds impeccable records of all that happened. The APRS today, after more than 60 years of excellent work, goes from strength to strength and had as its Patron the 10th Duke of Atholl who was also a Vice President of the NTS.

Amongst the Executive and Council Minutes of the APRS there are two extracts worthy of comment. The first is one of 19 December 1930 when it was noted that the preliminary expenses in connection with the proposed formation of the NTS amounted to approximately £10 and it was agreed that this somewhat modest sum should be shared equally between the Trust and the APRS. In the second, an extract of 28 October 1931, Sir Iain intimated to the Council of the APRS that the newly formed NTS had received a bequest of £5,000 and gratification was expressed at so substantial a gift to the new Trust – 'for whose formation the APRS had been responsible'. This was a very large sum in those days and there must have been many sitting round the table of the APRS Council who thought that but for the formation of the NTS that £5,000 might have come to the APRS.

The APRS continued to keep a close eye on the NTS and referred to its progress in their annual reports of 1930, 1931 1932 and 1935 – all references making glowing reference to the new Trust's progress. The 1935 APRS Annual Report referred to the fact that Scotland had looked like being in the first stage of a new movement of progressive development with regard to the problem of conserving and preserving amenity both in country and in town and with the preservation of old buildings of architectural of historic interest. It went on to refer to the work of the NTS 'which was brought into being as a holding body at the instigation of the APRS some few years ago and is now proving an influential and effective ally'.

But to return to the actual formation of the NTS. Matters proceeded to the end of 1930 and into early 1931 with Arthur Russell acting as Law Agent, working closely with Sir Iain Colquhoun as the designated Chairman of Council from the office at 14 Melville Street.

On 1 May 1931 the new Trust was incorporated as a company limited by guarantee and not having a share capital with the name of 'The National Trust for Scotland for Places of Historic Interest or Natural Beauty, Limited'. This remained the constitution of the NTS until 20 December 1935 when the 'National Trust for Scotland Order Confirmation Act 1935' was passed by Parliament to confirm the Trust's provisional order annexed to the Act. 1 May 1931 can therefore be looked upon as the first day on which the NTS had a legal identity.

Following the incorporation of the company on 1 May, Sir Iain wrote a letter calling a meeting of the Provisional Council for 27 May 1931. The minutes of this meeting of the Provisional Council have not been preserved but it is clear that the business included a report on the incorporation of the company and centred round the arrangements for the First Ordinary General Meeting of the Trust. It would also appear that at this meeting, Arthur Russell was appointed Acting Secretary and Treasurer in place of Mr Ferguson of the APRS, who had held the fort up till then.

The First Ordinary General Meeting of the Trust was arranged for 21 July 1931 (see formal circular of June 1931: Appendix 1.b) and people were invited to become annual members by subscription; '10 shillings or more' (this sum was not increased until 1963, to £1). The report of the Provisional Council was submitted to the First Ordinary General Meeting on 21 July 1931.

The question of the publicity for the new venture was well looked after and articles appeared in *The Scotsman* on 2 May 1931.

At the First Ordinary General Meeting on 21 July

Invitation to join the Trust as members

1931, which was held in the City Chambers in Edinburgh, the Duke of Atholl remarked, that although it was only two and a half months since the Trust had been incorporated, it had paid off all its preliminary expenses and had a balance of £100. It also possessed the historic old Crookston Castle with 2.5 acres of ground (now under the guardianship of the Secretary of State), a gift from Sir John Stirling Maxwell.

The Council met on 14 October 1931 and appointed an Executive Committee with Sir Iain Colquhoun as the Chairman along with Sir D Y Cameron, Mr A O Curle, Professor Baily, Mr Leadbetter, Kenneth Murray, Miss Murray and Dr David Russell, who was later knighted. Arthur Russell was appointed Secretary and Treasurer for the period up to December 1932. The Trust was not in a position to offer a salary but it was hoped there might be an honorarium. Lord Elgin was invited to become a Vice President and Harry McRobert to join the Council.

The Trust opened its bank account with the Royal Bank of Scotland at the West End Branch where it has remained to this day. At the same time discussions were already taking place with the Pilgrim Trust who had offered to give all the support they could to the new body. The Council and the Executive must have decided that the Trust should seek more publicity throughout Scotland and in December 1931 a formal paper was prepared and widely circulated, seeking members of the Trust and setting out the list of bodies who were to be invited to appoint representative members to the Council.

Dr David Russell, a cousin of Arthur Russell, was one of the first Life Members, together with Sir Steven Runciman and Lord Wemyss, an early Council Member and a lifelong supporter. His son, David, followed in his father's footsteps and is now a Councillor Emeritus. Their family charitable trust, the Russell Trust, continues to help the Trust in countless ways.

Meantime, the Pilgrim Trust generously made grants of £500 in each of the years 1932/1933 for administration purposes and discussions took place with regard to Culross, Culloden and Bannockburn as well as continuing discussions about Burg and Crookston Castle. In 1932 it was noted that Arthur Russell was moving from Messrs Pringle and Clay WS at 14 Melville Street to Strathern and Blair at 12 South Charlotte Street and it was agreed that Strathern and Blair WS would be Law Agents to the Trust. Arthur Russell remained Secretary and Treasurer and a sum of 100 guineas was paid to him for his services for the past year as Secretary, Treasurer and Law Agent.

The Annual General Meeting was held in the City Chambers on 29 June 1932. It cannot have taken long to produce the first Annual Accounts as the assets then were under £500. The meeting was, legally speaking, the First Annual General Meeting of the newly formed Trust, as the meeting on 21 July 1931 was in fact the First Ordinary General Meeting to report on the establishment of the Trust and was not a formal annual meeting as such. The meeting held on 29 June 1932 should be looked upon as the first AGM – held once again in the City Chambers in Edinburgh.

The minutes of the AGM were very formal and need not be referred to in any particular way but of course the Report of the Council which was prepared for that meeting is now part of the Trust archives and included with all the other annual reports from then onwards. Bannockburn, Bruce's Stone near New Galloway and Culross Palace were the main subjects discussed. The total expenditure for the year to 30 April 1932 was the princely sum of £570. 14s and the assets of the Trust at 30 April 1932 were just under £500. Applicants were sought for the new post of Secretary and Treasurer in view of Arthur Russell wishing to remain as Law Agent in his firm of Strathern and Blair; in due course Captain E D (Teddy) Stevenson was appointed and took over as Secretary and

The National Trust for Scotland for Places of Historic Interest or Natural Beauty Limited

In 1895 an Association was formed in England entitled "The National Trust "for Places of Historic Interest or Natural Beauty" for the purpose of acquiring by gift or purchase and holding on behalf of the Nation lands and buildings of special natural beauty or historic interest. The idea which gave birth to the Trust in England, as expressed in a recent circular of that Trust, applies surely with equal force to Scotland : "That there are in this country many buildings of "such historic interest and much land of such exceptional beauty as to demand "and require permanent preservation."

Prior to 1895 however there was no body either governmental public or private appropriate for that purpose and as indicative of the need of such a Body and how greatly its value when formed was appreciated it is only necessary to point to the rapid growth of the National Trust to its present position of power and responsibility throughout England and Wales and to its general recognition as the natural custodian or trustee for property or buildings to be held for the Nation. The Trust was originally formed under the Companies Acts as a Company limited by guarantee and not having a share capital, but by 1907 it acquired for itself a special Act of Parliament and now holds invested funds of over £30,000 and has an annual revenue of over £7500 which includes fully £1700 in annual subscriptions. Apart from these invested funds the Trust owns a very large number of properties of all kinds throughout the length and breadth of England and Wales; these include Scafell and some of the finest areas in the English Lake District, Stonehenge, Runnymede of Magna Charta fame, Housesteads Camp on the Roman Wall, Commons, Downs and Parks in many parts of the country as well as historic castles and buildings in cities such as York and Winchester.

Thus there has been preserved in England as the permanent property of the Nation and under conditions which ensure that they shall be properly looked after and maintained a large number of the most interesting historic landmarks and many of the finest tracts of country and the number of these is ever increasing, the annual Report for 1929-30 showing a considerable number of new properties handed to the Trust together with some large sums of money for general purposes, special purchases or the endowment of properties already held. The Trust however has never functioned in Scotland and indeed is unwilling to do so, having its hands very full with its large and ever-growing domains and properties in England.

It has been felt by many that as there was no appropriate body in Scotland to carry out the work so successfully carried out by the National Trust in England the formation of such a Trust in Scotland would be of great value, fill a similar want and meet with ready response, especially at the present time of rapid changes taking place in the ownership of land in Scotland. Accordingly a small Committee

First page only of circular for the First Ordinary General Meeting on 21 July 1931

Treasurer on 25 October 1932 when the administration of the Trust was transferred from 12 South Charlotte Street to 4 Great Stuart Street.

Sir John Stirling Maxwell presided at the AGM and the minutes say that Sir John considered that 'the Trust served the nation as a sort of cabinet into which could be put some of its valuable things where they would be perfectly safe for all time and where they were able to be seen and enjoyed by everyone'. This paper does not deal with the work of the Trust but only with its formation and constitutional changes. It was in April 1934 when it was agreed that a Royal Charter should be sought. This was carried forward with great vigour and a formal petition was drafted. The matter is referred to for historic reasons only as the petition for a Royal Charter was not proceeded with, although it was forwarded to the Clerk to the Privy Council. For some reason, however, it was reported at an Executive Committee meeting on 14 November 1934 that a communication had been received from the Lords of the Council that they had found themselves unable to recommend to His Majesty to grant the Charter prayed for. It was minuted that Sir Iain Colquhoun hoped to pursue the matter. Sir Iain later reported that he felt no useful purpose would be served by doing so and it was agreed to consider following the lines of the National Trust and seek a Private Act of Parliament.

The issue then proceeded in the hands of the Law Agents for the purpose of dissolving the Trust as then constituted under the Companies Act and to reconstitute the Trust by Act of Parliament by means of a Provisional Order. A Provisional order confirmed by Parliament as an Act is the Scottish equivalent of an English Private Act of Parliament. In due course an Act was passed on 20 December 1935 known as 'The National Trust for Scotland Order Confirmation Act, 1935' which confirmed the Provisional Order.

The first accounts of the Trust were audited by Bryson & Craig CA. The Partner concerned was Archibald G Bryson CA who was not only the first Auditor of the Trust Accounts but also the first subscriber. His family is proud to hold the first membership receipt.

A G Bryson was a very public spirited man who took a keen interest in his native City of Edinburgh, was involved in the affairs of the Royal Blind Asylum and of the Scottish National Institution for the War Blinded. He presented to the city the clock at Canonmills as a thanksgiving gesture on the return of his four sons safe and sound at the end of the 1939-45 War. It must have been natural for him to take a keen interest in the work of the NTS – whenever the idea was first discussed – especially as his office was at 7 Forres Street – almost next door to the APRS offices at 3 Forres Street. A G S Bryson gradually took over the Audit after the War from his father and their firm continued as Auditors until September 1963 having held the appointment for 32 years

The resignation of Bryson & Craig was accepted with regret when Mr Bryson said that the volume of work involved in the Audit of the Accounts of the Trust was becoming beyond the resources of his firm. Messrs Lindsay, Jamieson & Haldane CA (James Haldane and Lindsay Brown) were subsequently appointed.

I must thank the members of the NTS staff who have helped me with the production of this paper. Mr Robert Smith, the Director of APRS, who so readily made available to me all the early records of that body. My daughter Barbara Cairns who did all the original typing, photocopying, setting out etc. W J Cairns and Partners for the office facilities they so generously provided for preparing the first edition.

FIRST PREPARED BY GEORGE S RUSSELL
IN 1989 AND REVISED 2000

IMPORTANT AND HISTORIC DATES

1927	12 April	Inaugural Meeting of APRS
1929	6 June	Executive Committee of APRS makes first mention of the desirability of a National Trust for Scotland being formed.
1930	22 July	APRS formally agreed to proceed with formation of a National Trust for Scotland.
	6 August	Letter sent out by the Earls of Crawford and Haddington and Sir John Stirling Maxwell and Sir Iain Colquhoun seeking support from suggested Trustees.
	10 November	First meeting of Provisional Council of NTS and formal resolution passed to set about registering a company limited by guarantee.
1931	1 May	The company incorporated. First property given to NTS – Crookston Castle by Sir John Stirling Maxwell.
	21 July	First Ordinary General Meeting of members of NTS and Statement of Accounts tabled and approved from 1 May 1931 to 8 July 1931.
	14 October	First Council Meeting.
1932	29 June	First Annual General Meeting of the Trust when the accounts from 1 May 1931 to 30 April 1932 were presented and approved.
1935	20 December	Passing of The National Trust for Scotland Order Confirmation Act 1935

NTS ACQUISITIONS
1931-2000

1931-1944

1931   Crookston Castle*

1932   Bruce's Stone. Burg. Culross Palace including the Study. Souter Johnnie's Cottage

1933   Glenluce Abbey Glebe*

1934   Gladstone's Land. Calanais Blackhouse†

1935   Glencoe

1936   Balmerino Abbey. Black Hill. Caiy Stane. Thomas Carlyle's Birthplace. Castlehill* Dumbarton. Cunninghame Graham Memorial

1937   Barrie's Birthplace. Glencoe & Dalness. Hamilton House†. Mote of Mark & Rough Island, Rockcliffe. Culloden including Leanach Cottage

1938   Bachelors' Club. Glenfinnan. Hugh Miller's Cottage. Antonine Wall*. Provan Hall*. Linlithgow Houses†. Stenhouse Mansion†

1939   Strome Castle

1940

1941   Falls of Glomach

1942

1943   Bucinch and Ceardach. Culloden: King's Stables, Clan Graves, Memorial Cairn and Cumberland Stone

1944   The Hermitage. House of the Binns. Kintail & Morvich. Linn of Tummel

1945-1950

1945   Bannockburn. Corrieshalloch Gorge. Culzean Castle & Garden. Leith Hall & Garden. Clava Cairns*

1946   Balmacara Estate

1947   Craigower. Pass of Killiecrankie. St Mungo's Chapel, Culross. Boath Doocot

1948   Threave House, Garden & Estate. Threave Castle*

1949   Hill of Tarvit Mansionhouse & Garden & Scotstarvit Tower*. Parklea Farm*

1950   Ben Lawers. Dollar Glen & Castle Campbell*. Preston Mill. Sailor's Walk†

1951-1960

1951   Crathes Castle Garden & Estate

1952   Falkland Palace & Garden. Inverewe Garden. Pitmedden Garden. Provost Ross's House*

1953   Plewlands House†

1954   Dunkeld*. Fair Isle. Weaver's Cottage. Balmacara, Lochalsh House & Woodland Garden

1955

1956

1957   St Kilda Archipelago. Kirkwynd Cottages, Glamis, acquired for the Angus Folk Collection

1958   Brodick Castle, Garden & Goatfell. Stanley Hill, Dunkeld. Lamb's House*

1959   Inveresk Lodge Garden

1960

1961-1970

1961

1962   Grey Mare's Tail. Phantassie Doocot, Preston Mill

1963   Craigievar Castle. Macquarie Mausoleum**. Abertarff House†

1964

1965 Muckle Lands, Jubilee Path, Rockcliffe

1966 5, 6, & 7 Charlotte Square, Edinburgh

1967 Branklyn Garden. Torridon

1968 Malleny Garden. Wester Alligin, Torridon

1969 Auchenvin House†. Rockcliffe. Preston Tower*

1970 Kellie Castle & Garden. Shieldaig Island

1971–1980

1971 Rockcliffe coastline near the Merse

1972 Achnacon, Glencoe. Dob's Linn,
Grey Mare's Tail

1973

1974 Pineapple. Priorwood Garden

1975 Culross Town House. Angus Folk Collection,
later renamed Museum

1976 Castle Fraser & Garden. Drum Castle &
Garden. Greenbank Garden

1977

1978 Haddo House. Cammo Estate*.
Craigievar fields

1979 Isle of Iona except Abbey & sacred buildings

1980 Brodie Castle. House of Dun. St Abb's Head

1981–1990

1981 Isle of Canna. Culloden (part). Venniehill.
Dirleton Castle*

1982 The Hill House. Hutchesons' Hall.
The Tenement House. Kippen Smiddy†

1983

1984 Ben Lomond. Fyvie Castle. St Abb's Head –
Lumsdaine coastal strip

1985 South banks of the Rivers Tay & Braan,
near Birnam

1986 Robert Smail's Printing Works. Isle of Staffa.
Town House, Falkland

1987

1988 Barry Mill. The Old Granary†, Perth

1989 Atholl Memorial Fountain, Dunkeld. Geilston
Garden. Culloden, Field of the English

1990 Rockcliffe coastline near the Merse

1991–2000

1991 Cameronians' Regimental Memorial.
Murray Isles

1992 Arduaine Garden. Moirlanich Longhouse.
Wester Kittochside.

1993 Finavon Doocot. An Torr Woodland, Glencoe.
Old Schoolhouse, Cottown†. West Affric.
Land at Castle Fraser.

1994 Holmwood House. Blackpotts grazing,
St Abb's Head

1995 Mar Lodge Estate

1996 Alloa Tower**. Harmony Garden.
26–31 Charlotte Square, head office,
exhibition, retail & catering. Northgate House†.
Morenish, Ben Lawers

1997 Broughton House & Garden. Balnain House*.
Beaton's Croft House†. Newhailes†.
Kittochside, additional land for Museum of
Scottish Country Life

1998 Pollok House**. Unst & Yell Estate, Shetland

1999 The David Livingstone Centre**

2000 The islands of Mingulay, Berneray, Pabbay &
Rosinish. 14 Ramsay Garden†, Edinburgh

* 17 properties owned by NTS and under
Guardianship Agreements or leased to others

† 15 properties owned by NTS but not open
to the public

** 4 properties managed but not owned by NTS

Over 120 properties owned and managed by NTS

The above dates of property acceptance, some of which
may vary with the dates of legal disposition, are derived
from *The National Trust for Scotland Guide*. The guide
also contains descriptions of all categories of properties.

GEORGE WATERSTON AWARDS

* These recipients are more fully described
in Chapter Seven

1982 BASIL SKINNER*

1983 STEWART AND ANNIE THOMSON OF FAIR ISLE

The Thomsons were integral to the welfare of the island in an abundance of ways, notably in organising numerous work parties from the UK and abroad to benefit the community. They were voluntary representatives for the Trust on the island for 34 years.

1984 BETTINA, LADY THOMSON

Bettina was the principal inspiration behind the setting up of the dried flower enterprise at Priorwood Garden, Melrose, at that time unique among gardens in the Trust, and in leading a stalwart band of volunteers to run the operation from 1974 to 1992. They raised considerable sums of money for the Trust in the process and with enthusiasm and commitment ensured a reputation for the quality of the dried flowers they produced.

1985 PETER WRIGHT*

1986 ELIZABETH GILLIES

Elizabeth Gillies was a 'character' who with other volunteers organised the shop at Hutchesons' Hall for some eight years. Entirely volunteer run and ruled with a rod of iron, the shop was an outstanding success. Elizabeth also catered for events at the Hall.

1987 CHRISSIE MCGILLIVRAY OF BURG

'Chrissie Burg' was born on the remote Ardmeanach peninsula on the west coast of the island of Mull. As the Trust's representative, Chrissie spent all her long life in the small cottage at the end of the rough road, apart from occasional visits to the mainland. On their return from the Wilderness and MacCulloch's Fossil Tree, on the coast well beyond her cottage, weary visitors would be welcomed with a cup of tea and freshly baked scones and pancakes!

1988 DOROTHY ROBERTSON

As one of the first volunteer guides at Hill of Tarvit Mansionhouse in Fife, Dorothy joined the Needlework and Conservation Group when it began in 1979, shortly after the house was opened to visitors. Dorothy was the enthusiastic and talented leader who with some 20 other volunteers made and repaired an extensive range of items for Trust properties over many years.

1989 THE REV CHARLES B EDIE*

1990 WALLACE S JONES*

1991 JOHN FOSTER

Following a notable career as Director of the Peak District National Park, John Foster was the first Director of the Countryside Commission for Scotland. He became associated with the Trust from 1968 and as a professional planner helped to advance the cause of countryside conservation in Scotland and the Trust. After his retirement in 1985, John acted as the Trust's Countryside Adviser.

1992 GEORGE RUSSELL*

1993 NINIAN BRODIE OF BRODIE

The warmth and friendliness of Brodie Castle is largely due to the personality of Ninian Brodie, who personally did much to welcome visitors from the first day it opened its doors to the public in 1980. He has been of inestimable value in advising the Trust's managers and staff at the property and has ensured that good relations were maintained between the Trust and the local community.

1994 LEA MACNALLY

In 1969, Lea at Torridon was the first ranger naturalist appointed by the Trust. An obituary written by Jamie Stormonth Darling in *The Scotsman* of February 1993 described him as 'quiet spoken, unassuming and gentle yet a dynamo for hard work, often out on the hill in all weathers before dawn until late; a sensitive and observant naturalist with poetry in his pen and a brilliant photographer. In his 25 years at Torridon he epitomised the countryside work of the Trust'.

1995 KATHY RICE

Kathy received the Award in recognition of her leadership of the 45 Friends of Greenbank Garden who were established in 1981, although there were a few volunteers before that date. The Friends devote their energies to the property and are involved in the shop, helping in numerous ways in the garden, as well as using their sewing expertise for other properties in the West Region. Kathy continues in her capacity as Chairman of the Friends.

1996 BETTY JESS AND BETTY MOIR

The 'Two Betties', as they were affectionately known by many in the Trust, became shop manageress in 1978 at Culzean and Crathes respectively. At separate ends of the country they significantly raised the sale of Trust goods. For sheer hard work cheerfully carried out they were difficult to beat and visitors were always assured of a warm welcome. They died within four days of each other in February 2001.

1997 THE VERY REVEREND DR JOHN PATERSON

John succeeded the Reverend Charles Edie, a previous winner of the George Waterston Memorial Award in 1989, as the Trust's Special Adviser. In this capacity he travelled Scotland far and wide getting to know the many Trust properties and their staff and acting as discreet counsellor and/or friend to everyone he met.

1998 CAROLINE VEVERS*

1999 WILLIAM (BILL) MURRAY

Bill was a committee member of the Tayside Group of Conservation Volunteers, and had special responsibility for managing their tools. All tools have to be numbered, ordered, kept in clean working order and assembled for tasks of each of the five groups of volunteers. A time-consuming and labour intensive job, it ensures the efficient and safe working of the groups. Bill enthusiastically managed the tool store for over 5 years.

2000 TOM HALL*

PATRON AND OFFICE-BEARERS

PATRON

Her Majesty Queen Elizabeth,
The Queen Mother
1953–

1931–2001
PRESIDENTS

The 8th Duke of Atholl 1931–1942

Sir John Stirling Maxwell 1944–1956

The 12th Earl of Wemyss and March 1967–1991

The 6th Marquess of Bute 1991–1993

The 10th Duke of Atholl 1994–1995

The 13th Earl of Airlie 1997–

CHAIRMEN

Sir Iain Colquhoun 1931–1946

The 12th Earl of Wemyss and March 1946–1968

The 6th Marquess of Bute 1969–1984

William M Cuthbert 1984–1988

R Charles Tyrrell 1989–1994

I Hamish Leslie Melville 1995–1998

Professor J McC M Cunningham 1998–2000

Professor Roger Wheater 2000–

SECRETARIES AND TREASURERS

Arthur W Russell 1931–1932

Edward D Stevenson 1932–1939

Arthur W Russell (interim) 1939–1944

Edward D Stevenson 1944–1947

Jo Grimond 1947–1949

Jamie C Stormonth Darling 1949–1963

SECRETARY

Jamie C Stormonth Darling 1963–1971

DIRECTORS

Jamie C Stormonth Darling 1971–1983

Lester Borley 1983–1992

Douglas M Dow 1992–1997

Trevor A Croft 1997–2001

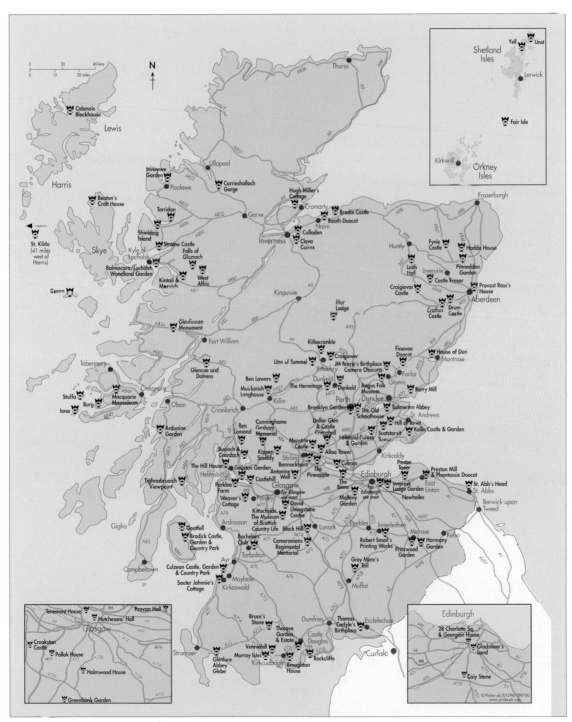

MAP OF
SCOTLAND
SHOWING NTS
PROPERTIES

Shetland Isles

Yell · Unst

Lerwick

Fair Isle

Kirkwall · Orkney Isles

Thurso

A836

A9

Calanais
Blackhouse

Lewis

Harris

Ullapool

A837

Inverewe
Garden

Poolewe

Corrieshalloch
Gorge

Hugh Miller's
Cottage

Cromarty

Brodie Castle

Boath Doocot

Fraserburgh

A832

Beaton's
Croft House

Torridon

Garve

Nairn

Culloden

Clava
Cairns

Inverness

Fyvie
Castle

Haddo House

Huntly

A96

Shieldaig
Island

Skye

Strome Castle

Falls of
Glomach

Leith
Hall

Inverurie

Castle Fraser

Pitmedden
Garden

Provost Ross's
House

St. Kilda
(41 miles
west of
Harris)

Kyle of
Lochalsh

Balmacara/Lochalsh
Woodland Garden

Kintail &
Morvich

West
Affric

A887

Craigievar
Castle

A944

Aberdeen

Canna

A9

Kingussie

Crathes
Castle

Drum
Castle

Glenfinnan
Monument

Mar
Lodge

A93

Fort William

A82

Killiecrankie

Craigower

Finavon
Doocot

House of Dun

Montrose

Glencoe and
Dalness

Tobermory

Ben Lawers

Linn of Tummel

Pitlochry

JM Barrie's Birthplace

Camera Obscura

Forfar

Glamis

Staffa

Burg

Macquarie
Mausoleum

Muirlanich
Longhouse

The Hermitage

Dunkeld

Angus Folk
Museum

Barry Mill

Iona

Oban

Craignure

Arduaine
Garden

Crianlarich

Killin

Branklyn Garden

Perth

Dundee

The Old
Schoolhouse

Balmerino Abbey

St. Andrews

Hill of Tarvit

Kellie Castle & Garden

Ben
Lomond

Cunninghame
Graham
Memorial

Dollar Glen
& Castle
Campbell

Falkland Palace
& Garden

Scotstarvit
Tower

Menstrie
Castle

Alloa Tower

Kirkcaldy

Bucinch &
Ceardach

Kippen
Smiddy

Stirling

Bannockburn

Antonine
Wall

Culross

Preston
Tower

Preston Mill
& Phantassie Doocot

The Hill House

Geilston Garden

The
Pineapple

Edinburgh

For
Edinburgh
see inset

Inveresk
Lodge Garden

East
Linton

St. Abb's Head

St. Abbs

Helensburgh

Castlehill

The Binns

Malleny
Garden

Newhailes

Berwick-upon-
Tweed

Tighnabruaich
Viewpoint

Parklea
Farm

Weaver's
Cottage

Paisley

For Glasgow
see inset

David
Livingstone
Centre

Peebles

Innerleithen

Melrose

Harmony
Garden

Kelso

Ardrossan

Goatfell

Kirtochside,
The Museum
of Scottish
Country Life

Black Hill

Lanark

Robert Smail's
Printing Works

Priorwood
Garden

Gigha

Brodick Castle,
Garden &
Country Park

Bachelors'
Club

Cameronians
Regimental
Memorial

Grey Mare's
Tail

Campbeltown

Ayr

Tarbolton

Moffat

Culzean Castle, Garden
& Country Park

Maybole

Souter Johnnie's
Cottage

Kirkoswald

Tenement House

Provan Hall

Hutchesons' Hall

Glasgow

Crookston
Castle

Pollok House

Holmwood House

Greenbank Garden

Bruce's
Stone

Dumfries

Thomas
Carlyle's
Birthplace

Ecclefechan

Threave
Garden
& Estate

Castle
Douglas

Edinburgh

28 Charlotte Sq.
& Georgian House

Gladstone's
Land

Stranraer

Vennelhill

Murray Isles

Glenluce
Abbey Glebe

Kirkcudbright

Broughton
House

Rockcliffe

Carlisle

Caiy Stane

© Pindar plc (01296) 390100
www.pindar.com

ORIGINS OF QUOTATIONS

FOOTNOTE NUMBER   PAGE NUMBER

CHAPTER ONE

1 *'... all too common a feature of Scottish institutions,'*   11
   SIR IAIN COLQUHOUN, CHAIRMAN OF COUNCIL, NTS ANNUAL REPORT, 1933

2 *'since its inception rapid development would be dangerous and injudicious.*   12
   We have therefore pursued a policy of considered caution.'
   SIR IAIN COLQUHOUN, CHAIRMAN OF COUNCIL, NTS ANNUAL REPORT, 1933

3 *'The National Trust for Scotland serves the Nation as a cabinet into which it can put some*   16
   of its valuable things, where they will be perfectly safe for all time, and where they are open to
   be seen and enjoyed by everyone.' SIR JOHN STIRLING MAXWELL, VICE PRESIDENT AT THE NTS
   FIRST ANNUAL GENERAL MEETING, 29 JUNE 1932

4 *'... to cut our coat according to our cloth'*   22
   J S LEADBETTER, ACTING CHAIRMAN OF COUNCIL, NTS ANNUAL REPORT, 1939

CHAPTER TWO

5 *'The Trust must remain independent and flexible, for therein lies its strength'*   25
   THE EARL OF WEMYSS AND MARCH, CHAIRMAN OF COUNCIL, NTS ANNUAL REPORT, 1950

6 *' "We are thinking of giving the house, which in the normal course of events when we die would*   27
   belong to you, to an organisation called The National Trust for Scotland" (which in effect for them
   was Scotland itself). My parents said they could not know what I would do in life, but they were very
   clear about the importance of the family in Scottish history.'
   LETTER FROM TAM DALYELL TO THE AUTHOR, 21 NOVEMBER 1999

7 *'I became famous in the school for having been the only boy ever allowed to use the headmaster's*   27
   fountain pen!' LETTER FROM TAM DALYELL TO THE AUTHOR, 21 NOVEMBER 1999

8 *'... it is even possible that the accounts may break even in the current year and no longer show a deficit'*   35
   NEWS LETTER NO 3 JUNE 1950

9 *'... a perfect walled garden kept up to a high standard, famous for its apples and visited*   43
   by keen gardeners and garden societies from all over Britain.'
   COMMENTS ON THE GARDEN AT THREAVE BY MRS ALISON CHANDLER TO
   THE REGIONAL OFFICE, 29 MARCH 1999

SELECTED REFERENCES
AND GLOSSARY

Robert Hurd, *Scotland under Trust*. Adam and
Charles Black 1939.

Jennifer Jenkins and Patrick James, *From Acorn to Oak
Tree, The Growth of the National Trust 1895–1994*.
Macmillan 1994.

J Laughton Johnston, *Scotland's Nature in Trust. The
National Trust for Scotland, and its Wildland and
Crofting Management*. T & AD Poyser, Ltd. 2000.

Agnes Mure Mackenzie, *Scotland in Modern Times
1720–1939*. WR Chambers Ltd 1942.

Howard Newby, Editor, *The National Trust, The Next
Hundred Years*. The National Trust 1995.

National Trust for Scotland Annual Reports
1931–2000. National Trust for Scotland
archives and publications.

Robin Prentice, Editor, *The National Trust for
Scotland Guide*. Jonathan Cape Ltd 1976.

Sir John Stirling Maxwell, *Shrines and Homes in
Scotland*. Alexander Maclehose & Co 1937

Kenneth Williamson, *Fair Isle and its Birds*.
Oliver & Boyd 1965.

compositor: a person whose work consists of hand-setting type for printing

corbelled: projection of stone or wood, jutting out from a wall to support weight

feu: land formerly held in perpetuity, or for 99 years, generally in payment of a yearly rent

inalienable: not capable of being transferred or removed, except by Act of Parliament

in-bye: land near the farm dwelling

muniments: documents kept as evidence of rights or privileges

pedimented: triangular part crowning the portico in the front of a building

policies: pleasure grounds round a mansion house

prebendary: a resident clergyman who has a prebend or share of the revenues of a cathedral or collegiate church

quinquennial survey: (often of buildings) completed every five years

roup: a sale by auction

sarking: an underlining for slates or tiles traditionally in timber planking

sasine: traditional form of transfer of land ownership in Scotland

servitude rights: rights of access which pass to successive landowners

superiorities: interests in the land entitling the owner to enforce title conditions

upset price: lowest selling-price of property at auction

vernacular: often relating to buildings native to the district

INDEX